"Adam Gearey's marvelous new book is a leading entry in a new and emerging field of critical legal scholarship that speaks from the heart about one of the most important questions in all legal studies: how is it possible to live an ethical life in the law? Gearey's decision to tell the story of 60s poverty lawyers in America, including the roads not taken by them (and subsequently barricaded by politics) is brilliant. But this is not just an American story, for there are universal lessons to be drawn from the journey that the author describes. The book will strike a chord for readers eager to hear more about actually *being* a progressive member of the legal profession."

Louis Wolcher, Professor Emeritus, Charles I. Stone Professor of Law,
University of Washington School of Law.

"At a time of burgeoning inequality, intensified threat to democratic inclusivity, and renewed neoliberal assault on the welfare state, *Poverty Law and Legal Activism: Lives That Slide Out of View* refocuses attention on poverty and "poverty law" through the lens of critical theory and practice. Surveying diverse strands of the progressive response to poverty in the United States over the past several decades, Gearey draws novel connections, surfaces contradictions in the deployment of law for social change and offers a wide-ranging analysis of a field that defies easy categorization. A timely and thought-provoking study at a critical moment in the struggle for social and economic justice."

Stephen Loffredo, Professor of Law, CUNY Law School.

"*Poverty Law and Legal Activism: Lives That Slide Out of View* is really a magnificent piece of work, a true excavation and scholarly assessment that traces the tendrils of poverty law and CLS; in essence a return to what used to travel under the name of existential Marxism; but broadened through Buber and Christian radicalism to become a bricolage of humanism, poetry, music and theory. These modes of self-recognition in others suggest the possibility of overcoming alienation, degradation, pure poverty and pain"

Peter Goodrich, Professor of Law and Director of Law and Humanities,
Benjamin N. Cardozo School of Law.

Poverty Law and Legal Activism

Linking critical legal thinking to constitutional scholarship and a practical tradition of US lawyering that is orientated around anti-poverty activism, this book offers an original, revisionist account of contemporary jurisprudence, legal theory and legal activism. The book argues that we need to think in terms of a much broader inheritance for critical legal thinking that derives from the social ethics of the progressive era, new left understandings of "creative democracy" and radical theology. To this end, it puts jurisprudence and legal theory in touch with recent scholarship on the American left and, indeed, with attempts to recover the legacies of progressive era thinking, the civil rights struggle and the Great Society. Focusing on the theory and practice of poverty law in the period stretching from the mid-1960s to the present day, the book argues that at the heart of both critical and liberal thinking is an understanding of the lawyer as an ethical actor: inspired by faith or politics to appreciate the potential and limits of law in the struggle against economic inequality.

Adam Gearey is Professor of Law at Birkbeck College, University of London.

Poverty Law and Legal Activism

Lives that Slide Out of View

Adam Gearey

Routledge
Taylor & Francis Group
LONDON AND NEW YORK

First published 2018 by Routledge

2 Park Square, Milton Park, Abingdon, Oxfordshire OX14 4RN
52 Vanderbilt Avenue, New York, NY10017

Routledge is an imprint of the Taylor & Francis Group, an informa business

First issued in paperback 2019

British Library Cataloguing in Publication Data
A catalogue record for this book is available from the British Library

Library of Congress Cataloging in Publication Data
Names: Gearey, Adam, author.
Title: Poverty law and legal activism : lives that slide out of view / Adam Gearey.
Description: Abingdon, Oxon ; New York, NY : Routledge, 2018. | Includes bibliographical references and index.
Identifiers: LCCN 2017055109 | ISBN 9781138556058 (hbk)
Subjects: LCSH: Legal assistance to the poor--United States. | Public interest lawyers--United States. | Public welfare--Law and legislation--United States.
Classification: LCC KF336 .G43 2018 | DDC 344.7303/258--dc23
LC record available at https://lccn.loc.gov/2017055109

ISBN: 978-1-138-55605-8 (hbk)
ISBN: 978-0-367-86266-4 (pbk)

Typeset in Galliard
by Taylor & Francis Books

Contents

Acknowledgements

It seems fitting that a book about working on the self should be written on a sabbatical; or, rather, in a space in between work and the peculiar form of not-working called writing. The inspiration for *Poverty Law and Legal Activism: Lives that Slide Out of View* in fact came out of an earlier sojourn at University of California, Berkeley. The energies stored in the Social Protest Archive – in particular documents on the new left – crackled with ideas that seemed both distant and incredibly present. More recent digging in New York Public Library also revealed exciting xeroxed pamphlets that mixed social science, utopianism and practical organising. *Poverty Law and Legal Activism* was completed during a period spent as a visiting fellow at the University of Sussex. I would like to thank the Law School for its hospitality. I am writing these acknowledgements against the background of a resurgent Labour campaign for the General Election (and Bernie Sanders speaking at the Brighton Dome). Doorstep persuasion is a far more difficult discipline than academic argument – and more pressing.

My thanks to Peter Goodrich, Louis Wolcher, Maria Grahn-Farley and Lucy Finchett-Maddock. Their comments on earlier drafts of this text were exemplary of the generous, creative thought that this book hopes to celebrate. Lou Wolcher's comments were pondered walking through a wheat field at dusk on the way back from the Gun Inn under a crescent moon (Lou made me a gift of his copy of *People of the Abyss*; stock withdrawn from the Belle Isle Branch of the Oklahoma City Library). Anthony Farley, Gavin Clarke, Piyel Haldar, Marinos Diamantides, Mark Perryman, Costas Douzinas, Michelle Everson, Bella Dicks, Kev Monroe, Angela Paccini, Peter Finnemore, Scott Vietch, Dan Matthews, Peter Fitzpatrick, Mark Griffiths, Gilly Schapiro, Tanya Shadrick, Paul Virr, Illan Wall, Gil Leung and Benjamin R. Gearey all provided much-needed support and encouragement in various forms, optics and measures. Thanks also to Hannah Lovelock at Routledge, and Niamh Gearey for the back cover art. Colin Perrin – a publisher, thinker and editor of style and nobility – my sincere thanks and gratitude. Mary Gearey, the Dorothy Parker of de-growth; divine interlocutor, my love and thanks. Arthur and Niamh, Dionysians, Corbynites, trouble makers – I love you guys. Finally, my comrades at Birkbeck and the Critical Legal Conference, I salute you.

La Lutte continue.

07/06/17

Abbreviations

ACORN	Association of Community Organizations for Reform Now
AFDC	Aid to Families with Dependent Children
AIM	American Indian Movement
BLS	US Bureau of Labor Statistics
BPP	Black Panther Party
CED	Community Economy Development
CEP	Conference on Economic Progress
CLS	Critical Legal Studies
CRT	Critical Race Theory
CWRO	Chicana Welfare Rights Organization
ELAWRO	East Lost Angeles Welfare Rights Organization
ERAP	Economic Research and Action Project
FAP	Family Assistance Plan
LID	League for Industrial Democracy
LIHTC	Low-Income Housing Tax Credit
LSC	Legal Services Corporation
MFY	Movement for Youth
NMI	New Markets Initiative
NWRO	National Welfare Rights Organization
OEO	Office of Economic Opportunity
PBJI	Program for Better Jobs and Income
PLDC	Progressive Liberal Democratic Constitutionalism
PPEHRC	Poor People's Economic Human Rights Campaign
PRWORA	Personal Responsibility and Work Opportunity Reconciliation Act
SDS	Students for a Democratic Society
SNCC	Student Nonviolent Coordinating Committee
TANF	Temporary Assistance for Needy Families
WIN	Work Incentive

Chapter 1

Lives that slide out of view

Vivas to those who have fail'd.

(Walt Whitman, "Song of Myself", 1885)

Poverty Law and Legal Activism: Lives that Slide Out of View concerns the origins and fates of Critical Legal Studies (CLS).[1] Against the usual conventions, the

1 Thus, we are very much concerned with a way of re-thinking CLS, its location and cultural legacies. CLS is perhaps best conceived of as a left-leaning grouping of scholars based in university law schools. Standard accounts of CLS trace one line of inheritance back to American Legal Realism and the historical context of the New Deal, but this does tend to obscure the relationship between the new left and CLS. Although the first Conference on Critical Legal Studies at the University of Wisconsin did not take place until 1977, CLS was rooted in the radical politics of the 1960s (Duxbury, 1995, p.432). CLS scholars tended to see law as political; claims to legal autonomy and neutrality effectively concealed law's role in social control and the ideological construction of private property, the market and bourgeois order. This thesis took a slightly different form in arguments about legal indeterminacy. Not only could legal doctrine be considered fractured and ambiguous, but law itself could never be properly delineated from politics. Our main concern in this footnote is not to define CLS, but to look at a particular theme in the history of the movement. The conventional account of CLS presents it as prone to splits that began with the creation of a distinct group of feminist critical legal scholars. Feminist critical legal thinking has its roots in feminist streams organised at a 1983 conference on CLS, but its proper origins can be traced to a specifically feminist CLS conference in 1985. Critical legal feminism "began in reaction to a radical and mostly, but not exclusively, male vision of an alternative conception of society" (Menkel-Meadow, 1988, p.63). Feminist scholars were keen to develop their position against "classic" CLS. For instance, Menkel-Meadow argued that the feminist approach is committed to the "experiential point of view" as seen from the perspective of the "oppressed, dominated, and devalued" (Menkel-Meadow, 1988, p.63). The next significant split came in the late 1980s. Critical Race Theory's (CRT) founding moment can probably be traced to its first conference in 1989. Scholars of colour reacted to the "white patriarchs" who ran "the movement" (Goldfarb, 1992, p.685). White feminism was also a target of critique. CRT can thus be seen as a "critique of the critique". Consider Williams's celebrated criticisms of CLS. She castigated "classical" CLS as stemming from "the white left's" inability to know what it means to be black. Critical Race Theorists wanted to "look to one's own" (Cook, 1990). This argument itself breaks down into two positions: one which sought to build

book presents CLS as a philosophy of activism, located on a particular fault line that runs through American radical culture from the new left[2] to the welfare rights movement. The central argument is that the politics of the movement are essential if we want to grasp a peculiar continuation of CLS, tentatively called critical legal theory.[3] If there is such a thing as critical legal theory then it might be seen as a political and philosophical engagement with the constitutive social divisions that articulate market capitalism.

For the purposes of our argument we will follow the various "splits" in the American critical legal tradition between feminism, Critical Race Theory and Latino/a Critical Theory (LatCrit) – but we want to suggest that mainstream accounts of CLS misunderstand the fundamental continuity of critical legal thought. Indeed, it is now necessary to read the critical tradition in reverse from

black consciousness, and one whose energies went into identifying the interests and "essence" of racist oppression. However, in the mid-1990s, CRT was itself subjected to a "fracturing" by LatCrit (Frug, 1992, p.1051). LatCrit subjected CRT to critique – in particular its focus on discrimination as a "black white binary" as a way of understanding discrimination and marginalisation (Gines, 2013). LatCrit's own "inward turn" further questioned "subdivision within outsider groups that at one time saw themselves as unitary" (Delgado, 1993, p.753). LatCrit scholarship is also marked by a distinct turn to Queer Theory in order to understand the homophobia of Latino cultures (Valdes, 1997a). Histories of CLS, CRT and LatCrit can be found in West (1986), Dalton (1987), Delgado (1987), Matsuda (1987), Goldfarb (1992) and Hernández-Truyol et al. (2015). Bauman presents a slightly different approach. Not only has "the story of the critical legal studies movement's genesis and growth … not yet been definitively told" (Bauman, 2002, p.4), but "the place of the Movement" has been downplayed (Bauman, 1988, p.352). We would thus follow Bauman and take issue with Cornel West's positioning of CLS. West accused CLS of parting company with "nonacademic prophetic and progressive organized efforts to transform American culture and society" (West, 1988, p.270). He argues that CLS required a turn to Gramsci and a movement away from Foucault. This is certainly a compelling approach. However, the genealogy presented in this book suggests a different cultural location of CLS. Whilst we touch upon certain themes that might resonate with West's notion of the prophetic, this concept is not used to organise the argument of this book. There is, nevertheless, an ongoing dialogue (explicit or implicit) with Cornel West that runs through its pages, particularly around the relationship of critical legal thought to liberalism and West's reading of Unger. The engagement with Dewey owes a debt to West (1989), as does the reading of Marx and the Marxist tradition and the orientation to existentialism (West, 1991).

2 We will concentrate on Students for a Democratic Society (SDS]. Whilst the SDS was not entirely synonymous with the new left, it was arguably the most influential. See Chapter 2 for a more extended discussion of the SDS and the new left.

3 The movement was a term used by those involved in the SDS, the National Welfare Rights Organization (NWRO) and CLS as a way of identifying themselves. The fact that this term extends from new left and anti-poverty activism to CLS suggests the peculiar kind of genealogy that this book sets out to study. However, this is not meant to suggest that there was any real continuity between these different groupings, other than passionate modes of self-identification. Critical legal theory is not as recognised a term as Critical Legal Studies. Chapter 10 attempts to sketch out how critical legal theory might be understood.

the perspective of LatCrit and ClassCrit.[4] To this end, we will also follow the boundary that exists between critical legal thinking and its nearest cousin or neighbour, progressive constitutionalism.[5] For example, we can hear the dim echoes of street protests in Michelman's sophisticated moral philosophy. The critical legal tradition and progressive constitutionalism share a fundamental concern with poverty. Poverty is the leading edge of a movement of thought that holds together engagements with welfare rights, democracy and activism.

4 ClassCrit can be traced back to workshops held at the University of Buffalo in 2007. A grouping of scholars drawing on the legacies of CLS and CRT, the ClassCrits also have ongoing associations with LatCrit. Thus, ClassCrit can be seen as one of the mediating "points" between critical legal traditions of thought, and a key site for creative thinking on Marx. For a general overview of ClassCrit, see Grahn-Farley (2008), Mutua (2008), Kessler (2008), Mutua (2008a) and Mahoney (2009).

5 Although the concept of progressive constitutionalism is somewhat disputed, there is sufficient agreement to make it a useful term – if only to catch a certain mood in constitutional scholarship. As a general, catch-all definition, Lipkin offers the idea that progressive approaches to the constitution seek "to improve the chances of authentic self-definitions for all Americans" through "interventions in both private and public affairs that neither liberals nor conservatives would be happy to countenance" (Lipkin, 1999, p. v). In keeping with at least some of the arguments presented in this book, progressive constitutionalism communicates with legacies of new left thought. Perhaps West's view of progressive constitutionalism resonates most clearly with the values that can be associated with the new left. She asserts that: "[p]rogressivism is … a particular moral and political response to the sadness of lesser lives" that have been "unnecessarily diminished by economic, psychic and physical insecurity in the midst of a society or world that offers plenty" (West, 1999, p.1). Progressive constitutionalism, as a "moral response to suffering" draws its energy from "collective action" and is aimed at "ameliorating the suffering that is consequent to private maldistributions of wealth and security" (West, 1999, p.3). Thus, the "normative antiauthoritarian aspirations" that characterise at least one of the anima of progressive constitutionalism could be traced back to the new left (Cohen and Alberstein, 2011, p.1086). At the same time, the progressive fear of "backlash" and distrust of the Supreme Court might also suggest that the concept of progressive constitutionalism is itself a critical response to the militancy of the movement (Spindelman, 2011, p.1116). Progressive constitutionalism is a broad church. Some scholars associated with progressive constitutionalism distance their work from any links with the new left. For instance, Tushnet's nuanced version of progressive constitutionalism shares with scholars like Robin West the concern with "racial justice" and forwarding "public policies aimed at improving the material conditions of those suffering "severe deprivation" (Tushnet, 2011, p.1074). However, Tushnet also argues that progressive constitutionalism need not be egalitarian, provided it takes seriously the question of how "severe material deprivation" can be reduced as far as possible (Tushnet, 2011, pp.1075–1076). We will follow these concerns throughout the book. We will bracket Michelman's work under the general rubric of progressive constitutionalism, even though he is somewhat critical of the term. This approach is justified in terms of our argument as it indicates the complex legacies at play in Michelman's constitutionalism. It is also worth pointing out that our argument does not assert that the NWRO must be seen as central to either progressive, popular or democratic constitutionalism. Our point is merely that these currents of scholarship carry forward certain memories of the movement, repressed or otherwise.

The book's argument is organised around three key terms: alienation, praxis and ethics. Activism is understood through this network of themes. Our approach to alienation takes its basic orientating points from Marx.[6] In crudest summary: to understand poverty it is necessary to grasp alienation. Alienation, and the closely related term reification, have largely disappeared from contemporary legal critique. One objective of this book is to re-open debate around these ideas.

Alienation must be located within a particular critique of American monopoly capitalism. In distinction to the forms of mechanised mass production that defined classical capitalism, decent wages and expanding consumer markets are essential to cycles of production/consumption in monopoly capitalism. Thus the new problematic of alienation is that of the worker as consumer in a post-scarcity society.[7]

6 In the discussion that follows, we make a distinction between Marx's understanding of a capitalist mode of production and a more precise understanding of American capitalism as monopoly capitalism. A capitalist mode of production operates to specific and immanent logics. From an historical perspective, we are concerned with a process that can be dated to the sixteenth century and the creation of "a world-embracing commerce and a world-embracing market" (Marx, 1975, p.247). From a more technical and economic sense, the process of self-valorisation is peculiar to capitalism. This is itself a complex idea, but can be simply put as follows. The capitalist does not seek to make a profit on a single transaction but to realise the "restless never-ending process of profit-making alone" (Marx, 1975, p.254). The capitalist throws his money into circulation, in the hope that it will be endlessly augmented. Capital itself thus appears to be "an independent substance, endowed with a motion of its own, passing through a life-process of its own, in which money and commodities are mere forms which it assumes and casts off in turn" (Marx, 1975, p.251). This is clearly an inadequate description of Marx's understanding of capital. However, in very general outline it traces the fundamental relationship between a capitalist mode of production and alienated labour. A capitalist mode of production "subordinates human needs to the profit motive". This has certain economic effects: "trigger[ing] crises and contradictions" that, in turn, "limit the scope for the reproduction of capital" (Saad-Filho and Fine, 2004, p.89). Capitalism articulates a form of human being defined by a capitalist mode of production. This analysis is based on a reading of *The 1844 Manuscripts.* The concept of alienation comes out of a reflection on the social degradation of a world reduced to a form of economics: "the devaluation of the world of men is in direct proportion to the increasing values of the world of things" (Marx, 1977, p.68). In most general terms, the worker is alienated from the product of his/her labour (as something produced for someone else); alienated from the process of production, or from work itself and, as a "deduction" from these first two features of the phenomenon, alienated from species being. This is the most central part of the theory of alienation we want to carry forward. Species being addresses the problem of meaning, or, more specifically, human meaning. See below in note 8.[8] In general, our argument follows Mészáros, Sayers and Ollman to the extent that it sees alienation as a theme that runs through Marx's work. Whilst its presence in *Capital* is not as pronounced as certain earlier texts, this does not mean that the concept is absent in Marx's mature critique of political economy – or even in the work of those, such as Baran and Sweezy, who develop a more contemporary understanding of monopoly capitalism (Mészáros, 2005).

7 The concept of monopoly capital was important to the new left as it appeared to identify the nature of the massive surplus of wealth created by American capitalism in

Baran and Sweezy provided the basic forms of the critique of consumerism: the more one consumed, the more one sought satisfaction through further consumption (Baran and Sweezy, 1964). Alienation is thus linked with a network of phenomena around the numbing loss of meaning in an administered society. Consumerism also conceals the racism and sexual division of labour that define a particular social structure of waged and unwaged work. Drawing on Baran and Sweezy, and compressing a great deal of analysis of poverty and class, new left theorists argued that – despite their ethnic diversity – "the poor were united by deprivation or near-starvation levels of income" (Gilbert, Gottlieb and Tenney, 1967, pp.116–117). Whilst the "unity" of the poor was somewhat overstated, the basic insight remains sound. We can follow this approach and see America's quasi welfare state as central to the management of poverty. Welfare provides a mode of bureaucratic control that disciplines those unable to commodify their labour.

It is important to stress that this approach to poverty and alienation relates to the time and place studied in this book. A proper understanding of alienation and reification[8] has to be sensitive to the complex assemblages that articulate modes of

the post-war period: "always too much never too little" (Baran and Sweezy, 1966, p.114). The engines "that produce[d] [the] surplus" are "giant corporations", no longer under the control of single families but a managerial elite (Baran and Sweezy, 1966, p.58). The monopolistic tendencies of giant corporations prevent markets operating rationally. The key concern is thus the "generation and absorption" of corporate profits (Baran and Sweezy, 1966, p.77). Provided that corporations can divide up the market to their own satisfaction, the surplus they generate from their activities can continue to grow (Baran and Sweezy, 1966, p.77). However, the "contradiction" in monopoly capitalism is that whilst it produces "ever greater surpluses", it "fails to provide the consumption and investment outlets" that would "absorb" the surpluses and allow the economic system to continue functioning. This leads to various pathologies such as unemployment and business failure (Baran and Sweezy, 1966, p.114). The state has a central role in ensuring that the economy serves the interests of powerful economic actors. Baran and Sweezy's discussion of the changing form of the American state in the period of the New Deal suggests that government spending was a way of dealing with the crisis of the Great Depression. Despite the liberal argument that "inadequate surplus absorption could be solved by … increased government spending for welfare purposes", the New Deal in fact failed as a "salvage operation". It was only the war that dragged the country out of depression (Baran and Sweezy, 1966, pp.162–163).

8 Recent scholarship has found in reification an understanding of a "stance" or an attitude of mind that can be understood as "empathetic engagement" or a "qualitative experience of interaction" (Honneth, 2008, pp.56, 57). We reify other people to the extent that we do not recognise them as human beings and, indeed, we suffer from reification to the extent that we forget or limit our own emotional responses to others. This re-orientation of the concept of reification stresses that it is necessary to re-read Lukács's Marxist understanding and also to observe the resonances between certain Heideggerian notions of care and Dewey's arguments about experience. One important upshot of this argument is that it expands the meaning of reification beyond a narrow account of "the sphere of commodity exchange" and allows us to engage with a more sophisticated understanding of the interior effects of reification (Honneth, 2008, p.24).

production.[9] We thus draw on the work of Mészáros (1970), Ollman (1971) and Sayers (2011), as it holds together the dialectical relationship of economics, society and culture.[10] Particularly useful in this respect is West's understanding of Dewey as a major progressive philosopher (West, 1987), and the more general re-positioning of Marx as a philosopher rather than the dour ideologue of failed state socialism (West, 1991). It is important to appreciate the inherent complexity of alienation: one must study genealogies, intersections, combinations and mediations.[11]

9 A problem bedevilling the study of alienation has been the translation of the original terms used by Hegel and Marx. *Entfremdung* has been translated as estrangement but also carries the specific sense of alienation. In *The 1844 Manuscripts* Marx argues that under the social conditions of a capitalist mode of production, one is alienated from *Gattungswesen*, "species-essence" or species being. Rather than offer an elaborate argument about this term, we will suggest that it can be associated with "being with" (explained presently). This does not make *Gattungswesen* an understanding of a human essence, for reasons given in the text of this book. "Being with" as *Gattungswesen* is our being with each other: our social being. A second issue is the relationship of alienation to reification. This relationship will be explained in greater detail in the text. However, the following preliminary observations might be useful. *Verdinglichung* can be translated as "thingifying" or turning something into a thing. Bringing these terms together, we get at the general idea that reification/alienation are parts of a complex that can be understood as a failure to find oneself in the world. In alienation one's response to the world (and sense of self) has become reified – frozen out – no longer a process or a becoming; no longer experience in a meaningful sense. To get at this idea we need to look at what the word experience actually means. The root of the word is "per": "to lead, pass over", which in turn can be linked to *peritus*: "tested", even a reflexivity, the sense of testing the self, and perhaps into *perius*: peril, putting something at stake; risk, anxiety and living dangerously. It would seem, then, that the process of experience, of putting in question, of becoming an activist, is an opening of one's self to experience and personal change. In very brief overview, our argument links together the notion of species being with an account of social recognition and "being with". Admittedly, this conjunction of terms is somewhat problematic, but it allows the critique of political economy to be linked to an account of social being and a notion of ethics and praxis.

10 The contemporary reconstruction of Marx's theory of alienation has the notion of system (or assemblage) at its core. This is perhaps one of the fundamental ideas behind Mészáros's ground-breaking defence of the rigour of Marx's theory of alienation (see Mészáros, 2005).

11 This study of intersections and combinations is a form of genealogy. Rather than engage in a complex attempt to mediate the relationships between two seemingly antagonist traditions of social and political thinking, we will merely suggest one possible (and useful) point of agreement between Foucauldian or Nietzschean genealogy and studies in the spirit of Marx/Hegel. Arguably both traditions are interested in the historical study of the forces that seize hold of phenomena. Depending on the play of forces, certain themes disappear or become obscured only to re-appear in a different configuration at a different historical juncture. As a form of critical history, genealogy brackets any notion of an ultimate telos. In terms of our arguments below, it should be clear that our borrowings from Marx and Hegel do not require a closed history or a unified historical subject (Mészáros, 2005).

The most basic terms for understanding alienation are thus a concept of capitalist economy and a notion of consciousness.[12] Consciousness is created and sustained in the dialectic of social recognition. Grasping consciousness will take us to terms that are definitional of socially recognised selves. Alienation describes the subtle way in which selves are constituted: inner and outer, body and soul folded together in the creation of a self-conscious thinking substance. As we will see, Du Bois's understanding of race is of great relevance in defining a colour line that runs through American culture and determines forms of racialised consciousness. Du Bois's approach is based on a Hegelian insight: we are how others see us. Black philosophers have taken this theme very seriously and have shown how ideas of character and personality provide a structure for the study of alienation. These concerns run through our engagement with James Baldwin's midnight fiction.[13] They also connect with our reading of Unger and intersectional analysis. In most basic outline, character is a manifestation of self – a complex bound up with notions of action and social recognition; an insight most succinctly articulated by Marcel Proust: "our social personality is the creation of other people's thoughts" – a sentiment with which Ellison's invisible man might also agree (Unger, 1976, p.146). Bridging between Baldwin and Unger we will also suggest that

12 As it would further complicate our thesis, these ideas are not developed through psychoanalysis. However, it is worth noting that psychoanalysis was important for new left thinking on alienation. For instance, in *Eros and Civilisation*, Marcuse drew on Fromm's work to provide an account of "socio-psychological phenomena" or "processes of active and passive adjustment of the instinctual apparatus to the socio-economic situation" (Marcuse, 1955, p.241). The individual is trained to fit into society, to accept its codes and values as legitimate. Psychoanalysis finds this process playing itself out in the psyche, through the harnessing of primarily libidinal forces to what Marcuse called "economically structured relationships of domination and subordination" (Marcuse, 1955, p.242). Social tensions manifest themselves as the level of individual psychic dis-function; outer antagonisms become inner antagonisms. In *The Sane Society*, Fromm engaged explicitly with alienation in terms that resonate with ideas developed in this book. Alienation is a "mode of experience", where a person becomes lost or "estranged" from him (or her) self" (Fromm, 1955, p.120). These ideas are also important to Castoriadis's treatment of alienation (although Castoriadis plays down the role of instincts). Like Marcuse, Castoriadis sees the unconscious as a social phenomenon: the internalisation of an imaginary that defines both "reality and desire" for the subject. Alienation is "instituted" in this imaginary construction of reality. Psychoanalysis seeks to restore the "autonomy" of the subject, or rather to provide a form of "self-regulation" where the subject comes to understand the "construction" of the real (Castoriadis, 2005, p.103). Much more work would be necessary to provide a proper psychoanalytic understanding of alienation that could make the most of the different traditions of psychoanalytic thought (in particular the Lacanian elements of Castoriadis's philosophy and their relationship to those of Marcuse). This demanding feat is not attempted here.

13 These themes are informed by black existentialism. Gordon's (2014) understanding of "double consciousness", drawn from the work of Du Bois, is central to the argument of this book. Cornel West's work is compelling because it reads between black existentialism and other traditions of thought. Gines's (2011) approach to intersectionality also feeds into the general approach to this term. See, in particular, chapter 10.

recognition is a major component of Dewey's social ethics.[14] In other words, if we accept that these themes underlie both black and white radical thought (and LatCrit, which seeks to break out of this binary), we can begin to appreciate how different critical traditions have communicated with each other. Moreover, we can engage with the granular substratum of a particular mode of radical thought – with all its different nuances, tension and over-determinations.

Alienation is immanent to consciousness. One might posit a necessary alienation that is actually the condition of thought, the social form of consciousness that is bound up with the realisation of the self. Necessary alienation can be opposed to bad alienation. The latter term describes frozen or reified forms of consciousness that hold in place modes of recognition. These modes of recognition are themselves embedded in hegemonic ideologies structured by a capitalist mode of production. In the terms suggested above, hegemonic social and economic forms define pseudo-realities that limit the creative human desire to transcend the limits of specific contexts. The critique of alienation proceeds dialectically to the extent that one can untangle one's consciousness from the forms that it has assumed.[15]

14 For William James, "identity is only a loosely constructed thing", something that exists "on the whole", and which rests on the basis that whatever one is thinking, one is always aware of "my self" and "my personal experience". Self for James is thus "duplex" – partly knowing and known; grammatically the "I" and the "me". However, the I which knows is neither "an aggregate" nor "an unchanging metaphysical entity like the Soul, or … transcendental ego", existing "out of time" (James, 1910, pp.215–216). Such an approach is not unique to James. For example, in the work of Cooley the self is no more than what is "designated" by the first person singular and "something known to experience" (Cooley, 1902, p.136). Cooley also talks of the "social self" or the "looking glass self". Just as we have a visual sense of the self from looking in the mirror (a sense associated with feelings that the mirror reflects "my attributes"), the social self is the sense of what "I" seem to be in "another's mind". The looking-glass self thus has three essential attributes: our imagination of how we appear to the other; our imagination of the other's judgement, and "some sort of feeling" that can range from "pride" to "mortification". The worst thing for the social self is to "lack the support of the other". Closed in on itself, the "I" becomes "unhealthy" – loses its "vigour and plasticity" and becomes reified (Cooley, 1902, p.155–157).

15 Although we will not use the Hegelian term Spirit (for reasons outlined below) the presentation of the problem of social consciousness in *The Phenomenology of Spirit* provides the basic terms for our argument. Spirit can be understood as consciousness that, mediated by self-consciousness, underlies any individual act. Spirit is, then, a form of self-reflexivity which creates the self as a fold in thought where "I" appear to myself. Spirit is no more than the "plurality of distinct consciousnesses definitely existing" or the way in which reflexivity is a social phenomenon (Hegel, 1967, para. 447). To put this slightly differently: self-reflexivity is both "for itself" as it recognises itself in the rational acts of others, and "in itself" to the extent that this recognition is a form of self-consciousness. Hegel argues that the social world is constituted by consciousnesses relating to each other through their common productions. Marx elaborates this point, and argues at length in *The Paris Manuscripts* that any proper critique of Hegel requires an engagement with political economy. As Marx himself affirms: "[w]ithin the framework of speculation Hegel … makes distinctions that really grasp the vital point" (Marx, 1977, p.665). It should thus be clear, even if only in outline, how Marx's

Philosophies of alienation are also accounts of praxis. Praxis overlaps with its nearest English cognate, practice, but rendering practice as praxis stresses that our concern is with particular forms of self-conscious practice that contest the terms of social recognition. This is a somewhat general definition, precisely because the contestation of social recognition must be studied in context. The development of these themes in the Marxist tradition has tended towards essentialism. For instance, from the perspective of Lukács's *History and Class Consciousness* (1923), the proletariat are capable of becoming the subjects of history and destroying an alienating social, economic and political reality through the collective realisation of their own political agency as a class. Our understanding of praxis is much more modest.[16] As we argue below, it actually parts company with classical Marxism. A proper account of praxis should eschew readymade concepts. Praxis is best conceived as an ongoing work in progress, an infinite conversation.[17]

New left praxis can be traced back to forms of community organising and the politics of the civil rights struggle. We will be particularly concerned with the

account of alienation both borrows from Hegel's terms and locates them in a new context: a critique of political economy.

16 An account of praxis does not require a "theory of history", absolute knowledge or a smooth dialectical circuit. If praxis is always a doing, then the theory that informs it is best thought of as clarification of the terms in which things are done. This approach borrows from Gramsci, Castoriadis and Cornel West. Praxis is understood as the reciprocal involvement of thought and action in particular historical contexts. A particularly influential statement of these themes, important for social movement theory, and for critical legal theory in general, is that of Laclau and Mouffe (2001). *Poverty Law and Legal Activism* departs from this text. Although our arguments follow a line that passes through Mouffe and Laclau, they connect with currents of thought that were not part of Laclau and Mouffe's project. We do not offer a "model" of radical democratic practice. Theory, in the sense used in this book, is "the always uncertain attempt to realise the project of clarifying the world" (Castoriadis, 2005, p.74). To elaborate this argument in detail would require extensive discussion of themes central to the philosophical tradition. Whilst we cannot provide anything like a detailed engagement with understandings of *techne, episteme, phronesis* and praxis inherited from Aristotle, we can suggest one important concern: different ways of acting have their own ways of working out how to achieve the goals they seek. The carpenter and the geometer have their own ways of going about things. It is not that we are compelled to a choice between "geometry and chaos" (Castoriadis, 2005, p.72). This does not mean that one cannot have a general account of praxis. It means that a general account of praxis is fairly useless when it comes down to doing something rather than writing or thinking about it abstractly.

17 In this respect Bernstein's arguments are an important influence, particularly on the relationship between Marx, Dewey and Hegel. However, Bernstein's position is mediated by an engagement with Gillian Rose. This encounter produces a different understanding of the line of thought coming out of Hegel and Marx. For Rose, dialectical philosophy does not result in coherence and redemption. It is the agonistic form of a kind of thought that attempts to grasp "the absolute", or the inter-relationship of different, but interlocking levels of social reality (Rose, 1981). In Rose's later work, ethics is related to the difficulty of remaining in this broken middle.

activism of the NWRO and the links between the new left and this late offshoot of the civil rights movement. In reconstructing the transport of ideas between activists from the SDS and anti-poverty militants we will argue that (at least for the former), John Dewey's understanding of creative democracy was a major point of reference. Dewey's engagement with themes around social recognition and alienation can be traced further back to the influence of Hegel on his work (and also his desire to develop a social ethics; a project that brings together Dewey and Jane Addams's philosophy of activism). The understanding of alienation and praxis put forward by this book thus borrows from a line of thought that moves from Hegel to Marx, through Arendt and (in its American manifestation) to Dewey. It is worth stressing at this stage that ideas of alienation and praxis are not linked to a vulgar operation of dialectics. Rather than an immanent pattern working to an inevitable conclusion, dialectics describes thought struggling with itself; or, perhaps more precisely, thought grasping itself through reflection on social action. At this level there is an overlap between Dewey's pragmatism, dialectics and contemporary understandings of intersectionality.

Poverty Law and Legal Activism does not seek to provide an elaborate philosophical defence of this thesis. Rather, our approach is based on the observation that certain philosophies overlap and can be *used* in similar ways. This argument takes us to the concept of intersectionality and to understandings of CRT, feminism and LatCrit. Intersectionality is rooted in "the social movement politics of the 1960s and 1970s" (Collins, 2012, p.443). It has a fundamentally dialectical organisation, focused on ideas of double-ness, hybridity and combination (without resolution). Our understanding of intersectionality relates back to the dialectical description of consciousness. Class, gender and race are fundamental to the positioning of selves within a socio-economic order. However, class, gender and race are open to creative re-appropriation that resists and redefines dominant norms. As Agnes Heller has pointed out, "[i]t is not obligatory for every person to receive the world" in the way that it is given (Heller, 1984, p.19).

Our understanding of praxis moves through this engagement with intersectionality to open onto an encounter with an idea of ethics. How do these ideas fit together? Praxis creates, in a hesitant way, the new. It does not simply reproduce a "pre-established order" – a "stable, limited, dead artefact" (Castoriadis, 2005, p.77). A great deal could be said about this theme, but we want to concentrate on praxis as a work on the self. As will be explained later in the book, self carries the meaning of character or personality. Given the complexities of this theme, the following brief statement from Castoriadis will have to suffice. We are not concerned with the "absolute Self" – the "monad" that retains its core through "contact with others" (Castoriadis, 2005, p.77). Nor are we particularly concerned with Foucauldian notions of the work on the self. We are concerned with the self as the "active" agent that "constantly reorganises" itself throughout its experiences (Castoriadis, 2002, p.106). Personality and self are therefore plastic; it is this plasticity that allows alienation to be instituted in the self, but also for the self to realise its alienation.[18]

The ethical charge of the theory of alienation is based on the assumption that life, one's values and the roles that one plays, are not givens. You can change. Arguably this concern was part of the ideologies of engagement animating new left groups and those working for civil rights. Certainly for the former, living differently tapped into notions of creative democracy (and earlier ideas of social ethics that stressed the importance of working with the poor as a way of coming to know the self and its limits). The theme that we want to concentrate on has been well described by Katz (1982): how does one "become" a poverty lawyer – especially when, as Sylvia Law has pointed out, lawyers "have a dangerous capacity to disguise political choices as technical givens" (Law, 1984, p.426)? How a professional life becomes dedicated to a way of "being and living" is a major theme of this book (Law, 1984, p.428).

The work on the self requires us to study a somewhat complicated relationship between "middle-class" radicals and those with whom they worked: the problem of the "white ally". It is important to stress that praxis is not based on some idea of "middle-class" leadership. A recurrent theme in philosophies of praxis, from Gramsci to Freire, is that praxis does not come out of teaching or the effect of gifted leaders or philosophers on the masses. Praxis is found in communal endeavour (Gramsci, 2005, pp.333–343; Freire, 2017, pp.35–43). Reconstructing the

18 A brief study of the etymologies of self, personality and character suggests interesting points of overlap between different but related concepts. The common sense meaning of all these terms relates to what is distinctive of an individual, but going deeper reveals some intriguing mysteries. Personality can be traced back to Greek words meaning *prosopon* or mask. Congruent Latin words relate to *persum* (hand or face) and *per se una*, or self-containing. There is also a relationship with *per-sonare*: to sound through. This complex of meaning suggests something "put on" that allows one to play a public role; a mask through which the actor's voice can be heard. The Latin sense of "self-containing" is a little strange in this context. If the general sense is one of *persona* or of a dramatic mask, then presumably what is "self-contained" is the actor playing a role. To be self-contained, then, is already to be double (Allport, 1937). Pushing this further, the idea of personality suggests a double-ness that is the public form of something that talks through a *persona*. The mask as a public face through which one talks is thus the way in which the actor appears to others. The face is thus not so much the otherness of the other, but the way in which one becomes visible (even if there is something behind the role or the public face that is held back). Character comes from an entirely different etymology that can be traced back to the sense of scratching, marking or scraping. Character and personality can be linked together to the extent that they describe a defining trait, even if this trait is plastic and capable of change. Self has a third line of derivation. Its earliest sense is that of a pronoun. At root, then, it is a grammatical term. Character and personality exist in and through language and reflection. We cannot pursue the philosophical or psychological meaning of these terms in any great detail. Indeed, we can but allude to the Hegelian subject and the ego or subject of psychoanalysis. Our working thesis is that all these words offer different insights into the forms of embodied social reflexivity that define us as thinking and acting beings.

myriad conversations and encounters between activists and poverty lawyers is impossible; the documents and texts used in the pages to come are mere proxies for countless intense, passionate meetings in streets, offices or on demonstrations, occupations and picket lines. Perhaps some talked about Marx, Ellul and Marcuse; undoubtedly others didn't. However, it is indeed interesting that one of the most important statements of a philosophy of praxis stresses that one's "personality" comes out of the "ensemble" of social relations into which one enters (Gramsci, 2005, pp.352–353). You are who you hang out with.

In the terms developed in this book, the ensemble of social relations that create and re-create one's personality (one's self and sense of values) is described as a form of "being with". "Being with" (*mitdasein*) is a term developed in Heidegger's *Being and Time* (1962). Contemporary understandings of *mitdasein* can be traced to the influential philosophy of Jean-Luc Nancy, and the beginnings of a kind of "left Heideggerianism".[19] Identifying broadly with this "tradition", this book offers a creative appropriation of "being with", reading the term through references to Martin Buber, Louis Wolcher, Ed Sparer and William Stringfellow. In short, "being with" is used to describe the open-ended work on the self that is occasioned when one does things with others.[20] This book does not seek to give a

19 In brutal summary, Martin Buber's work mediates between that of Hegel and Heidegger and provides one possible way forward for "left Heideggerianism". For the relationship between Buber and Hegel, see Hudson (2010) and Williams (2000). More precisely, Buber's I-thou relationship can be seen as a critical elaboration of Hegel's dialectic of recognition, and as a particularly interesting appropriation of Heidegger's world of "the they" where, one might say, passion is replaced with the statistics, gossip, common sense and the management of information (Heidegger, 1962, p.165). These themes are developed throughout this book. The jumping-off point is Heidegger's notion that the "information" which "comes in the night" is "nothing" (Heidegger, 1962, p.318). For Buber the encounter with the other cannot be understood as an exchange of information. In the they world there are no secrets worth knowing; the encounter places the secret in circulation (Buber, 1937, p.5). It is also worth noting at this point that there is no real engagement with Levinas in *Poverty Law and Legal Activism*. For Levinas's position on Buber, see Bernasconi and Wood (2002). There is only a brief discussion of Levinas in Chapter 9. Any proper defence of this position would have to stage an encounter between alterity, and a notion of negative dialectics. Suffice to say that the understanding of the dialectic of recognition presented in this book does not lead to a community of sameness, and ethics remains in the trauma of the self's relationship to the other. Developing this point in any detail would require an engagement with Levinas's reading of Hegel (see Bernasconi and Critchley (1991). And a turn to the idea of negative dialectics in the work of Gillian Rose: Moscow, Athens and Jerusalem. Whilst there is a sophisticated critical, legal literature on Levinas, there does not appear to have been a great deal of scholarship on the relationship between Levinas and Buber. But, see Wolcher (2016, 2005). Essential works for understanding Levinas's impact on critical legal theory are Douzinas (2000), Wolcher (2003), Diamantides (2007), Manderson (2007) and Stone (2016).

20 Being with – or *Mitdasein* – is an idea taken from Heidegger's *Being and Time* (1962) and elaborated by John-Luc Nancy (2000) and others. Within the terms of this book, "being with" is linked to an understanding of ethics. This can be elaborated as follows. *Mitdasein* tells us something about *Dasein*. *Dasein* is untranslatable, but means

full theoretical defence of this term; rather it sets out a provisional analysis of how "being with" might be used; in particular, a valence of "being with" that will be called "working with". The argument will take us to a certain understanding of the "white ally". In summary, the problematic of the "white ally" comes out of the politics of new left activism. Our critical approach takes us to questions of anxiety that re-frame the issues thrown up by the analysis of "the white ally". We will argue that these anxieties are associated with the call of conscience[21] and a practice of successful failure that informs the sensibility of the radical lawyer.[22]

something like "being there". *Dasein* tells us something about our social life. The "who" of *Dasein* is established through the way that *Dasein* lives. *Dasein*'s "who" can be defined by asserting that *Dasein* is "in every case I myself". However, the "who" takes us towards the problematic of the others amongst whom *Dasein* lives – an issue inseparable from sense, meaning and language. The "who" of *Dasein* is the "primordial" fact that being is always being with others. Primordial, in this context, describes the fundamental structure of being: a being with, or even a being between others. There is at least some relation between this notion of being with and the account of social recognition: we are because we are with others. This understanding enables others to appear as a matter of concern to *Dasein*, and, arguably, allows some notion of ethics to be appropriated from *Being and Time*. This argument is set out in more length in Gearey (2012, pp.20–21 and 150–167). It does not presuppose a true or authentic self (even though we use the latter term): only an anxiety that one can resist, or attempt to articulate as some kind of ethical relationship in the sense of attempting to justify one course of action rather than another. An action is authentic if it appears to the deliberating self that it is the best way of dealing with the demands of one's "being with".

21 This understanding is drawn from *Being and Time*, and there is a clear sense in which this analysis links with themes in understandings of alienation. Crudely, in the everyday world of the they, *Dasein* (or "us" to the extent that we question our Being) flees from itself, or fails to grasp itself. *Dasein* is anxious, and turns away from being in the world. Anxiety, as something in the world, has an enveloping quality, it is both "there" and "nowhere". This peculiar quality means that the world itself is that which *Dasein* is anxious about: perhaps it is the worldhood of the world that is the cause of anxiety; not so much "this" or "that" but the world in its entirety. Indeed, when anxiety dies down, one reflects that it was "really nothing" – but this "nothing" is the world itself (Heidegger, 1962, p.232). Anxiety discloses the world as world. But, although anxiety reveals the world, it also allows the world to slip away, and as such, produces a kind of singling out of anxious *Dasein*, which becomes "thrown back" on itself and can no longer fall away: "Anxiety individualises *Dasein* for its ownmost Being-in-the world." If *Dasein* is to understand or interpret this experience, then, it must seek to "project" itself into its own possibilities. So, the most essential revelation of anxiety for *Dasein* is its own "being possible" (Heidegger, 1962, p.232). *Dasein* is confronted with the need for "choosing itself and taking hold of itself". This is described as a movement away from the public and the they, into the "uncanniness" which also exists as a possible mode of being.

22 Admittedly, this runs the Heideggerian notion of being with into the Hegelian notion of *sittlichkeit*. In outline, the argument works in the following way. In *The Phenomenology of Spirit*, ethics is bound up with *sittlichkeit*. *Sittlichkeit* can be realised only when individual consciousness is united with all other consciousnesses and thus finds its own reality reflected back to itself, to the extent that it is possible to say "I see them as myself, myself as them" (Hegel, 1967, p.378). This is the "realm" of the "Social Order" (Hegel, 1967, p.375), or the "essential substance of individuals in their

This range of references – this play of different themes and philosophical methods – may seem somewhat idiosyncratic, but eclecticism is part of the legacy of the new left. In comparison to the somewhat austere modes of contemporary critical theory, the new left were happy to mix Marx with Dewey, Buber with Heidegger, Marcuse with Ellul; existentialism with phenomenology and Marxism.[23] But why return to this moment? The answer is that contemporary theory has lost sight of its inheritance from the new left. A related problem is the presentation of certain false choices between post-modernism (and identity politics; bad), and transcendental historical materialism (something like class politics; Marx and Lenin; good). This distinction is not sustainable. Perhaps the problems of contemporary theory have also come from the jettisoning of existentialism (or what is taken to be existentialism). This has made it difficult to understand why people act, and, indeed, how action is the communal making of the self. This is why themes drawn from contemporary black existentialist philosophy are so important for the thesis of this book.[24] Black existentialism inherits at least one of the spirits of the new left. So, CLS (and indeed critical legal theory, if such a thing exists) should perhaps be understood as essentially *bricolage*. This book, then, is an exercise in a way of thinking; a rhythm, an anxious amalgam of joyous despair.

Before we embark on these arguments, it is worth giving a definition of poverty. Poverty is a mobile concept. The definition of a term relates to the forces that seize it at any given time. Our concern is thus with the mutations of a definition

independent reality" realised most completely in the "life of a nation" (Hegel, 1967, p.376). In the nation, the individual feels at home because the community has been produced through the "actions of [citizens]". Common life is expressed through the "laws" of the community (Hegel, 1967, p.377). Law is not experienced as something up against which the individual finds himself. The laws give "expression" to the part of the individual in the social whole. The whole problem of ethics, for the critical legal traditions, is that this coherence of self, nation and law does not take place. Ethics become de-coupled from conventional norms – especially if these norms serve to deny being to certain groups within the national community. Thus, in a problematic inherited from the new left, self-understanding comes through activism in the cause of egalitarian politics. Our development of this problematic appropriates themes from Buber and Heidegger to articulate an ethics of encounters with others.

23 Within the context of the new left, Ellul's ideas fed into a wider sense of "social and spiritual alienation" that was articulated in terms of a Christian existentialism (Rossinow, 1994, p.319). Rossinow puts it well: "[e]xistentialism gave a name to feelings of meaninglessness and incoherence that some young white people sought to assuage, and that name was alienation. Christian existentialism searched for ways of replacing alienation with feelings of wholeness, authenticity and community" (Rossinow, 1994, p.330). Existentialism stressed the need for action, especially if action was risky and came out of a crisis of personal belief. Action was precisely the way in which one tested oneself and affirmed one's faith.

24 Consider, for instance, Gordon's notion of the situation at this point. The situation is the sense in which one is confronted by a "question" or "an inquiry" that raises a compelling matter of concern; a serious provocation of one's "being in the world" (Gordon, 1997, p.3). The readings of Heidegger and Buber are particularly influenced by Gordon's understanding of the situation.

over a period stretching roughly from the early 1960s to the present day.[25] We do not pretend to trace these mutations in great detail but we do try to follow the shifting political and economic circumstances in which the term is understood.

Poverty and activism

Moving from a discussion of philosophy to an engagement with poverty and political activism is only strange if one sees philosophy as primarily an academic concern. Quite to the contrary, questions of poverty and activism can only be understood if framed through philosophy. It is, though, necessary to engage with the historical context of anti-poverty activism. Our point, for the moment, is not so much poverty lawyering (this is examined in the next two chapters) but grass-roots organising around poverty and welfare. We will return to these issues in

25 The measurement of poverty is a complex and developing field of study. This note only gives some basic references. An important starting point is Michael Harrington's estimation that there were 40–50 million living at "levels" below "those necessary for human decency" (Harrington, 1962, p.4). Harrington was rather vague about the poverty line, arguing that it was "somewhere between $3,000 and $3,500 a year for an urban family of four" (Harrington, 1962, p.4). Dwight MacDonald's *New Yorker* review criticised Harrington's "impressionistic" use of statistics whilst praising the "moral" elements of his argument (MacDonald, 1963). MacDonald's point was that Harrington rightly identified the way in which manipulation of statistics could be used to conceal the reality of poverty, an argument similar to Rainwater's understanding of the techniques used to neutralise responses to human suffering (Rainwater, 1967). Mollie Orshansky, whose work developed the poverty thresholds used for government research, offered a similar reflection on poverty statistics: "unlike some other calculations, those relating to poverty have no intrinsic value of their own" (Orshansky, 1967, p.28). Harrington's book certainly gave a sense of the scale of the problem and refuted Galbraith's influential argument that poverty had more or less disappeared in the United States and existed only in isolated "pockets" or individual cases of personal misfortune or incapacity (Galbraith, 1958, p.62). Harrington also provided some sense of the composition of the population living in poverty – drawing attention to the rural and urban unemployed, the relationship between poverty and old age, and the scale of black poverty. We get a slightly different sense of the statistics from the 1962 report of the Conference on Economic Progress (CEP), a think tank committed to furthering public spending for economic growth. The CEP report estimated that in 1960 there were 77 million people living below the poverty line, which it set at between $4,000 for a family of any size, and $3,000 for an individual (Joint Economic Committee, 1959). Clearly, the extent and depth of poverty depends on how one defines the poverty line. Since 1964, the official poverty level has been set by the Department of Agriculture (West, 1981, pp.41–42). In 1964 this gave $3,220 a year for the minimum income of a family of four. On these figures, 34 million people were below the poverty line. Researchers for the NWRO argued that the Department of Agriculture figure for the poverty line was too low, as the median income was $7,500. The NWRO made use of figures based on publications from the US Bureau of Labor Statistics (BLS). The BLS lower standard budget referenced the annual cost of living and was used to produce the figure of $4,000 as the minimum income for a family of four to "live in dignity, meeting all its basic needs".

more detail in Chapter 5, but for the moment it is necessary to sketch out a general overview of the work of the NWRO and CWRO.

The later phases of the civil rights struggle were significant in articulating a politics of poverty. Before his assassination, Martin Luther King had urged the Southern Christian Leadership Conference to turn their attention to organising around economic justice. As the successes in achieving formal rights for African Americans did not appear to have made significant changes in their living standards, a movement for economic justice and poverty appeared to make sense. The Economic Bill of Rights gave shape to these arguments, and the mass protest camp in Washington lent it an organisational and social form. Despite the dispersal of Resurrection City, and the refusal of Congress to take up the Bill, the campaign did show that it was possible to sustain an alliance of poor people's movements (Jackson, 2007, pp.245–329; Mantler, 2013, pp.90–186).

How can we conceive of the political agency of the poor? Oscar Lewis noted that whilst Marxists like Castro and Fanon grasped the revolutionary potential of the lumpenproletariat, his own studies suggested that "radical ideology amongst [those of] low income" could not be taken for granted (Lewis, 1969, p.195). This issue relates to a central theme in new left thought: "the [driving] issue [for] the development of a radical movement [was] the forging of a new identity" (Frost, 2001, p.110). However, even those organisations like the NWRO who saw themselves as poor people's movements were aware that the term carried a sense of stigma that did not well serve purposes of political mobilisation. Certainly anti-poverty organisers found that those groups that they thought could be identified as poor were held together (and divided) by rival forms of identification around ethnicity, language or locality. Whatever interests people shared by virtue of their poverty were often not enough to produce viable long-term modes of political identification. For instance, the NWRO showed that it could organise black women on AFDC (Aid to Families with Dependent Children), but it was much less successful in appealing to unemployed or poor men.

Whatever the wisdom of using poverty as a political identifier, poverty has to be understood in the context of the restructuring of labour markets and the organisation of employment around divisions between gender and race. The operation of the welfare state is itself a significant factor in determining how these forces play themselves out. The interplay between these factors will be examined in Chapter 5, but some salient points can be outlined by means of an introduction.[26]

26 Although black women made up the majority of rank-and-file members of the NWRO, and some of the leadership, in percentage terms, the ethnic breakdown of those groups in poverty showed that black women were not the majority. That willingness of black women to organise and take part in social protest has been explained by different ethnic understandings of femininity, but the influences of the civil rights movement must also be taken into account. Commentators have suggested that whilst white women tended to remain somewhat isolated and to see poverty as a matter of personal shame, black women were much more willing to take part in political action. Organisers frequently attested to the importance of the social networks that women had

Ideologies of work and gender play a significant role. Scholars have drawn attention to the shifts in understandings of motherhood and work that went on throughout the middle part of the twentieth century. The terms of the Social Security Act of 1935 that related to AFDC were originally based on the "right" of women not to seek employment and to remain at home and look after their children. As women entered into the labour force in increasing numbers in the 1960 and 1970s, it became harder to sustain this distinction between waged work and state benefits. Concerns around the sexual morality of welfare mothers and the "failure" of the black family also fed into the sense in which AFDC provisions appeared to be responsible for the growth of welfare rolls and the social problems that were thought to stem from female-headed households. Scholars of poverty stress that work incentives pressured women to find precarious "low paying dead end jobs" and largely ignored issues of childcare and training (West, 1981, p.88).

A point of agreement between NWRO leader George Wiley, Frances Fox Piven and Richard Cloward was that dependency on welfare was a result of economic pressures. Asserting that all women should have the choice to work or to look after their families, NWRO activists saw that the real problem was to do with the paucity of jobs and the inadequate training provisions under the WIN (Work Incentive) programmes. However, NWRO ideologues did not believe that women on AFDC would become "economically mobile" even though the evidence suggested strong motivation and the desire to work (West, 1981, p.89). Beulah Sanders, chair of the NWRO in the early 1970s, stressed the difficult situation that women were put into: working in low-income jobs and paying for childcare. Hence, the only viable solution was a "right to life" or a minimum income guaranteed by the state. Minimum income arguments were supported by redefining the very idea of work. Even though it was unwaged, childcare was work – as important and meaningful as waged employment. As Johnnie Tillmon put it: "women's work is real work" – a right to minimum income would effectively be "wages for housework" – the productive task of "child raising and housekeeping" (West, 1981, p.91). We will return to these points in Chapter 5.

The Chicana Welfare Rights Organization

The CWRO is somewhat sidelined in histories of the welfare rights movement.[27] The movement was a response to particular patterns of stigmatisation and

created. Such networks not only provided social support but were useful for mobilising welfare mothers. The greater willingness of black women to engage in social protest may also be explained by broader ideologies of black power. Certainly, there was cooperation between the NWRO and local branches of the Black Panthers.

27 See Bermúdez (2014); Mantler (2013); and Garcia (2014). The CWRO needs to be understood in the context of the Chicano movement more generally. The Chicano movement can be seen as animated by energies similar to the black civil rights struggle. It had distinct regional foci. In California, efforts were made by figures such as Cesar Chavez and Dolores Huerta to organise farm workers into a trade union. In New

discrimination visited upon Chicana welfare mothers. A brief review of the literature on poverty amongst Latino/a communities suggests that there were distinct historical and cultural patterns that defined the cultural, legal and social experiences of these groups, and fed into the experiences of the CWRO. There was a growing sense of the need for political and communal organisation that would deal with problems of discrimination and marginalisation suffered by Mexican American and other Latino/a communities throughout the United States.[28]

Latino/a poverty is bound up with patterns of immigration from the Caribbean, Southern and Central America. It is arguably the case that immigration tends to be seen from the perspective of white immigration from Europe (Moran, 1997). Whilst white immigrants were "invited" to live and work in the United States, and expected to commit to its cultural norms, Latin immigration was different: for instance, in the first years between 1940 and 1950, the majority of Mexicans who came to America did so as either "temporary contract workers" or "without documents" (Moran, 1997, pp.117–118). Lacking the correct documents for citizenship, immigrants existed in a twilight world of informal work and limited opportunities. Despite relatively high levels of workforce participation, employment opportunities were concentrated in low-waged, precarious jobs (Reyes, 2004, pp.42–43).

These are, of course, snapshots of broad historical patterns. Experiences of Latino/a poverty are culturally differentiated. For example, the welcome shown to Cuban refugees in the 1960s contrasts with the hostility shown to those from Guatemala or El Salvador in the 1980s, and later, that of Mexicans in the 1990s (Iglesias and Valdes, 1998, p.29). Latino/a cultures are also further articulated around "hetero-patriarchal" norms that condition and affect ways in which poverty is experienced and perceived (Iglesias and Valdes, 1998, p.31). Thus, it would be wrong to homogenise Latino/a experiences of poverty and to ignore the role that class, as well as race, gender and sexual orientation play in the construction of particular experiences of poverty (Iglesias and Valdes, 1998; Hernández, 2000). Echoing Harrington, Latinos/as are "forgotten Americans" whose status as

Mexico, Reies Lopez Tijerina agitated for land grants. Out of the Crusade for Justice, a civil rights organisation based in Denver, Rudolfo "Corky" Gonzalez emerged as a main mover in Chicano student organisation and the militancy that fed into the east Los Angeles high school "blow outs". Another central feature of the Chicano movement was the formation of the La Raza Unida, active in Texas, California and Colorado. Inspired by black nationalism, this political party enjoyed considerable success in 1970–78, contesting municipal and gubernatorial elections and developing alongside its electoral campaigns, grass-roots movements and an increasingly revolutionary ideology. In the later phase of its operations, La Raza Unida made much of the notion of *Aztlán* – a semi-mythic notion of a homeland stretching between Mexico and Texas, and – for some – the justification for a new nation: *República del Norte*.

28 Certainly, from the perspective of the courts, cases such as *Hernandez v Texas* 347 U.S. 475 and *Mendez v Westminster* 161 F.2d 774; 1947 U.S. App, showed that Mexican Americans could be protected from discrimination by the law.

"outsiders" within the polity is, at least in part, defined by their poverty (Johnson, 1997, p.135).[29]

To study the Chicano/Chicana Movement is to examine a particular form of Latino/a radicalism. The Chicano/a community sees itself as an indigenous people of North America. The dispossession of La Raza from lands straddling what became the Mexican–US border, lends a specific quality to their politics, and, indeed, opened up cooperation between Chicano/a groups, and American Indian activists around poverty activism. Most notably black, Chicano/a and participants in the American Indian Movement (AIM) came together at the Alianza Conference in 1967, but failed to agree a coordinated programme of action (Mantler, 2013, p.67). Some stressed that poverty was primarily related to jobs and income, others saw poverty in terms of marginalised cultural heritage, land and fishing rights (Mantler, 2013, p.87). Given limitations of space, we cannot pursue an analysis of AIM, and our engagement with Latino/a struggles is, of necessity, rather narrowly engaged with the CWRO. The CWRO ultimately has to be seen as an expression of a particular form of political sensibility that, whilst sharing a great deal with black struggle, assumed its own forms and dynamic.[30]

Overview of the book

We now want to map the development of the book over the remaining nine chapters. Chapter 2 examines a number of intellectual traditions that were to influence lawyers involved in the war on poverty. One tradition that fed into later activism came out of the new left's adaptation of ideas whose origins can be found in the work of John Dewey and Jane Addams. At the heart of Dewey's and Addams's work are profound ethical questions about how one acts and how one is orientated to the world. In following these issues through we will sketch out a more general understanding of the character of the radical lawyer at odds with the disconnection between professional work, politics and life. Tracing these themes

29 Census data from 2014 show that Hispanic earnings remained well below the median. Other indicators of poverty and low-waged work, such as receipt of welfare benefits, food stamps and poor health insurance, also suggest that Hispanic groups experience poverty with greater frequency than white groups – although black poverty remains most marked in recent national figures. Nearly a quarter of the Hispanic population of the United States are living in poverty (with evidence that this is in-work poverty), with a strong correlation between poverty, disadvantage and those who were born outside the United States. Hispanic women figure disproportionately in the statistics: they earn much less than white women, and much less than Hispanic men. See www.pewhispanic.org/2016/04/19/statistical-portrait-of-hispanics-in-the-united-states/ and www.jec.senate.gov/public/_cache/files/96c9cbb5-d206-4dd5-acca-955748e97fd1/jec-hispanic-report-final.pdf.

30 Whilst the movement was briefly affiliated to the NWRO, and, indeed, both the NWRO and Chicano/a activists (as well as Puerto Rican and American Indian groups) participated in the Poor People's Campaign in 1968, a "rainbow alliance" was not forthcoming.

forward from Dewey and Addams, we will be particularly interested in the ideology of SDS activists involved in the Economic Research and Action Project (ERAP), and at a later point with the work of activists involved in the war on poverty. From the former, we will see how important practices of participatory democracy were in community organising work. From the latter we will be particularly concerned with how those lawyers and organisers linked with Movement for Youth (MFY) in New York City understood their work. Activists concentrated on the everyday challenges of working with the poor – activities requiring self-examination and personal transformation.

There is, however, a difficult question to ask about the nature of this radicalism. To what extent could white activists understand the reality of lives lived in poverty? This is the leading edge in an argument that addresses the problem of the "white ally".

We will use the idea of the "white ally" (a term so contested that it must appear in quotation marks) to explain certain tensions in new left politics. Taking some orientating points from Marcuse's critique of the new left, we will suggest that Martin Buber's philosophy of the encounter, also influential in activist circles, offers a way forward: an engagement with the difficulties of working with others towards a shared goal. However, Buber's philosophy needs to be supplemented with themes from Fanon, Du Bois and Newton. The problem of alliance across the poverty line and the colour line (to say nothing of the gender line) moves towards our understanding of the broken middle, a term that will be introduced in this chapter but not developed properly until the end of the book. The notion of the broken middle will be used in Chapters 9 and 10 to frame the sense of poverty law theory as a radical openness: a creative and anxious praxis that informs social justice projects and working with the poor.

Chapter 3 continues to trace the philosophies that fed into anti-poverty activism and extends the argument to the reception of these ideas by the Critical Legal Studies movement. The chapter begins with a recap of some key themes around SDS organising with particular reference to ERAP. The chapter follows these concerns into the work of Ed Sparer. Sparer drew on Hegel, Marx and Buber to provide one of the first consistent attempts to theorise a radical account of poverty law. Sparer also picked up on and developed themes relating to movement lawyering and ethical praxis. However, his ideas largely failed to enter into the mainstream of CLS. The end of the chapter is an exercise in reconstruction that reads back from later CRT scholarship and feminist accounts of alienation to sketch out a theory of social ethics that the crits failed to develop. This will be presented as an account of the consciousness of the poverty lawyer working with poor clients and open to social and personal transformation.

In Chapter 4, we turn from the crits to progressive constitutional theory and examine another split in poverty law theory. The chapter begins with Michelman's analysis of the 14th Amendment and his adaptation of Rawls's moral philosophy to provide a theory of constitutional welfare rights. We then turn to study Michelman's re-working of his position around republicanism. The final parts of the chapter weigh up Michelman in the light of more recent radical constitutional scholarship.

Chapter 5 returns to the crits and examines the way that we can creatively respond to the legacy of NWRO and CWRO militancy. We will work with three key terms: the social reproduction of capital, reification and poverty. These terms are rooted in the insights of the ClassCrit "turn to Marx" – a moment in which certain legacies of 1960s poverty activism re-enter contemporary critical thought. Linking Piven and Cloward's work with ideas of reification, the chapter argues that the NWRO can be understood as resting on a street philosophy of social recognition that rejects the reifying determinations of class, race and gender. We will read these themes into studies of Alicia Escalante, Johnnie Tillmon, Jeanette Washington and Beulah Sanders, leading figures in the welfare rights movement. Their work offers a principled and articulate response to the alienation and reification brought about by the social reproduction of capital. The chapter concludes with a final question: what did the NWRO mean for activist lawyers? Answering this question takes us to Chapter 6.

In Chapter 6, we engage with the work of William Stringfellow, and themes of vocation, conscience and freedom. These ideas are central to the fundamental problematic of the engaged lawyer involved in social struggles. We propose to follow Sparer's promptings and to open a dialogue between Buber and Stringfellow. This raises questions about Heidegger's influence. In Stringfellow's writing we can find the outline of an account of "being with" or caring for the fate of the poor. We will see that Stringfellow's concept of "being with" the poor is rooted in his Christian faith. However, whilst one can aid and sympathise with others, one cannot stand in the other's place. The question thematised by Stringfellow and performed through "being with" is thus an assumption of responsibility from within radical freedom. One does not need to respond, to work with the poor or be alongside them. "Being with" the poor is a path that is chosen as a vocation, a calling of conscience. To answer the call of conscience, one must be involved in the travails of everyday life, even if the proximity to poverty occasions a certain anxiety about one's own commitment and motivation.

Elaborating this theme takes us to the new poverty law scholarship in Chapter 7. Most critical accounts of the new poverty scholarship stress its concern with the power relationship between lawyer and client. There is something about the nature of poverty law that means the lawyer's relationship with his/her client is distinct from that of corporate, commercial or business relationships. As White has pointed out, the plaintiffs in celebrated welfare cases rarely met the lawyers who represented them once the depositions had been filed (White, 1987, p.536). However, this problematic conceals another way in which the new poverty law can be understood. Our approach stresses the way in which the new poverty law scholarship can be read as inheriting and carrying forward an ethics of anxiety.

In Chapter 8, we will go on to show how the ethics of anxiety are bound up with a legacy of the new left and CLS that cast a long shadow over law and activism in the decades between 1980 and 2017. The final parts of Chapter 8 argue that LatCrit is the inheritor of new left ideas on poverty, democracy and praxis. This is precisely why LatCrit offers such an important perspective on critical legal theory. Praxis is understood as a form of intellectual cooperation with "activists" and other "outside scholars" (Valdes, 1999, p.102). But praxis is also an orientation to LatCrit's own positioning in the critical legal tradition. LatCrit stresses that critical legal theory is a work in progress; a self-critical reworking of the jurisprudential tradition, as well as an investigation of its own identity. A long way from a form of identity politics, LatCrit eschews essentialisms and concentrates attention on the play of forces that define phenomena, and, indeed, can bring about social change. Sylvia Law put it well: "legal doctrines" are changed only through "larger change in social organization and consciousness" (Law, 1984, p.426). In bringing these themes together, we hope to suggest a somewhat different way in which we can understand the future of critical legal theory.

Chapters 9 and 10 seek to show how the concept of "being with" the poor relates to the sensibility of the radical lawyer. To describe this radical openness we will make use of Rose's "concept" of the broken middle. The work of the broken middle presupposes no final answers, fixed identities or final resolution of its informing tensions. The broken middle of poverty law gives onto the anxious practice of critical legal theory.

Chapter 2

Something happening

Activism and the problem of the "white ally"

> We begin now. Our philosophy is redemptive.
>
> (Michael Harrington, "Review of Martin Buber's Paths in Utopia", *The Catholic Worker*, 1951)

> When racism in all of us is finally out and gone ...
>
> (Ralph Chaplin, "Solidarity Forever", 1915)

> So we've got to stick together in fine or dirty weather.
>
> (Joe Hill, "Where the Fraser River Runs", 1912)

Introduction

Borrowings from diverse traditions fed into the efforts of the new left to define their work as community organisers. Dewey's social ethics provided important orientating points, as did the experiences of the civil rights struggle. These ideas went on to influence activists engaged in the war on poverty, and intensified certain issues. How could white activists understand experiences of alienation and discrimination? Did the belief in democratic participation lack a proper engagement with the reality of life in poverty ghettos? These questions defined the figure of the "white ally" (Boyd, 2015; Brown, 2002; Kendall, 2013). To frame these themes, we will refer to Marcuse's account of the new left. Working through Marcuse will take us to another important reference point: Martin Buber's philosophy of the encounter. For Buber, the encounter with another has the potential to utterly transform the self. Reading Buber alongside Fanon and Newton will allow us to address a world where racism destroys the dialectic of social recognition (Buber, 1937, p.43). The latter parts of this chapter go on to describe the primordial difficulties of working alongside others in mutual respect. We hope to sketch out the term of a creative anxiety that re-inscribes the "white ally" in the problematic of commitment to a cause that crosses the colour line and the poverty line: a creative, democratic struggle against poverty and degradation.

Take a step into America

New left understandings of alienation, poverty and ethics can be traced back to John Dewey and a particular elaboration of social ethics in the settlement house movement. We will go into this relationship in much more detail in Chapter 9. The main issue that we address in this section relates to the difficulties in holding together our central thesis.

In a piece written in 1939, Dewey articulated a creative notion of democracy. His argument begins with a distinction between the historical definition of the term and the present "moral" understanding of democracy opened up by the poverty of the Great Depression (Dewey, 1981, p.225). A compelling theory of democracy must have at its core a response to the withering of human life in poverty. To this end, democracy must go beyond what happens in the polls in "Washington … or some other state capital" and become a "habit of thinking" about "political duties" (Dewey, 1981, p.226). Democracy is thus "a way of life". Conceiving of democracy in this way is "hardpan" (Dewey, 1981, p.226). Dewey is in pursuit of a way of living that defines character. What, we might ask, is character, and how does it relate to the theory of social recognition outlined above? Four themes interlock.

Firstly, the democratic character is founded on the recognition of an underlying commonality that is "exhibited in every human being irrespective of race, color, sex, birth and family, of material or cultural wealth" (Dewey, 1981, p.226). Democratic citizens must recognise each other as of equal value and worth. If the democratic sensibility is anything it is thus openness to this experience, a way of life "controlled by personal faith in personal day-by-day working together with others" (Dewey, 1981, p.227). The stress is on working with others as work on the self is a social activity. This does not, of course, resolve difference into similarity. Working with others gives "differences a chance to show themselves". Being with different people refines "one's own life-experience" (Dewey, 1981, p.228). Dewey is thus talking about a spirit or sensibility. He denounces "[i]ntolerance, abuse, calling of names" as this turns "differences of race, color, wealth or degree of culture" into divisions that are "treason" to the animus of the "being with" of democracy (Dewey, 1981, p.228).

Secondly, it was important to discover what creative democracy means. Dewey uses the word "faith" (Dewey, 1981, p.227). He evokes a "Belief in the Common Man", but the common man will only appear if the conditions are right. The right conditions are "consultation … conference … persuasion [and] discussion, in [the] formation of public opinion" (Dewey, 1981, p.227). Underlying the right conditions for creative democracy are "effective guarantees of free inquiry, free assembly and free communication". Dewey has in mind "free gatherings of neighbors on the street corner" and "gatherings of friends in the living rooms of houses and apartments to converse freely with one another" (Dewey, 1981, p.227). Democratic commonality is thus allergic to the "barriers that divide human beings into sets and cliques". The democratic spirit moves between boundaries, travels freely, talks with its equals. Talk is the genuine token of its openness to all men and women (Dewey, 1981, p.227).

Thirdly, we can say that this complex of democratic recognition is rooted in an ethical praxis. Ethical praxis takes as a "moral commonplace" the understanding that a relationship changes one's perspective on the world and on one's self. Dewey, writing with Tufts, provided a clear statement of the orientating framework of this ethics: "the good for any man is that in which the welfare of others counts as much as his own" (Dewey and Tufts, 1908, p.315). However, the good cannot be defined outside of contexts of cooperation, mutual endeavour and persistence where people work towards the realisation of the good. The good might be difficult to determine in advance but it is still possible to provide a general outline of its form. The good relates to what we would call positive freedom: securing to all citizens a "standard of living" that "makes possible a full moral life" (Dewey and Tufts, 1908, p.496). To the extent that we can talk of the good as happiness, it is the realisation of a decent social way of holding wealth to enable the general development of personality. This can be understood as a growing awareness of one's own power as it is the realisation that the end of social life is meeting the expectations and requirements of others. When one works for the ends of others, one develops one's own sense of self. This development of the self is inconsistent with endemic poverty and to the torpor and idleness that perverts the mind and destroys the affections. If my good is related to your good then a social vision of the good must take on the causes of poverty. A democratic sensibility must object profoundly to the poverty of others and struggle against it.

Fourthly, Jane Addams made a major contribution to this articulation of social ethics. From Addams we want to take a notion of "conviction" and "genuine emotion" that expresses itself as a feeling of the disconnection that comes with privilege. A particular social training leads people into "cultivated unnourished, oversensitive lives" (Addams, 1912, pp.116–117). Social differentiation leaves people both physically and emotionally separated from each other: "shut off from common labor ... which ... is a great source of moral and physical health" (Addams, 1912, pp.116–117). This labour is a source of health or well-being because it addresses an internal split, an inner unhappiness: "a lack of coördination between thought and action" (Addams, 1912, pp.116–117). Recovery of the self comes through work on the self with others. Addams, like Dewey, locates ethics in a praxis and a vision of the good. She asserts that through "common intercourse" we can ensure that the good can be secured in "common life" (Addams, 1912, pp.116–117).

Note that Addams sees this "subjective pressure" towards work with others as "primordial" (Addams, 1912, pp.116–117). Quite strangely the immediacy of the primordial in social engagement with others is lost once Addams starts to speak of "ancestral memories" (Addams, 1912, pp.116–117). We will try to reclaim the notion of the primordial and the pre-political not as "the life of the race" but through the idea of connection with others. This is perhaps not just "sympathy" but the "longing" for a "fuller life" – "Intimations of Immortality" – that as yet lacks its "ode" (Addams, 1912, pp.116–117). We will follow these traces and pre-political understandings of social life into the term "being with" and argue that the "ode" has been written; or rather, a poem by William Carlos Williams can be understood as the text of social ethics that Addams imagined. However, this is to run forward to Chapter 6. The remainder of this chapter shows how it might be possible to carry forward the legacy of social ethics.

Working with the poor

The new left committed itself to a kind of experiential politics that had its immediate roots in the work of the Student Nonviolent Coordinating Committee (SNCC) amongst the black poor in the southern states of America. The reception of these ideas was mediated by the League for Industrial Democracy (LID) of which John Dewey had been president. Students for a Democratic Society (SDS) emerged from LID.[1] Those involved in reflection on SDS projects tended to think in terms of social ethics and the pragmatic idea of "what works". SDS activists also showed a commitment to participatory democracy, as the SDS slogan "let the people decide" suggests. The basic approach of SDS strategy was to "convince people that the search for orientating theories and the creation of human values is a complex but worthwhile" task (SDS, 1968, p.29). The SDS thus opposed "the depersonalisation that reduces human beings to the status of things" (SDS, 1968, p.29). These ideas (in particular, concepts of alienation and reification) were themselves intensified by a later phase of new left social action.

1 Following Gosse (2005), the new left as a whole can be seen as "a confrontation with the existing political, social, and cultural consensus in American life during the 1950s" (Gosse, 2005, p.5). Particularly influential were groups like the SNCC and the role that they played in voter registration and civil rights campaigns. The Free Speech Movement active from 1964/65 created a focus for radical politics at the University of California, Berkeley. The primary targets of activism were "arbitrary restrictions on student political expression" (Flacks, 1966, p.401). Events in Berkeley served as an inspiration for the founders of the SDS. The SDS was formed in 1960, and *The Port Huron Statement*, which was to become its manifesto, published in 1962. The SDS defined itself through the "face to face" of participatory democracy (Breines, 1989; Sale, 1973; Gitlin, 1993). *The Port Huron Statement* links the foundation of the SDS to "the establishment of a democracy of individual participation, governed by two central aims: that the individual share in those social decisions determining the quality and direction of his life" and, that "independence" and "common participation" are brought together. Participatory democracy is thus central to complex ways of living and acting that perform the "value" of the human being. The "system" is denounced precisely for being "dehumanizing" (see Greg Calvert, in *White America: Liberal Conscience v Radical Conscience*, www.sds-1960s.org/Calvert-WhiteAmerica.pdf). Significant points of both fracture and identity in the new left existed between black and white radicals. The Black Panthers can be understood as a new left organisation, but see Wilson (in Laerow and Williams, 2006). Wilson points out that there were "two movements on the left" and they largely failed to "find enough common ground" to work together (Wilson, 2006, p.193).

In 1963, the SDS leadership announced a controversial initiative. The Economic Research and Action Project (ERAP) was an ambitious attempt to organise the poor in the ghettos of cities such as Chicago, Cleveland, Newark and Boston. The dynamic of this theme appears if we appreciate that ERAP was conceived as a "movement of all the poor" (Wittman and Hayden, 1963, p.27). ERAP organisers stressed that "moral reconstruction" could be found in "cooperation" between middle-class activists and the white poor. The "forms" that this cooperation would take could not be anticipated as they would come out of "doing". It was precisely this collaborative, exploratory form of social work that would create the "social basis for democratic America" (Wittman and Hayden, 1963, p.26).

Consider the pamphlet *Take a Step into America*. This SDS text describes a process of education outside the law school and the university that was markedly "different from social work school courses and OEO [Office of Economic Opportunity] training manuals". The pamphlet stresses that the experience of working with and for the poor is a slow process "filled with personal hurts". It goes on in slightly different terms to present poverty work as a way of:

> coming aware … understanding and knowing of people known in every bar on the Avenue: guys who know most people on most corners, key hustlers in many scenes; the matriarch in a group of buildings on a block … what all-night restaurants of blue vinyl that catch a hodge-podge of comers on main thoroughfares are all about, as well as those restaurants with steamed windows, single brand music jukeboxes, and home cooked-specialists whose customer, waitress and owner all know one another, and if you don't, at least it reminds you of the place you hung out in your home town.
>
> (SDS, 1968, pp.11–12)

The poetic register of this writing immediately stands out. It is an attempt to write against alienation. If not reminiscent of Kerouac, it has something of a beat sensibility in its celebration of "small town[s]" where everyone knows each other. The writer is thrown back on his/her own memories, less an outsider than a participant. Do we not find here something of the innocence and dynamism of the movement? The text celebrates the joy to be found in making connections and the energies that come from crossing social boundaries, discovering or inventing a new language that can give voice to personal and social experience:

> In all our organizing work, in slums and on campuses, we aim to involve everyone equally and openly in the making of decisions, to break down social machines that bestow power undemocratically and withhold it in the same sorry way … for the only power available to any of us is the power of good sense and humanity.
>
> (Rothstein, 1965, no page numbers)

This passage is about empowering people to make their own decisions. The author evokes a kind of powerless power – a mode of association based on the assertion of the worth of the individual:

> Today, an ERAP community union meeting is probably the only institution in the world where a destitute alcoholic can stand up and give a lecture, occasionally brilliant but usually incoherent, on political strategy and be listened to with complete respect.
>
> (Rothstein, 1965, no page numbers)

The peculiar rationality of ERAP expresses itself in this desire to hear all people speak, and to value their words. It is a form of anti-organisation that avoids the deadening effect of bureaucracy and hierarchy: "[t]he power of good sense" aims at authentic human "relatedness" (Rothstein, 1965, no page numbers). Borrowing from the rhetoric and practices of the SNCC, "relatedness" took the name the "beloved community", evoking the idea of black and white Americans working together in difficult and dangerous circumstances in a movement dedicated to ending racial discrimination and, in the context of ERAP, contending with the human cost of poverty.

Although we cannot establish in detail the precise relationship between ERAP and those who became involved in the war on poverty, it is possible to note a number of close associations between SDS ideas and themes that began to figure in the legal literature when President Lyndon B. Johnson's initiative was rolled out. Lawyers involved with the war on poverty saw poverty as an attack on "human values" (Brager and Purcell, 1967, p.297).[2] Activists were not so much concerned with statistics and figures as human problems. They did not identify with social workers and other government agents (dismissively dubbed poverty pimps), but with the poor themselves.

2 President Johnson's war on poverty was announced in 1964. A number of currents of thought fed into this major federal initiative. Johnson picked up on and continued policies of Kennedy's administration. The "rediscovery" of poverty in the 1950s had been turned into a political issue by Democratic senators such as Paul H. Douglas and Hubert Humphrey who objected to the more limited approach of Eisenhower's government (Brauer, 1982, pp.98–101). When Kennedy took office it appeared that America was losing ground to the Soviet Union. Social and economic problems had been ignored. During Kennedy's first two years in office, poverty and unemployment were not priorities. There was, however, a growing awareness that government action would be necessary. Whether or not one accepts Moynihan's assertion that the war on poverty was driven by social scientists, sociologists and economists stressed the impact of poverty on social breakdown and slowing productivity. Government research began to uncover evidence that problems were more deep seated than otherwise suspected. Official explanations began to make use of the "culture of poverty" thesis that drew attention to the pervasive and generational effects of deprivation. Human capital theory backed up these findings and supported arguments that the poor were to be rehabilitated and made economically productive. The effects of the civil rights struggle in the South and Kennedy's conversion to civil rights legislation were also important factors.

Rather than thinking in terms of a culture of poverty, ideas inherited from organisers and activists tended to present poverty as alienating the poor from participation in society. The poor were people in intolerable situations, coping as best they could.

Stigmatised as "less than" proper citizens, the poor were subject to what tenBroek called a parallel legal system. Sylvia Law, then a law student working for MFY and soon to be involved in *Goldberg v Kelly* (missing Woodstock to prepare a brief in "the dreadful stacks of Columbia Law School"), later furthered this analysis, describing "the pervasive meanness and incompetency" of welfare bureaucracy (Law, 1983, pp.805, 807). The welfare system itself was the problem. Cahn and Cahn wrote that poor "[p]eople are faced with a scale of events and new powers that dwarf them ... a world in which impersonal forces operate over which they have no control – a vast complex of communal regulations that impinge on their lives ..."[3] Poverty crippled character with the "mentality of despair, apathy, passivity, and the vulnerability to exploitation, harassment and manipulation" (Cahn and Cahn, 1964, p.1322).[4]

The activism of radical lawyers was rooted in a response to the disabling clientistic relationships between the welfare authorities and the poor. The poor had to be helped to organise against their poverty and to break out of "a self-perpetuating system of dependency and dehumanization" (Brager and Purcell, 1967, p.78). Working in poor neighbourhoods, poverty lawyers placed themselves "at the disposal of a community" (Cahn and Cahn, 1964, p.1333), advocating, as

3 Sir George Haines, quoted in Zucker (1964, p.333).

4 Brager and Purcell published an essay that stressed that "public welfare" is "the right to life – the right of an American citizen to live and not to die because of starvation or lack of housing, clothing or medical care ... [it] means the right to life, the right not to die, the right not to be a beggar". Welfare is linked to the very idea of American values: "[i]t was for the preservation of human values that our democratic nation was founded, and only by the preservation of human values can it survive" (Brager and Purcell, 1964, p.291). These sentiments are not far from Reich's seminal essay on property rights. Reich argued that property marks the "troubled boundary between the individual man and the state" (Reich, 1964, p.733), and, in so determining this boundary, property has to be understood as a "particular portion of well-being" that actually defines the individual. Reich offers a subtle re-theorisation of central themes in political and legal theory. How is individuality possible under the government of the administrative state – a giant "syphon" that sucks in taxes and re-distributes them as "money, benefits, services, contracts, franchises and licences"? What claims can an individual make over such largesse when they appear to be replacing "traditional forms of wealth held as private property"? Most importantly, Reich sees "unemployment insurance" as a species of the new property. Comparing the worth of a job with the status of being unemployed, Reich observed that "for the jobless, their status as governmentally assisted or insured persons may be the main source of subsistence" (Reich, 1964, p.738). He went on to argue a case for welfare rights: "[t]he aim of [welfare] benefits is to preserve the self-sufficiency of the individual, to rehabilitate him where necessary, and to allow him to be a valuable member of a family and a community" (Reich, 1964, pp.785–786). We will pursue these themes into Michelman's writing in Chapter 4.

Clinton Bamberger, head of the OEO's Legal Services Program put it, not for the "status quo" but for "change" (Bellow, 1996, p.30).[5]

For activist lawyers, the movement expressed the possibility that social degradation could be repaired through social action and political mobilisation. This approach appeared to work. One organiser, drafted from the ranks of the poor, spoke in the following terms about her experiences:

> I learned I am somebody. Welfare Rights meant a right to life – it freed me from emotional slavery. I am a person you can't push aside; I have a right to be. Welfare Rights showed me that my counterparts are all around; knowing this, I no longer feel alone. Welfare Rights lives – me and other people are still active, struggling for a better life.
>
> (Burson, cited in Mobilization for Youth, 1966)

Note the way in which "Welfare Rights" are talked about in a manner that goes well beyond conventional jurisprudential understandings. Rights are located in a struggle for social recognition. If this corresponds with the notion of the "dignity and worth" of those in "slum communities", then rights are an expression of the worth of individuals. We could thus say that the struggle for rights has an ethical dimension. What is at stake is a right to be – the right to be considered a human being – a recognition that a minimally decent human life requires certain resources.

For the lawyers involved, the response to the plight of one's fellows is an immediate, visceral issue and a struggle for the meaning of law. Organisers and activists saw their work with the poor as an exercise in creative or participatory democracy and as an antidote to alienation.[6] However, we need to appreciate that

5 Fiscal limits, political opposition and ideological commitments to a culture of opportunity meant that poverty could not be addressed through transfers of wealth or redistributive policies. Government planning thus drew on the experience of those involved in initiatives on delinquency and other, earlier programmes. Anti-poverty projects were to be based on encouraging community activism and popular motivation. Government funding would be focused on "service orientated, coordinated efforts" in places where the poor were concentrated (Brauer, 1982, p.109). After Kennedy's assassination, misgivings about the nature and direction of anti-poverty initiatives were put aside as Johnson bullishly announced a war on poverty – a call to idealism and traditions that went back to the New Deal (Brauer, 1982, p.113). Sargent Shriver was given responsibility for overseeing operations and made director of the newly created Office for Economic Opportunity. In the celebrated words of the Equal Opportunities Act, the war on poverty would require the "maximum feasible participation" of poor people in the campaigns ahead. Federal initiatives sought to "utilize and mobilize the entire power structure of the community to attack such evils as slum housing, illusory social welfare services, credit or other business abuses, and lack of responsiveness by elected and appointed officials" (Cahn and Cahn, 1964, p.1323).

6 It was observed that a noted left-wing journal of the time had a "special type writer" with "alienation stamped on every key" (Feuerlicht, 1978, p.6). Feuerlicht also refers to Feur's argument that alienation provides "the basis for student movements" (Feur,

the reality of anti-poverty activism was not as straightforward as our arguments above might suggest. Contemporary scholars have been critical of the way in which radical lawyers sought to dominate grass-roots organisations and direct the welfare rights struggle (West, 1981, pp.24, 41, 77, 80, 194–195; Kornbluh, 2007, pp.179, 153–154; Nadasen, 2005, pp.129, 150, 213, 87–88). These criticisms can be related to other points about the politics of the SDS. Historians have stressed that the SDS actually failed to articulate the concepts that were so central to their identity; in particular, to the way in which participatory politics often failed (Young, 1977, pp.8–24; Evans, 1980, pp.149–154). Meetings were dominated by cliques or the most vocal members of a group. Feminist scholarship has drawn particular attention to the way in which the anti-organisation of the SDS effectively led to the dominance of faction and personality – problems that were appreciated by some at the time.[7] Behind the rhetoric of participation lay unexplored assumptions and practices that marginalised women (Breines, 1988, pp.146–153; Evans, 1980, pp.220–221; Trimberger, 1979, pp.431–450).

So, building the beloved community was not easy. As well as critical examination of the relationships between men and women,[8] radical practice required confrontation with "white skin privilege" (a term credited to Theodore "Ted" Allen).[9] Whilst the contemporary debates around Noel Ignatiev and Ted Allen's pamphlet *White Blindspots* (1969) certainly anticipated many contemporary debates on the intersectionality of race, class and gender, it was also specific to the politics of the period.[10] The key point is that the new left's failure to deal properly with these issues, despite the sincerity of their self-questioning, created profound difficulties (Barber, 2006, p.225).

From this perspective, should we consider the SDS a failure? This would seem a rather harsh conclusion. For all the SDS evasions on matters of race, class and

1969, p.503). Also influential in contributing to discussions of alienation were C. Wright Mills (1958) and Kaufman (1973). Also, see Seeman (1961, pp.753–758). Seeman enumerates four categories of alienation: "powerlessness, meaninglessness, isolation, self-estrangement." Rotenstreich offers an alternative categorisation. Alienation relates to two forms of psychic phenomena: "the loss of personal identity"; and "loneliness, self-isolation from, or loss of contact with, others and society, as well as the replacement of emotional reactions and relations by a callous, mechanical attitude" (Rotenstreich, 1989, p.78). However, a "negative evaluation of alienation" is "not warranted" as "one aspect" of alienation "is concomitant with the very position of man in the world" (Rotenstreich, 1989, p.103). Rotenstreich is working with a broadly Hegelian understanding of the term. Alienation is "the rhythm of human existence" (Rotenstreich, 1989, p.86), bound up with "acts of identification" and the "reflexivity" of consciousness (Rotenstreich, 1989, p.89). See also Bell (1976, pp.189–191).

7 Casey Hayden and Mary King, *Sex and Caste*, www.historyisaweapon.com/defcon1/sexcaste.html

8 We return to this point in Chapter 3.

9 See Allen (1994, 1997).

10 There were particular tensions between the SDS and the Progressive Labor Party around the "correct line" on student activism, working-class politics, and the relationships with the Black Panthers, the Young Lords, and other radical nationalist groups.

gender, a contemporary reader of ERAP publications does get the impression that the young men and women who committed themselves to organising in the ghettos were serious about their activities and the challenges they faced.[11] We will take this as a token of the commitment to living differently. In order to get any real purchase on these questions, it is necessary to examine in a little more detail the social alienation against which both the SDS and anti-poverty militants were struggling.

Marcuse provided a useful account of the general situation of new left thinking – poised between the social ethics tradition, and something more; struggling to understand its own contradictions. For Marcuse, SDS activists and community organisers were in search of those moments of vision when exploitation, loneliness or social disconnection became visible. Activism was a praxis, an attempt to articulate forms, ways of acting that would make for "the conscious transcendence of … alienated existence" (Marcuse, 1964, p.63), and show how human beings could be liberated from "toil and poverty" (Marcuse, 1964, p.8). Precisely because the working class could not be relied upon to take up the revolutionary struggle, it was necessary to look to a "great refusal" from "the substratum of outcasts and outsiders, the exploited and persecuted of other races and other colours, the unemployed and the unemployable" (Marcuse, 1964, p.260).

Whilst there are problems with Marcuse's analysis, he did realise (perhaps more than C. Wright Mills) that there was no settled analytical language to get at the "living, human negation" of the system (Marcuse, 2005, p.64). He sensed that the shift from the class-based analysis of the old left, to the revolutionary potential of the "outsider" was a "preparation" for a much broader struggle that would go on to create new forms of radicalism. In grasping the "real nightmare" for "classical" Marxists, Marcuse named one part of the problem with which we are trying to come to terms (Marcuse, 2005, p.56). The vocabulary of classical Marxism lacked the analytical terms to describe the contradictions of social ethics. The idea of a "great refusal" had some purchase, but, aside from identifying a radical potential in the lumpenproletariat, Marcuse does not close in on the real tensions that resulted from educated middle-class radicals committing themselves to welfare struggles.

If we want to use Deweyan notions of commonality, and to mobilise Addams's practice of crossing class divisions in order to promote creative democratic practices, then it is essential to engage with the fraught reality of creating the beloved community. We will follow a response to this problem that drew on the work of the Jewish philosopher and theologian, Martin Buber. Buber presents the social encounter as a tense and anxious moment. People meeting together may be able to address each other as "thou". Thou is the token of a singular humanity that

11 See, for instance, "Chester PA: A Case Study in Community Organization"; "Organizing Poor Whites" and "Chicago: Organizing the Unemployed". Published originally in *New Left Notes*, these papers are available in the online SDS archive at www.sds-1960s.org/documents.htm.

comes out of mutual respect. Whilst Buber is some way from Dewey, the possible relationships between these two different traditions in ethical thought does present itself. In order to set up an engagement between different traditions of ethical thought, and, indeed, to pick up on other contemporary ideas that are still useful, it is important to retain something of Marx. Ethics has to take account of the structural, material inequalities that make for social alienation. In the next sections we will argue that bringing together themes from black Marxism and Buber provide a necessary engagement with social recognition and the problem of the "white ally".

Black Marxism and the problem of the "white ally"

How, then, can we talk meaningfully of social encounters when recognition has to take place across the poverty line and the colour line? We can clearly see how the problematic of recognition operates if we look briefly at Fanon's reading of Hegel, and then trace this theme into black radical thought. The basic form of discrimination is the reduction of another being to the status of "an object in the midst of other objects" (Fanon, 1986, p.109). One experiences one's being through the recognition of others. If others withdraw that recognition one ceases to exist as a subject. The struggle for recognition is the struggle against non-being. This account of consciousness shows how resistance to racism emerges from racism itself. The experience of being an object of discrimination has the potential to turn the object back into a subject. For Fanon, this is the coming into being of a "black consciousness" (Fanon, 1986, p.109). Black consciousness is not imposed – it is worked towards through struggle.

Fanon's philosophy of struggle gives a radical turn to the notion of praxis that we studied in relation to social ethics. We will see that especially for black poverty activists the complex of self-interpretation and social action defined a form of thought and action. We will read some passages from Huey P. Newton's autobiography, *Revolutionary Suicide*, as it gives a good sense of how these ideas went into action. Newton is writing about how one confronts alienation. How is it possible to engage with the ways in which you have been demeaned, dehumanised and degraded? These questions are at the heart of Newton's desire to bring together "street philosophy" and "academic work" (Newton, 1973, p.76). The answers that Newton provides pull in themes from Marxism and existentialism. Newton's draft of the Black Panther Party (BPP) manifesto makes this absolutely clear. The concept of "the community" replaces the pejorative and loaded term "ghetto". The demand for "full employment" or a "guaranteed income" is very similar to that of the NWRO, but the BPP's conclusions are unashamedly revolutionary (Newton, 1973, p.76).

Newton's arguments become clearer still if they are located in contemporary understandings of the ghetto. We can borrow from some earlier scholarship on black political economy (Tabb, 1971). One of the most striking and productive approaches saw the ghetto as an internal colony of the United States. The ghetto as internal colony was both physically and geographically separated from the sites of national economic power but integrated into – and dependent upon – networks of political and economic power. This thinking drew on heterodox development economics, but also on black nationalism and its concerns with radical solutions to black poverty. Poverty in the internal colony is an effect of the ghetto's structural location: Malcolm X's "vicious cycle of economic, intellectual, social, and political death".[12] Black political economy, and Malcolm X's writings, identified the pathologies of an economic system in which ghettoisation provided a means for the control and exploitation of black labour. The nation-state and national government are part of this complex. It is in their interest to sustain poverty and low-waged work. This feeds into a political radicalism that links racialised capitalism to poverty.

Newton and the Black Panthers produced an understanding of race in ideological terms. Consider the frequent failure of antidiscrimination law to achieve substantive change. The necessary redistribution of wealth is prevented by a "white" perception that "they" would lose out to black interests. Race, in other words, unites whites across boundaries of class or gender. Ideology, in this sense, operates to create a hegemony of interests. For example, it is interesting that the labour unions primarily composed of immigrant white workers, excluded black workers as a means of displaying their compatibility with "the mainstream of American society" (Crenshaw et al., 1995, p.114). The removal of the more obvious aspects of discrimination does not mean that this hegemony has been broken. This takes us to W.E.B. Du Bois. Du Bois wanted to understand how power creates representations of the world that become the dominant interpretations of "reality". As Gordon stresses, Du Bois was driving at the "absence of true self-consciousness on the part of black Americans, the inability to recognise one's black self except through the mediated veil of the unacknowledging white gaze" (Gordon, 1997, p.52). In Anthony Farley's formulation, race and racism are "ideology made flesh" (Farley, 1997, p.530). Ideology makes economic differences signify in racial terms. Racism produces a form of "ghetto being" that extends beyond the ghetto, a constitutive wound to consciousness and the sense of self.

Hence the passion of Newton's thought. It appears to open a line that moves away from Buber to an assertion of armed struggle. However, this is not quite right. Newton is in fact much closer than some would allow to the new left's desire for a philosophy that privileges the transformation of character. Newton articulates something of a Deweyan ethics of creative democracy refracted through a politics of anti-racism. Black power, then, should be seen as a radicalisation of social ethics rather than their rejection. This returns us to the relationship between radical whites and black, working-class activists. A basic definition of the "white ally" suggests that it is someone who "vow[s] never to look away", and to engage with the experience of people of colour (Wilkerson, 2007, p.390). The anxieties of "white allies" address the contingencies of their own embodiment: the personal responsibility for social advantages conferred on them by white-skin privilege. The

12 "Racial Separation" – a speech given on 11 October 1963 at the University of California, Berkeley. Available at www.blackpast.org/1963-malcolm-x-racial-separation.

ethical register of language is clear – in particular the idea of a vow or a commitment based on personal responsibility. It is also clear that this vow binds together conscience and political action. To whom is the vow made? To the self? The other person? How can we get at these themes?[13] How might Buber help us?

Entering the "unbroken world" of the "thou" moves beyond the "alienation" suffered by an empty, "ghostly I" into a "solidarity" that come from mutual recognition" (Buber, 1937, p.100). The mutuality of the "thou" relationship should not be seen as mystical obfuscation, but a response to the problems of alienation that runs alongside that of Fanon and Newton. Whilst Buber had an understanding of the way in which racial difference disrupts the possibility of creative, critical relationships, his work is more important for its focus on the "cell" of face-to-face encounters (Buber, 1958, p.23). People can remain "ghostly" to each other. Alternatively, meeting together may evoke mutual recognition. The tension in the root meaning of the word cell, to cover or conceal, is active in Buber's analysis. The moment of the encounter, the coming into being of a "between", carries the chance of a revelation, an unveiling – or the collapse into separation that confirms our imprisonment in the "collective loneliness" that passes for life (Buber, 1958, p.14).[14]

13 As far as the new left period is concerned, there was a broad division between black nationalist groups who took the decision to exclude white members, and those like the BPP and the NWRO who actively sought alliance with organisations with predominantly white memberships like the SDS. Consider Newton's comments in his autobiography: "I felt that white people were criminals because they plundered the world. It was more, however, than a simple anti-white feeling, because I never wanted to hurt poor whites, even though I had met some in school who called me 'nigger' and other names. I fought them, but I never took their lunches or their money because I knew they had nothing to start with. With those who had money it was a different story. I still equated having money with whiteness, and to take what was mine and what the white criminals called theirs gave me a real feeling of freedom" (Newton, 1973, p.81). Newton's conduct is guided by a distinction between rich and poor, black and white. This is a paragraph from a fairly early point in the book and represents an early phase of Newton's thinking. The point is that it is yet to become a political ideology. Nevertheless, what Newton is wrestling with is how "correct action" can be guided once the idea that "all white people" are "criminals" has been bracketed. In its place the distinction between rich and poor operates. However, this distinction has to map onto yet another one that deals with the racism of poor whites. These people need to be fought, but, as they are poor, it would be "wrong" to take their money. Money makes all the difference. If richness is equated with whiteness (and implicitly) racism, then one can legitimately take action against them, and in this action find one's freedom.

14 A slightly more detailed articulation of Buber's philosophy and how it relates to ideas of "being with" could be set out as follows. The guiding theme is Buber's relationship to Heidegger. Buber asserts that Heidegger's phenomenology is unable to grasp the experience of interpersonal relationships as its fundamental ontology is flawed (Novak, 1985, pp.125–140). Buber allows that *Dasein* is thrown into a world of equipment (*zuhanden*), objects (*vorhanden*), and other persons in situations of care and concern (*sorge and fuersorge*). Buber also accepts that a thrown being may have a specific mode of being with others (*mitsein*). However, Buber asserts that neither relations with

Buber's work is based on a fundamental distinction between the "I", the "it" and the "thou". In a somewhat crude elaboration of this schema, we could say that what has been called ally-ship is actually a way of conceiving the relationship between I and thou. The ally resists the reduction of another I to the "it" of racism and commodification. Buber thus provides a further analysis of themes that we touched upon in Wilkerson's definition of the ally. The vow as a form of meaningful speech commits one person to another, and recognises both difference and shared commitment in a "bonding or binding" of mutual recognition (Buber, 1958, p.47).

At this moment in our argument we can appropriate another term that appeared earlier in our analysis. Addams's notion of the primordial. We have already suggested that this term needs to be understood in a very specific way.[15]

people nor relations with things are ways of "comprehend[ing]" the I-thou relationship. *Mitsein* is described by Heidegger as *Beistand* (or standing next to). *Beistand* relates to the solitude and finitude of the self that terminates in death. This contrasts with Buber's philosophical anthropology. Buber sees "[i]nterpersonal relationships" as *Beziehungen* or more immediate relationships in which the self encounters another. This is Buber's *Mensch zu Mensch*. *Mitsein* remains somewhat "epiphenomenal", "solipsistic" and "monological". Also at stake is Heidegger's reluctance to ground *Dasein* and *Mitsein* in the "divine unconditioned" (Novak, 1985, p.130). From Buber's perspective, then, Heidegger lacks a "theological ontology" and turns away from the "divine unconditioned". Unconditioned, *Unbedingt*, is the key term. Thus, in Buber's terms, to be unconditioned is to be capable of being a thou. God, for Buber, is the unconditional thou. In his dealings and encounters with others, man "aspires" to this "you sense" – yet often finds that the "you" collapses into an "it". The "you sense" "cannot be satisfied until it finds the infinite "you" which "can only ever be addressed" and "not asserted" (Novak, 1985, p.131). Thus "Buber counters Heidegger by reasserting the necessary theological grounding of true human being (Novak, 1985, p.131). Heidegger repeats Husserl's mistake, lending a "priority of thing relations over person relationships" (Novak, 1985, pp.130–132). Buber is quite different. Relations and relationships cannot be conflated. Rather than thinking of *Dasein* in the world, it is necessary to engage with "different manifestations of human personhood" where only the human being can be thought of as existing in a relationship of "I-you". Relationships with the world of things are thought of as "I-it". Rather than truth as the revealing of things, a philosophical discourse based on the Greek *aletheia*, personal relations are conceived in terms of the Hebrew *emet* (Novak, 1985, p.133; see also Jewula, 2013). The argument in this book does not follow Novak; in particular, it stresses *Mitdasein* rather than *Mitsein*. Distinguishing these two terms is outside the scope of this book. Crudely, *Mitdasein* is the mode in which "we" are with others. It might be said that *Mitsein* is its condition, but not its realisation. This approach perhaps coordinates with Buber's notion of the twofold: *Mitdasein* would provide the grounds for addressing the other as thou. As an extension of this argument, *Mitdasein* can be coordinated with Buber's approach to socialism. Whilst this is developed within a Jewish context, it could be extended into secular understandings of communal social organisation. See Löwy (2017).

15 Nothing in the "it-thou" relationship suggests that the authentic meeting between "I's" will realise the reality of being a thou for another. There is something about the meeting that is bound up with a "beyond" – something outside will and language; a "grace" that may or may not visit itself on the encounter (Buber, 1937, p.11). The

The relationship between ally-ship and the primordial can be studied through the etymological meaning of ally. The word derives from the Latin *ad* and *ligare*, to bind together. The primordial situation of the encounter is thus a vowing or a binding together that raises the question of the relationship of the self to the other.[16]

The other person, the one to whom the ally commits, may be differentiated from the ally by whatever is culturally significant enough to do the work of differentiation (Buber, 1937, p.64). These marks of differentiation may be arbitrary, but they are not unimportant in the constitution of the self. Buber does not mean that any sense of identity around difference is simply some sort of social construction. His point is that these fraught questions are precisely those at stake in an encounter where one addresses the other as thou. The problem is that the "I" can always function "emptied of reality" (the "ghost" at the centre of being). The energy that drives the dialectic of recognition is the understanding that I is a thou for another I, in the same way that s/he is a thou for me (Buber, 1937, p.70).

A clearer picture of this dialectic emerges from a point made by Charles McDew, a former chairman of the SNCC. McDew recounts coming across a rabbinical saying that had a profound influence on his politics: "if I am not for myself, who will be for me? If I am for myself only, what am I? If not now, when?" (Lewis, 2009, p.4). Borrowing from McDew, we can suggest that the moral intensity of the saying captures at least one meaning of the primordial binding of the vow. A "thou relationship" requires someone to be for themselves, but, unless one is also for the other, one falls into the alienation that Buber describes. The mutual binding together of self and other is thus much more than ally-ship. An ally might identify with another's struggle, but may not take seriously the parallelism of being for the self through being for the other. Indeed, the distance of ally-ship may be an ambiguity in the terms of one's own commitment, a failure to articulate the way in which the binding together of commitment compels a form of steadfast being with the other, and the difficult work on the self that this requires.

Within this complex we can find a further working out of the problem of recognition. If I do not recognise the other as a subject, then I am also profoundly limited by my failure to work through the reification of that other. The self

meeting can degenerate; the opportunity lost for any realisation of what might lie "between" (Buber, 1937, p.14). To return to the argument above, it may be that the culture itself is important in opening and preserving a real dialogue, but the spirit of the interlocutors is also a significant factor. In choosing to take certain risks, and to affirm the thou of the other person, the I realises its peculiar destiny, that it should be a thou for another (Buber, 1937, p.53).

16 Behind this meaning is the proto Indo-European verb to gather. This etymology can be traced through Norse into the word for "fixed or set". Studying these etymologies suggests that there might be a primordial meaning of the word, which suggests the act of choosing or fixing a course of action, or making a decision as to how one is to commit, fix or bind oneself.

remains insubstantial, lost in a solipsistic fantasy. It is indeed interesting that the rabbinical saying is framed as three questions, or demands addressed to the self and requiring immediate action. As Buber puts it, "we must create here and now the space *now* possible for the things for which we are striving" (Buber, 1958, p.13). The urgent and ongoing work of recognition is profoundly difficult; it cannot be reduced to a "rigid delineation of ways and methods" (Buber, 1958, p.50). Encounters with others are unpredictable. The encounter retains the "unknown and the unknowable" (Buber, 1958, p.50). There is no programme, no manifesto. The encounter opens to the "longest line" that might cross the space between us (Buber, 1958, p.50). There is nothing that compels one to vow, other than the decision itself to do so. Freedom is total and radical: "[o]nly when we can experience our life as our own in a demanding sense are we free" (Jaeggi, 2014, p.199). This knot of recognition, freedom and difficulty thus binds together the problematic of being with: a creative anxiety rooted in the "recalcitrant material" of the encounter (Buber, 1958, p.15).[17]

The decision to commit, to commence the work on the self that comes out of the recognition of others, shifts Deweyan social ethics into a slightly different key, and further modulates the politics of the SDS. We can carry forward Dewey's openness to others, the democratic intimation of equality that is, after all, a form of infinite conversation amongst people who have chosen to work together. There are always risks. Addams stressed the extent to which social ethics requires a change of character and position. The creative anxiety of commitment furthers the idea that in "going to" others, one has to be in dialogue with them. As far as the politics of race and class are concerned, this means that one has to be ready to work on the assumptions that might limit how one is alongside others. This is the difficult and intense responsibility for the creation of transformed social relationships. The "power" of the "good" that social ethics evokes is this movement between self and other that redefines the characters of those involved in common endeavour.

At stake is an account of social ethics that takes its direction from Wolcher's understanding of "the face-to-face relationship of mutual care and concern that subsists between one person and another person" (Wolcher, 2004, p.139). As Wolcher goes on to argue, a workable notion of ethics always requires us to move from this intense, perhaps inchoate response, to the world of "institutions"

17 Anxiety is related to the theme of care or solicitude as the constitution of *Dasein*. Stressing the importance of care to *Dasein* does not suggest that we are inherently ethical beings, but merely that we are beings amongst other beings. Thus, solicitude can cover, for instance, behaviour that may involve ignoring the plight of others or simply being indifferent to another person or not caring at all. We could say that it all depends on our mood. There is a "thrown-ness" to mood. Whether or not one has empathy or sympathy for another depends on how an individual relates itself to others and, indeed, how we relate to ourselves. In the everyday world that we share with others we can glean from the analysis of solicitude that we may or may not care (in a range of different ways) about the others whom we come across.

(Buber, 1937, p.43); to formal law and rights. In the first part of this chapter, we came upon a meaning of welfare rights that seemed excessive to conventional jurisprudential understandings. We want to pursue this understanding. As we will argue in the next chapter, rights can indeed be understood as "affirmations of human values" (Sparer, 1984, p.555). However, it is also necessary to stress that we should not fetishise rights, especially as the very idea of welfare rights came out of a political struggle (we retain at least some aspects of the classical CLS critique of rights). We are in pursuit of a radical political energy that takes form and achieves a kind of "[i]ntersubjectivity" that "is not just a sentiment of fellow feeling" or a formal structure of rights and duties, but is "constitutive of what we are" (Cornell, 1985, p.363). How does action in consort define us? Recuperating the etymology of the word ally, and arguing about the importance of being with, will not resolve the complex debates about the nature of correct action. It may be better to leave in place the fragments of the radical tradition. We will use the idea of the broken middle (rather than Buber's "unbroken world") to capture this element of critical thought, but this is to anticipate the argument of Chapter 9. [18]

Conclusion

In this chapter, we have studied a genealogy of the existential response to the poverty of others.[19] We could say that this is driven by an anxious question of how to work alongside the poor. The origins of this problematic have been traced back to the social ethics of John Dewey and Jane Addams. Dewey and Addams linked "economic", "legal" and "political phenomena" to "moral considerations" (Dewey, 1933, p.4). Somewhat later, the SDS were influenced by philosophies of social ethics, and orientated their ERAP programmes to organising the poor. The SDS's belief in participatory democracy was, however, subjected to crippling strains. Could the movement speak for the poor? The failures of the ERAP projects suggested otherwise. The politics of poverty were bound up with the politics of race and the problem of the "white ally". We turned to the work of Buber, Du Bois, Fanon and Newton to address this issue. In the words of Michael

18 For instance, one can be too precipitous in making claims to solidarity (see Mahoney, 1999, 2009).

19 The key point of reference is to Nietzsche's *Genealogy of Morals* (1887). *The Genealogy of Morals* is an examination of the origins of morality and good conscience in the training of bodies and minds. Nietzsche's notes for the guidance of philosophers of the future were developed by Foucault. Although we do not follow Foucault on many points, we do carry forward this concern with the material context out of which ideas of morality emerge. The genealogist studies those accidents and tensions that are the product of contending forces that define phenomena. We might say, rather elliptically, that writing a history of a critical legal sensibility is a study in how one can promise differently. The anxiety that defines the radical sensibility is thus perhaps the most recent manifestation of a logic that runs through much more ancient traditions of philosophical and religious thought.

Harrington, we have tried to sketch a redemptive philosophy. This can be understood as the difficult creation of forms of mutuality that involve negotiations of sameness and difference. Ways of saying thou to each other have to be defined and acted upon by those in dialogue around matters of mutual concern. We have argued that these ideas can be used to describe a radical response to alienation rooted in the realisation of a self transformed through political engagement.

Chapter 3

Come together one more time

Poverty and critical legal studies

Introduction

As we have seen, poverty law theory can be traced to the participatory democracy of the new left. In this chapter, we want to pursue understandings of activism into the writings of lawyers involved in the war on poverty. Practising poverty law meant recognising poor clients as human beings. Poverty lawyers rooted their practices in the experience of working with the poor. We will be particularly concerned with the work of Ed Sparer as it moves from an intense involvement in poverty law to an engagement with CLS. Sparer put forward a unique reading of Hegel, Marx and Buber that articulates the experience of social movement lawyering. However, Sparer's thinking was not taken up in the CRT literature on racism and the "double self". An ethics of poverty law was left an unfinished project. As Goodrich has pointed out, CLS "failed in its radicalism" (Goodrich, 1993, p.390). Towards the end of the chapter we offer an exercise in reconstruction, reading back from a second wave of CRT scholarship to recover what the crits had missed: a subtle, dialectical account of the consciousness of the activist lawyer.

This chapter will develop over six sections. The first reviews the experiences of lawyers working with the NWRO and other forms of community activism, sketching out the ideas that they used to articulate the significance of their work. We then turn to Sparer's sophisticated attempt to articulate the experience of practising poverty law before tracing congruent themes through the writings of CLS scholars. The latter parts of the chapter examine CRT notions of double consciousness that carry forward themes from Fanon and Newton. We also examine feminist accounts of alienation that run from Feminist Legal Critique (Fem-Crit) to more recent accounts of intersectionality put forward by LatCrit and critical race scholars. In the final part of the chapter, we exhume from the critical canon the basic outline of an ethics of praxis.

Back to the people

In this first part of the chapter our focus is on a group of lawyers and activists linked to Mobilization for Youth (MFY), an agency of the war on poverty. MFY was the first of a number of bodies set up in inner cities across the United States. Operating out of a storefront on Stanton Street in an impoverished neighbourhood in Manhattan's lower east side, MFY sought to initiate community action projects that would help local residents deal with their daily problems.[1] By 1967 MFY had helped coordinate the efforts of other community groups to feed into the creation of the NWRO.[2]

The movement lawyer had to be an organiser (Wexler, 1970, p.1049). In this milieu, poverty law is experienced by activists as a vital existential challenge, a way of living against the grain and challenging the staid norms of lawyerly professionalism. However, lawyers were confronted by the difficult realities of their clients' chaotic lives. Working with poor people required an acknowledgment of the complexity of the problems they faced. Although successful litigation might bring some form of immediate relief such as uprated benefits, winter clothes or a rat allowance, the fundamental problems of poverty remained. The poor continued to face the reality of struggling against welfare bureaucracies and the grind of day-to-day survival.

1 It was not long before the staff of MFY began to appreciate that the common problem of "lack of income" was due to failures in welfare administration alongside underbudgeting by welfare officials and delayed payments (Movement for Youth, 1962, p.291). MFY staff found that welfare officials had to be fought to ensure that benefits were correctly administered. Litigation became necessary. After early success, the welfare department chose to settle out of court. Welfare clients, centre attorneys and MFY workers began to appreciate that forcing settlement, whilst successful in individual cases, was not the best way to deal with the reality of group grievances. The solution was the Committee of Welfare Families. Under the auspices of MFY, welfare claimants were brought together to organise a coherent campaign around clothing grants. When this proved successful in compelling the welfare department to act on their own policies and issue winter clothing allowances, the Committee found itself organising campaigns that involved thousands of welfare families. Activists began to appreciate the potential of such strategies in building a broader movement and strenuous efforts were made to coordinate both welfare workers and claimants at a national level.

2 Although lawyers were involved in the NWRO, the movement was not formed around litigation strategies. The NWRO came out of the civil rights movement. After a founding meeting in 1967, the NWRO began to attract attention, organising protest marches, meetings, demonstrations and sit-ins. One noted event was the occupation of the Legislative Chamber in Wisconsin to oppose cuts in the state's welfare budget. Strategies developed by the NWRO included making available manuals of welfare policy to publicise welfare practices designed to deprive people of benefits, the ongoing organisation of mass campaigns to place pressure on welfare departments and occupations of welfare offices. The NWRO sought to become "a broad-based movement" of "civil rights organizations, militant anti-poverty groups and the poor" (Cloward and Piven, 1966, p.510). It is also worth stressing that the NWRO had an acute sense of the role that race and gender played in sustaining poverty. Its concern with rights can be seen as an attempt to forge a politics of citizenship where poverty or reliance on welfare payments did not make the recipient a lesser person. The NWRO insistence on dignity and respect can be seen as an intuitive understanding of what we characterised in Chapter 1 as the problematic of social recognition. NWRO activists objected to their social alienation and defined themselves as social actors through their activism.

Writers on poverty law were aware of the dilemmas that were faced by lawyers doing this kind of work. Poverty lawyers had come to terms with their own "shame and guilt"; their "middle class orientation" put to one side to allow them to understand "the grievances" of "slum communities" (Cahn and Cahn, 1964, pp.1346–1348). This approach to lawyering had not been taught in law school. The lawyer had to "daily tread the narrow line between representing and leading, between obeying and teaching, between heeding demands and educating the demander" (Cahn and Cahn, 1964, p.1349). If lawyer and client were to act together and be part of a social movement then law had to be understood in a new way (Bellow, 1966, p.30).

In the previous chapter we argued that Dewey's notion of the work necessary for creative democracy was an important precursor to new left thinking. The following passage suggests at least some evidence of Dewey's influence on the poverty lawyers:

> The lawyer, at least the lawyer who is true to his traditions, in serving as the client's advocate, affords the poor man an entirely new kind of relationship. For the first time, the poor person is told he is the principal and asked what he wants. He is told the range of his possibilities, the dangers, and the consequences. The lawyer tells him that he is his lawyer, no one else's, and that he will pursue his interest. Perhaps for the first time, the poor person has to be active, has to be a principal, and has to begin to recognize that he is a constituent in a democracy and has claims on the exercise of power.
>
> (Sparer et al., 1966, p.515)

This paragraph presents the nobility of the lawyer "true to his tradition" and involved in the kind of practice that animated the theory of creative democracy. Empowered by their lawyers, poor clients are no longer passive and can take steps to control their destiny. In contrast to the social worker, who sees the client as no more than a case, lawyers treat their clients as individuals who might prefer to "to be left alone … listening to jazz records rather than protesting against rats". The dynamic of the lawyer-client relationship nurtures the very form of "self-respect" that "will … generate those leaders and causes that will serve the war on poverty" (Sparer et al., 1966, p.240). Lawyers work to break down the "psychological inequality" that has been instilled in poor people (Sparer et al., 1966, p.240). The client, then, is an individual with specific problems. In understanding these problems and their social context, in acknowledging what law can and cannot achieve, the poverty lawyer begins to fashion a new practice.

Poverty lawyers were stumbling towards ideas for which they appeared to lack the concepts. It might be that, as Cornell put it at a somewhat later date, they wanted to talk about "[t]he experience of … being an I" (Cornell, 1985, p.363). However, this would be to credit these accounts with a register of language that they did not have. At the same time, we need to appreciate that the reflections on experience carry an acute awareness of the social self. Running through the accounts of the poverty lawyers is the sense that one's actions and words have weight. For movement lawyers this experience is bound up with the frustrations of the professional nature of lawyering. Being a lawyer both enabled and limited what could be done. The only way of proceeding was to face down problems, frustrations and failures in commitment to the cause.

The politics of experience

We now want to examine how these ideas were carried forward and mediated in the thinking of the lawyer/activist Ed Sparer. Writing some half a decade after the collapse of the welfare rights movement, Sparer brought together elements of Buber's existentialist thinking with his reading of Hegel and Marx. We find in Sparer a sophisticated attempt to frame the experiences of poverty law around the "open hearted" encounter with the other person. Addressing the Critical Legal Studies conference[3] and grappling with the CLS critique of rights, Sparer made a reference to the "existentialist" philosopher Martin Buber:[4]

> It is a struggle for life, to live one's own life and act out of a concern for others and for all of society. "All real living is meeting," Martin Buber taught, and I agree. Living is found in relationships and mutuality, between "I" and "thou," "we" and "them." Every effort to meet others results in some mutuality.
>
> (Sparer, 1984, p.549)

The grain of this way of thinking is quite peculiar. Sparer is mixing together themes from different philosophical registers. From Marxism comes the notion of the struggle. Read through Buber, class struggle becomes a struggle for "life". Note, in particular, the way in which life is defined as a way of living one's own self through a concern for others. The meeting or the encounter is at the heart of this experience. Living is defined as "mutuality" – an inescapable social experience. However, encounters between people are often fraught. There is no saying that the encounter will lead to cooperation or mutual appreciation. Sparer quotes Buber's assertion that "full mutuality is not inherent in men's life together" (Sparer, 1984, p.549). What Buber then goes on to say, and what Sparer does not

3 The context of Sparer's comments is a consideration of the fundamental contradiction. The fundamental contradiction posed by the welfare state to the lawyer should be fairly obvious. When a lawyer acts for a poor client, the very recourse to law may effectively legitimise the bureaucratic structures or the "system" that keeps poverty in place. Minor victories or indeed general advances in due process protections for welfare clients as a whole distract from political arguments for fundamental change.

4 Sparer pointed out that enforcing a rigorous divide between political and legal arguments is misconceived. The experience of the welfare rights movement was that both were necessary. Litigation strategies were developed with a view as to how they might be used to organise.

directly comment upon, is even more interesting. The mutuality that may result from an encounter is a "grace, for which one must always be ready and over which one never gains an assured possession" (Sparer, 1984, p.549). What does this mean? Moreover, how can we make sense of these theological ideas that emerge within a discussion of Hegel and Marx?

Sparer never returned to the notion of grace and indeed we will have to delay our own proper consideration until Chapter 6. Right now we need to work out what might be meant by the idea that mutuality is not an assured possession. The main sense of the argument seems clear. In social life we struggle to achieve mutual recognition with others. In Sparer's presentation there is a Hegelian and Marxian provenance to these themes, a reference to the writings on alienation in *The 1844 Manuscripts*. The fundamental idea is that of the "separation of man from man" (Sparer, 1984, p.529). This theme is related to Buber's thinking of the sense of what other people mean "to me". In order to elaborate this idea Sparer discusses the experience of coming across the other person, "the glances which strangers exchange in a busy street as they pass one another with unchanging pace" (Buber, 1974, p.21). Buber's idea is that whatever comes out of the encounter with the other person is not an "assured possession" – the encounter can simply confirm hostility and alienation as much as it might affirm connection or relatedness. We need to read its shifting terms. A glance may be particularly significant or "charged with destiny" (Buber, 1974, p.21). For something to happen the encounter has to be animated by "real speech" (Buber, 1974, p.21). This experience cannot be described, or rather, the request that is made in real speech is the medium through which "something has been said to me" (Buber, 1974, p.21). What does this mean? The "I" has encountered a mystery, although Buber is careful to specify that he is not describing a "mystical event" or a necessarily religious experience (Buber, 1974, p.21). The encounter in which the other addresses you does not have an easy resolution. The point is that one pauses before the other. Provided that you are "open hearted" there is the possibility that you might be transformed by something that happens in the encounter with the other person (Buber, 1974, p.21).

The open-hearted pause before the other person, the connection or the reflection on the experience of the encounter are elements in a theory of "social practice [s] concerned with changing the world" (Sparer, 1984, pp.532–533). No wonder that Sparer is critical of Marx. Marx was not radical enough. He failed to develop a sufficiently "reflexive" understanding of the relationship between "intellectual work" and "political practice" (Sparer, 1984, p.533). This does not suggest that class is irrelevant. Rather, it means that we need to think differently about class and pick up on earlier comments about the existential challenge of working with the poor. Quite how far one moves from Marx remains an open question. Given Sparer's own argument, it would seem unlikely that this is a rejection of Marx; rather, Marx's themes can be re-appropriated from Sparer's new perspective.

Is there not still a missing term? We know from our arguments that concluded the section above that the experience of poverty law points towards an ethics, but how can we make sense of this term in the context of Sparer's thought? Sure, we can show liberal doctrines and practices to be what they are – "oppression and domination" – but how should we act if we want to break out of these modes of behaviour (Sparer, 1984, p.556)? It is indeed interesting that this point takes us to the constitution of a radical sensibility. Important factors are the experiences undergone in the stiffing conservative environments of "law school in the late 1960's" and the coming of age in "the social struggles of the late 1960's and early 1970's" (Sparer, 1984, p.557). Committed to both legal practice and political activism, radical identity is forged in the frustrations of finding just how difficult it is to change "the system". Facing such problems, one looks for "more and deeper explanations" (Sparer, 1984, p.557). These explanations require us to engage with a number of interrelated concerns. Sparer goes on to quote the following long passage from Robert Gordon:

> Yet, if the real enemy is us – all of us, the structures we carry around in our heads, the limits on our imagination – where can we even begin? Things seem to change in history when people break out of their accustomed ways of responding to domination, by acting as if the constraints on their improving their lives were not real and that they could change things; and sometimes they can, though not always in the way they had hoped or intended; but they never knew they could change them at all until they tried.
>
> (Sparer, 1984, p.557)

This is undoubtedly about action: how we break out of the stultifying roles that define who we are, what we should value and how we should behave. The enemy is within as we have internalised the beliefs and understandings that control us. Encrypted in this passage is the link between ethics and practice. We "break out" when we act on the basis of an "as if". As if change is possible. This aligns with Sparer's thinking on the idea of the encounter that can force us to a limit and compel us to question ourselves. Might we even say that the "as if" is almost a mark of grace? Something might happen. We have little control over the happening. But it may profoundly alter our view of ourselves and the world. Furthermore, if this "taking place" is an interior event, a questioning of our own beliefs, then practices are works on the self. As we know from Sparer's reading of Buber, this is "social work" – a response to alienation and the dull repetition of the same thing. Clearly much more needs to be said. It will be necessary to build on Sparer's sketch of the encounter as a form of social recognition, and to examine the reception of these ideas by CLS.

Alienation and Critical Legal Studies

Around the time that Sparer spoke to the CLS conference about the experiences of poverty lawyers, other scholars associated with the movement were also developing accounts of law and alienation. One might have imagined that there would have been at least some reference to Sparer's work as this was part of the same dialogue around themes in continental philosophy.[5] However, CLS work was somewhat different. Gabel and Harris saw the "source" of alienation as socially hierarchical forms of organisation. Hierarchy prevents people from achieving authenticity through "the sustained experience of … egalitarian social connection" leaving them atomised and isolated. Alienation, then, is something that is lived and repeatedly lived, "a self-generating source of social repression that leads to the reproduction of class, race and sex hierarchies from generation to generation" (Gabel and Harris, 1982, p.371). It is worth noting the precise terms of this expression.[6]

Gabel and Harris drew on an account of reciprocity and social recognition similar to the one deployed by Sparer. They assert that "we are constituted as social beings by the desire to be recognised by others in an empowering, life-giving way" (Gabel and Harris, 1982, p.1566). This "desire" has become forgotten or obscured, covered over by the disconnections of modern life. "We" effectively "hide" from each other, or, at best, suffer from contradictory desires to be recognised yet not entirely present to the possibilities opened up by social encounters: "[w]e each become "one of the others" to each other thus helping to

5 Gabel and Harris rejected an instrumental Marxist approach that presents law as the tool of the ruling class. They were also critical of the liberal belief that legal systems protect people's rights. Their key argument is that law is dedicated to "the control of popular consciousness through authoritarian and ideological methods (one of which is the belief in "rights" itself). Legal practice can break out of the deadening routines of daily life and the forms of power that keep them in place: "the legal system is an important public arena through which the State attempts – through manipulation of symbols, images, and ideas – to legitimize a social order that most people find alienating and inhumane" (Gabel and Harris, 1982, p.370). The legal system legitimises the system by concealing this order, by turning endemic social conflicts into cases that can be resolved through court-based rituals that attest to the rightful authority of established institutions. The authority of law rests on its institutional nature and its rituals confirm and elaborate authoritarian modes of social life in which conflicts are framed and resolved in ways that leave the fundamental problems of the social, political and economic order in place.

6 Sparer's themes are repositioned. Now the social self is to be addressed through phenomenological philosophy. Phenomenology allows the critic to "re-experience the phenomena of everyday life", get at "hidden meanings" and describe how our experience of the social world can be understood. Phenomenology is not a form of disinterested philosophical description. It is philosophy in the service of a "progressive social movement". Phenomenological description, as a way of seeing again, or seeing properly, allows one to understand law and other powerful social practices and ideas as a "whole complex of images". The sense of "image" needs to be pinned down. It appears to mean "beliefs" or ideas. These beliefs and ideas inform institutions and practices that clearly can take a material form. If one does not see these institutions and practices for "what they are" then one has a false view of the world. One has fallen into false consciousness or become misled by images rather than the actuality of "ourselves as living beings" (Gabel and Harris, 1982, p.1565). Thus, phenomenological description can "get at" the grounding reality of our social being.

sustain "the very disconnection that we most wish others would allow us to overcome" (Gabel and Harris, 1982, p.1567). Alienation is this "paradoxical form of reciprocity between two beings" who desire "contact" and yet "deny" this same desire. Our alienation can be traced to "a fear of loss" that leads "intersubjective desire" to limit and constrain itself (Gabel and Harris, 1982, pp.1568–1569). The good news is that this self-limitation is itself a failure of a fuller sense of being. Intimations of our true selves come to us in moments of unconstrained communication when the mask we adopt in social life slips. Our true self thus seems to lie in the connections with others that somehow allow us to recognise ourselves.

Like Sparer, Gabel and Harris are struggling to find the point at which the authentic social encounter with others can be realised. To resist alienating hierarchy, the lawyer has to find "a way of working in the legal arena that consistently challenges the state's control over the way that we are to both feel and think about the nature of social reality" (Gabel and Harris, 1982, p.374). This, after Gramsci, is named counter-hegemonic struggle. Counter-hegemonic struggle is the task of the radical lawyer who seeks to challenge and delegitimise the legal system from within. Law is subordinate to collective political action. A good example of this approach would be the defence of the Chicago 8 or the various Black Panther trials where the defendants subverted the authority of the court. It is interesting that Gabel and Harris do not reflect on the activities of the poverty lawyers in any great detail. They offer the following brief passage. Examining how criminal cases might be radicalised, they point out that the best way forward may be a form of community activism: "[t]he aim would be to [work] … with existing neighbourhood groups to build consciousness about the way that the defendant's problem is actually the community's problem as an oppressed area within the socioeconomic structure" (Gabel and Harris, 1982, p.397). Despite the lack of an explicit engagement with poverty law, isn't this straight out of the poverty lawyer's handbook? In particular, it carries forward the resistance to alienation that comes from political lawyering and a creative sense in which such activities can give rise to a "movement" of "transformative" lawyers (Gabel and Harris, 1982, p.470).

What then do we make of Gabel and Harris's theory of alienation? The theme of recognition seems clear enough, as does the desire to be recognised by others. However, locating the problem in "hiding" from each other or positing a desire for anonymity that is somehow inauthentic misses out a whole level of analysis at which Sparer had hinted. Gabel and Harris offer no real advance on Sparer's analysis to show us how "something" gets covered up, hidden or obscured and so results in us somehow "holding back" or hiding from each other. We know from Buber that social encounters do not always lead to mutual appreciation, but it is not clear why we then need to go on to posit a true and a false self. Gabel and Harris do not quite get to the point that would clinch their arguments. Sparer was driving at some notion of inter-subjectivity or the constitution of character and the sense of self through the recognition that may take place in encounters with others. Gabel and Harris are certainly working within this broad problematic, but they seem to stop short of advancing the key theme: how does the analysis of false consciousness relate to an analysis of action? The theory of counter-hegemony might provide a broad orientating horizon but it would be necessary to know more about the problems encountered in counter-hegemonic practices for the term to be useful. It may even be the case that counter-hegemonic practice is severely limited by the unconscious repetition of learnt scripts. The "us" addressed by Gabel and Harris thus seems to be somewhat white and disembodied. Ignoring embodiment may also be related to a too simplistic announcement of sympathy or solidarity. Perhaps the point is not to stress some idea of "unconstrained communication" but the self-questioning work that constitutes an authentic response to social encounters.

Double consciousness and the midnight fiction

How do we address the "structures in our heads" that prevent decent forms of social recognition? The development of this analytic was severely hampered by the separation between CLS and CRT. CRT scholars began to develop arguments around social recognition that drew on earlier poverty research that parted company with the explicit analysis of alienation.[7] Consider the following passage in which Du Bois denounces a "world" that cannot sustain "true self-consciousness" because a person is "only" allowed to see him/herself through a world defined by others (Du Bois, 1903, p.3). Du Bois called this "peculiar sensation" that of "double consciousness". Double consciousness is defined as "the sense of always looking at one's self through the eyes of others, of measuring one's soul by the tape of a world that looks on in an amused contempt and pity" (Du Bois, 1903, p.3). "[T]rue self-consciousness" requires the rejection of

7 Du Bois's work in Philadelphia stands out. It is rooted in a very specific context. Drawing attention to the fundamental problem of racism, Du Bois showed that the cases of poverty amongst blacks in the city's seventh ward could be traced to low incomes, lack of opportunities to work, sickness and the continuing segregation of black communities. This went some way from the perceived wisdom that the solution to black poverty was integration into white culture and white norms (Du Bois, 1899, p.38). The cost of "pauperism" was linked to the "moral" failure to recognise the common humanity of whites and blacks (Du Bois, 1899, pp.394–397). The quality of Du Bois's work is suggested in its anticipation of later research on an area of Washington's inner city published in 1967 which studied the "inner" life of "the streetcorner Negro man". Liebow argued that "[t]he way in which [a] man makes a living and the kind of living he makes have important consequences for how [a] man sees himself and is seen by others". To suffer racism is to become reduced, to carry within one's self a sense of being degraded (Liebow, 1967, p.210). Liebow's conclusions were certainly somewhat different and more pessimistic than those of Du Bois. His study of the inner city reveals the development of a "shadow system of values" that reflect back, in an inverted form, the values of the white world (Liebow, 1967, p.213). Condemned to failure, the street-corner man attempts to "achieve many of the goals and values of the larger society" and, unable to do so, seeks refuge in a culture that "conceals his failure from others" and "from himself as best he can" (Liebow, 1967, p.222). Ghetto culture communicates this sense of personal and cultural failure.

"double consciousness" – of seeing oneself "through the eyes of others" – particularly when those others "seek to destroy, limit, belittle, insult or demean …" (Du Bois, 1903, p.3). The danger is that any reflection on the self – any story about the self or any voice speaking about the self – may simply reproduce (and reproduce in subtle and possibly hidden ways) the forms of the bogus self that racism has created. If one wants to see oneself differently, how does one reject the bogus self?

We can take some guidance from Newton's autobiographical study in resisting alienation. As the text points out: "[l]ife does not always begin at birth" (Newton, 1973, p.11). The birth of an individual is located in an historical pattern, the "history of all Black people" (Newton, 1973, p.11). The whole animus of the book is that of survival, the preservation of one's own dignity in a society that denies one's worth: "I was ashamed of being Black. This feeling followed me everywhere, without let up" (Newton, 1973, p.19). The text is attempting to trace the creation of a subordinate self. The site of the perpetuation of the norms and values of white society are the school system and an education that "rob[bed] me of the sense of my own uniqueness and worth" (Newton, 1973, p.22). Resistance to the values of the white world are found in the family itself and in relationships of male friendship. From his father and his brother comes the importance of fighting to preserve one's dignity, of facing down the disrespect of racist whites. His father's stories may be about "standing up to white men" but he also takes a sense of humour from his mother's ability to "look at things in another way" (Newton, 1973, pp.31, 13). The roots of Newton's thinking come from "standing one's ground" and persisting "in the face of bad odds" – but seeing differently is also an essential strategy.

Newton, like Du Bois and Sparer, is drawing on Hegel. The failure of social recognition, the breakdown of any correspondence between the self and its social form produces an unhappy consciousness that cannot find itself. It lives as a "duality" – a separation between being and thinking, between what it understands itself to be, and the social representations of this self. Unhappy consciousness arrives at a troubling but profound point: it discovers its own "self-existence" – the negating power of its own consciousness (Hegel, 1967, p.272). As we have seen, this deeply traumatic "splitting" of the self was a major theme in Fanon's thought. Whilst Newton was familiar with both Hegel and Fanon, these ideas took a little more time to filter into legal theory. Indeed, at this point we must move forward to a second wave of CRT thinking, and an essay by Anthony Farley.

Consider the following passage. It is a rather long quotation that has to be cited in full as we are interested in the relationship the passage articulates between an autobiographical short story and a commentary on the forms of consciousness it presents: "The black body is available for humiliation all of the time", or as Fanon put it, "[w]herever he goes, the Negro remains a Negro". In a short story about a black expatriate's fears regarding his impending return from France, where he had lived as a human being, to the United States, where he had lived as something less, James Baldwin describes the total availability of the black identity:

> Nothing was more familiar to them than the sight of a dark boy, singing, and there were few things on earth more necessary. It was under cover of darkness, my own darkness, that I could sing for them of the joys, passions, and terrors they smuggled about with them like steadily depreciating contraband. Under cover of the midnight fiction that I was unlike them because I was black, they could stealthily gaze at those treasures which they had been mysteriously forbidden to possess and were never permitted to declare.
>
> (Baldwin, 1965, p.138, in Farley, 1997, p.474)

Farley is using an extract from James Baldwin to develop an argument about Fanon's description of black consciousness. The black body is experienced as something to be humiliated. In the fragment from Baldwin, the narrator is expressing his misgivings about returning from France, where he had been accepted, to the United States. Farley is tracking Baldwin's description of his own experience. The colour line fixes this sense of self, the internalised understandings of how one is perceived and how one perceives oneself. The experience of being a black body or a black consciousness is bound up with the humiliations one suffers and the "pleasure" that racists take in inflicting humiliation. Note the play of consciousness in the fragment. Baldwin in describing himself observing himself in the way that the character in the story is being observed. There is a play between familiarity and unfamiliarity, between the seen and the revealed. What is familiar in different ways to the white and black observer is the spectacle of the black performer who is seen to bear a passion that the whites could not themselves possess. This is the "midnight fiction".

The midnight fiction names in a striking way the problem with which we are wrestling. The fiction is covered up, concealed. In this performance, something remains hidden: "[i]t was under cover of darkness, my own darkness, that I could sing for them ..." Baldwin is elaborating the metaphor of the fiction and appropriating it as a darkness in which he conceals himself. However, this is not a study in true and false selves. The main concern of the passage is with perspective and the movement between observer and observed. Both Baldwin and the whites (in different ways) remain hidden and concealed. They have disappeared from each other. This is the "thematic structure" of the colour line.

Baldwin the writer has taken control of the scene. The very presentation of the midnight fiction means that one may be able to achieve a critical perspective. This is hard fought and difficult to achieve. Whilst Baldwin could stand back and think, we need to follow the way in which this problem has been dealt with by others who are not perhaps as strong as Baldwin. How do we transform ourselves? How do we act? Farley's commentary on Baldwin is concerned with a general human situation, but his analysis is also relevant to the problem Sparer bequeathed to the critical tradition: the problem of an ethics. However, before we can think about these questions, we have to engage with another tradition of critical legal thinking.

Feminism and alienation

That the Fem-Crits came out of the new left is stressed by one of the earliest pieces that delineated a specifically feminist CLS. In the same way that it was necessary to resist the male-dominated new left, CLS needed to be reminded that radical thinkers were often blind to sexist behaviour and reluctant to question the norms that determined how men and women relate to each other (Menkel-Meadow, 1988, p.62). These themes are central to the first attempts to work out a critical feminist jurisprudence. Thus, West's leading contention that both liberal and critical forms of legal thinking fail to address an ontology that assumes "separateness" or individuality. Her argument would be misread if one saw it as an assertion of a female nature that was inherently connected to others. It is, rather, an elaboration of concerns with alienation. CLS has not been radical enough. It has failed to think through a hegemonic ontology because it has avoided questioning something that appears natural: the heterosexual construction of women as objects desired by men. Moving beyond these constraining norms (or re-appropriating them for those who feel that they do provide a form of ontological security) is the challenge for new critical thought. Thought has to grasp the gulf opened up by "subjective life" and "official value" (West, 1988, pp.43–45).

It is intriguing that the development of West's argument goes via a critique of Gabel. Gabel provides a one-sided analysis: a story told from the male perspective (West, 1988, p.45). West does not simply replace one perspective with another. She attempts to move towards a general understanding of the alienation of men *and* women. She is critical of Gabel and Andrea Dworkin's account of heterosexual intercourse as "collaboration" with the enemy. The intimate relationship between men and women is the site of struggle; a struggle to find those moments of "surprise, imagination[,] conscious intelligence [and] play that redefine gender roles as freely chosen" (West, 1988, p.47). However, things are not straightforward. West presses into service the concept of the fundamental contradiction to name an ontological precarity that is as much male as female. Undoubtedly, ontological precarity has been encoded in male and female terms (men as autonomous, fearing and longing for intimacy; women as nurturing, connected carers, fearing and longing for autonomy). Men and women remain alienated and trapped in inherited forms of social life to the extent that they do not open themselves to change. An immanent dialectic will not somehow work itself out. The re-creation of relationships between men and women will only take place through feminist projects that can re-figure the terms of social relationships.

The Fem-Crits were laying down paths out of alienation. This is exactly why MacKinnon was critical of different-voice feminism. Although different-voice feminists attempted to re-evaluate the very terms that were used to marginalise and subordinate women as care givers, MacKinnon saw this as "reification" (MacKinnon, 1987, p.39). Her early work had identified the alienating nature of heteronormativity with a bold argument that linked Marx's discourse on work to feminist discourses on sexuality. Women are alienated because of their sexuality.

Rather than being a natural substratum, heterosexuality is an institutional construction of domination and subordination. To be a woman is to be identified with a social category that is inherently alienating as it creates social roles and expectations that limit and constrain one's desire. MacKinnon deploys a move with which we are now familiar. Female experience may be the site of the construction of female subordination, but it is also the point at which consciousness of subordination and resistance to patriarchy becomes possible.

That MacKinnon's work was subjected to deliberate mis-readings suggests that her insights did upset male crits. Indeed, the reception of this wave of feminist work obstructs our ability to appreciate how it provided the essential supplement to CLS thinking. Consider Olsen's approach. Making use of Marx and the burgeoning concern with the ambiguous status of distinctions that were meant to define social roles, Olsen concentrated on the "market/family dichotomy". Her objective was to "counter the self alienation inherent in our present gender system". We can understand self-alienation as fundamental to both Marxist and feminist critiques of the negative internalities of market capitalism. The form of the family constructs and limits the terms on which an intimate relationship can take place (Olsen, 1983, p.1575). For an authentic "intimate sharing … between human beings", it is necessary to discover the real social and intimate needs between those defined as men and women and to "break out of the present dichotomized system" (Olsen, 1983, p.1575). These moments of vision come from our "occasional glimpses" of "power, sensitivity, and connectedness". Within the husks of the old, the new is waiting to appear: "a source of hope, a foreshadow of the human beings we can become" (Olsen, 1983, p.1578). Olsen is in search of those rare moments when we move beyond the social script – when something new happens.

How does this approach help us to think about the relationship of Fem-Crit to its own critique by women of colour? Just as the Fem-Crits provided a necessary supplement to CLS, their own account of authentic social relationships was subject to a further supplement. Intersectionality suggests that feminist thinking was itself insensitive to the experiences of women of colour, and that feminism was profoundly limited if it could not grasp the experiences of black women. A body of critical thinking that sought to articulate the social experience of the marginalised, effectively erased the experiences of those for whom it hoped to speak (Crenshaw et al., 1995, p.139). Crenshaw's influential articulation of intersectionality considered the plural modes in which the world is experienced. The experience of black women is here a token for those lives that had slipped out of an analytical vocabulary. Being is not "merely the sum of separate parts"; it has to be seen as "*multiplicative*" (Wing, 1991, p.194). Intersectionality is a way of thinking about the ontological thickness of a lived life. The question becomes: how is it possible to live authentically as an embodied person: a person of race, class and gender?

Answering this question requires us to bring into play all the aspects of our argument. We can make a brief reference to Adrienne Rich's *Women and Honour*. Rich defines a kind of dying relationship characterised by "manipulation" and "control" (Rich, 1979, p.193). Lively discourse between human beings has shrunk to nothing; the repetition of roles determined by routine and no longer capable of change. Creating something valuable does not require complete honesty or the sharing of everything, but a realisation of "the possibility of life between us" (Rich, 1979, p.194). Or, as Thom Gunn put it, the "arranging" of the "space between" by "love" (Gunn, 1973, p.55). The beginning of Rich's essay describes a relationship between two women. By the final paragraphs this has modulated into something stranger. Rich's "life between us" is something like an "honourable" solution to the midnight fiction. The text moves towards a statement that we must not forget ourselves in a world of empty talk and secrets that are not worth knowing. Rich draws the distinction between a "saying of anything" and actual speech with the other person. The honourable relationship is an opening to the other: a person to whom one could talk about anything, without, in some ways, actually saying anything at all. If the relationship is honourable, then the other person is similarly positioned: desiring to talk freely or to not talk, accepting a silence that might invite words. Strength is required from both parties. Authentic speech is "frightening" because it can contend with reification: with frozen positions that need to be thawed out (Rich, 1979, p.195).

We are thus concerned with a tentative dialogue that feels its way towards things that can be said and which resonate between self and other. How can we understand this strange idea? Feminist scholars have elaborated an ethics of care based on this relationship between self and other (Menkel-Meadow, 1994, p.114). Whilst this is not without its insights, we will not follow this approach as it collapses the "in between" – resolving a contradiction between self and other in a way inconsistent with the subtler thinking of West, Olsen, Crenshaw, Farley and Sparer. Making creative use of the "between" takes us back to Buber, and, amongst other points of reference, Cornell's contemporary thinking on social recognition.

Ethics, practice and social recognition

We can now pull together the various strands of our argument. This returns us to the issue of ethics. Ethics deals with the general problem of how one works on oneself to become something or resists being turned into an object by others. This is obviously a somewhat elliptical definition but we can sketch out its basic terms and connect our observations back to Sparer's thinking of the existential situation of the poverty lawyer. The poverty lawyer encounters a limit of the self which forces the question "how do I act?" How do I become true to my own actions? We have seen that these questions cannot be answered in narrowly professional terms. A proper response requires a new way of thinking, multiple perspectives, keeping things open. The dialectic of recognition cannot become jammed. This is a theme that runs through feminist critical legal thinking and critical race feminism. Perhaps this is also what Gabel and Harris were heading towards and what remains bound up with the study of alienated consciousness.

If, from the perspective of Fanon, Newton, Baldwin and Farley, the key question is how to resist the internalisation of the bogus self, the urgent question for the white radical is how not to be lost in the midnight fiction. This problem is as relevant to the radical opposed to what Lewis Gordon calls anti-black racism as it is to the lawyer working with poor people. As we saw in the previous chapter, it is also the problem of the "white ally". Radical thought and action risks the reproduction of those very schemas that it had hoped to escape. However, to repeat the question asked in the last chapter, would it be fair to say that the poverty lawyers that we studied at the beginning of the chapter were unaware of the way in which they were caught up in interchanges of power?

We can again make reference to Buber's thinking to engage with those encounters that cross the colour line and the poverty line. In the struggle against false consciousness, the other person must be recognised as such. This does not mean that the other is recognised as the same as the self. Buber is quite precise about this point. The awareness that is at issue cannot be thought of as merely encountering one's self in the other. Nor can it be confused with an anodyne resolution of difference into a primordial "we" or some pat articulation of a community of difference. Our concern is with ways of constituting viable versions of subjectivity that require both self and other to resist false consciousness and to be open to an ongoing process of transformation and becoming. To refer back to Baldwin's analysis, inverted forms of racism merely replay the original distortion and cement the hold of a world view in which we become invisible to each other.

Unreflective communication is the rehearsal of a script or the enactment of roles in which we lose ourselves. Such communication can run from merely not paying attention to the other person, to the deliberate use of language that insults, and to the contortions of the midnight fiction that we examined above. The "something happening" is the decision to "have done with" routines and social scripts (Buber, 1973, p.29). One needs to be "become aware" (Buber, 1973, p.27). These are necessarily general terms. Buber wants to get at the way that something might happen if one is open to its happening. The happening is not a once and once only experience. It is a struggle, an ongoing resistance to the "interlocking sterilized system" (Buber, 1974, p.28). We must therefore also be careful with claims to have found a true self. More accurately, we are concerned with how we reflect on ourselves, a process that can work with a shifting sense of true and false. To help us think this through we can refer again to the experience of the poverty lawyers working with others in the movement, actively engaging with new ways of doing things and new ways of relating to each other.

The becoming aware, the process, the opening to the other is a way of doing things. We might say that the sense of self is constantly constructed and reconstructed by subjects themselves, acting and thinking alongside other subjects: "the self [has to be] seen as constituted by and at the same time partially constitutive of a process of intersubjective interaction" (Cornell, 1986, p.297). Selves are created through social practice, the recognition of the reciprocity of subjectivity, of the "we that is I and the I that is we" (Cornell, 1986). The "I" and the "we" have to be understood as works in progress. We can see, then, that Buber's discourse on the encounter is a way of thinking an ethos where encounters with others are infinite and ongoing, and "serious speech" is a question of spirit and engaged intelligence. Working through the midnight fiction is a way of bringing together a praxis-orientated social ethics with a dialectical realisation of social recognition; a dialectic that is radically open and resists neat conclusions and resolution into sameness.

One final issue. It is easy for this kind of thinking to fall into self-congratulation or self-righteousness where the lawyer, the critical thinker, knows what it best. Stressing that the process of recognition is a difficult work on the self means that it is harder to fall into hubris and to replace dialogue with monologue. The entire problematic of recognition requires an ethics rooted in a certain spirit of experience of "being with" others. We thus come back again to the themes whose constituent parts we have encountered in the different thinkers that we have read in this chapter. What we can carry forward is an understanding of alienation and the struggle against alienation that takes place through the engagements of those who have chosen to dedicate themselves to the practice of a certain kind of activism, a certain way of working with others.

Conclusion

One thing I can tell you is you gotta be free

The critical response to poverty law requires a degree of reconstruction. It is only from the perspective of today that we can assess the way in which the legacy of the war on poverty was mediated by CLS and later waves of critical thinking. Sparer was a key figure. He focused on the idea of alienation. Social recognition is frustrated; people are trapped in a dull repetition of the same, a kind of script that constantly replays itself and limits democratic conversation. We followed these themes into feminist theory. Bringing together Buber and Sparer, West and Olsen, the argument attempted to define the dialectic between self and other as a struggle to become a human being amongst other human beings. CLS scholars worked in a similar direction, developing a phenomenological account of alienation. As the references to Cornell suggest, CLS and CRT were not finally able to pull together their insights into a coherent ethics of poverty law. In the next chapter we want to examine these ideas in much more detail. With the shift to progressive constitutionalism, the centre of the debate became a theory of social justice. Themes with which we are familiar from this chapter appear in a different key, as Michelman relates the constitutional order to "the process of self-government and to forms of reflexivity" (Michelman, 1986, p.42). Engaging with Michelman's thesis will show us just how much ground the crits ceded in failing to press forward the theoretical initiative, but also just how much radical thinking can still learn from an encounter with progressive constitutional scholarship.

Chapter 4

The poor and the constitution

> The proper aim is to try and reconstruct society on such a basis that poverty will be impossible.
>
> (Oscar Wilde, "The Soul of Man Under Socialism", 1891, p.292)

Introduction

This chapter sets up an encounter between radical thinking and progressive constitutionalism. Progressive constitutionalism carried forward certain energies from CLS and CRT, refining them in the light of the reactionary backlash against welfare rights. Whilst progressive constitutionalism sustained the case for welfare rights, did it concede too much political ground to the conservative ascendancy? What can a contemporary critical approach to welfare, work and poverty learn from scholars who have championed the interests of the poor in dark times?

Our starting point is Michelman's account of welfare rights and social justice.[1] Welfare rights require a polity in which people's self-respect and agency are recognised through their inclusion in social and political life. Responding to conservative and liberal criticisms, Michelman refined his position. He began to champion a radical republican philosophy of "citizenship-participation ... in public

1 Whilst Michelman has not wholeheartedly embraced the term progressive constitutionalism, he does not seem to have rejected it either. Addressing "Progressive Liberal Democratic Constitutionalism" (PLDC), Michelman argued that the words making up this portmanteau term must all do some work. Michelman has a "mildly unorthodox" understanding of liberalism as a "doctrine of ethics and morality" which is "humanist", "individualist" and "tolerant" (Michelman, 2011, p.187). In distinction to West's "progressivism" discussed in Chapter 1, Michelman's sense of the term is not founded on a "passionate enmity to suffering and domination". Rather, it is animated by an "anxiety" about "legitimation" (Michelman, 2011, p.188). Democracy is understood as "a doctrine of social structure and political process meant to bring public opinion to bear on the decisions of rulers" (Michelman, 2011, pp.196–197). Rather than get bogged down in a dispute over the precise meaning of progressive constitutionalism, it is perhaps not unreasonable to use it as a description of Michelman's work.

affairs" (Michelman, 1988, p.1503). However, the sophistication of Michelman's work ran into the simplicities of the Reagan revolution. We turn from Michelman to Peter Edelman. Edelman was acutely aware of the potential and the problems of Michelman's constitutional scholarship. He grappled with the idea that a democratic culture requires all people to be valued as self-respecting citizens. Leading with the notion of a survival income, Edelman put forward a robust defence of the use of moral philosophy in constitutional theory, even as the Supreme Court turned its back on welfare rights.

What conclusions can we draw from the limitation of the "thin constitution"? Whilst progressive constitutionalism and moral philosophy remain relevant and provocative, it is now necessary to present a new way of framing arguments about work and welfare. As McCluskey has argued, those working in progressive constitutional theory can no longer seek "accommodation" with market ideology (McCluskey, 2007, p.876). Not Rawls, but Marx; or, rather, a way forward that draws on Marx to develop an analysis capable of grasping the brutal subtleties of poverty amidst plenty.

First moves: use and abuse of the 14th Amendment

How can constitutional welfare rights be linked to a theory of social justice?

Start with the idea that the state has a "duty to protect [citizens] against certain hazards that are endemic in an unequal society". This duty must be carefully distinguished from the assertion that the state must ensure equality (Michelman, 1969, p.9). Whilst this argument might seem a little strange, it is on reflection an attempt to create a workable understanding of the state's duties towards poor citizens within the terms of the constitution. On first regard, one would imagine that under the 14th Amendment, it would be possible to assert that a group suffering discrimination has been deprived of the "equal protection", as they were, because of their poverty, unable to take up opportunities open to "the relatively rich".[2] However, one should be very careful in drawing general egalitarian principles from cases that support this approach. The equal protection clause does not cover "official act[s] of setting conditions of access" to essential services. The price of a service is a matter over which government officials have little control.[3]

2 The Supreme Court has made this kind of argument in relation to access to justice and voting rights. In *Douglas v California* 372 U.S. 353 (1963), it was held that an indigent defendant in a criminal case had a right to counsel under certain limited circumstances concerning appeal. The Supreme Court argued that to hold otherwise would draw "an unconstitutional line … between rich and poor". In the latter case of *Harper v. Virginia State Board of Elections* 383 U.S. 663 (1966), the Supreme Court held that making the right to vote conditional on the payment of a poll tax was unconstitutional.

3 We could change the terms of the argument. One might suggest that there are some goods that should not be provided in market terms but on the basis of need. Equality of access to such goods requires "assurance of access to universally needed amounts". Discrimination would take place whenever "uniform price or other impediment" means that some are prevented from "accessing the good" (Michelman, 1969, p.12).

Thus, we need to move away from the notion of equality and the legal doctrine of equal protection. To find welfare rights in the constitution we can make use of the idea of minimum protection. It is also necessary to reject the notion of discrimination. For a start, the more accurate term to describe poverty is "deprivation" (Michelman, 1969, p.13). The requirement that the courts provide "minimum protection against economic hazard" is thus distinct from some forms of welfare rights arguments, but it is still based on a theory of social justice (Michelman, 1969, p.13). Minimum protection arguments are not concerned with overall patterns of distribution or with "equal[ising] income". They serve to "specif[y] ... just wants" (Michelman, 1969, p.14). Just wants are understood as legitimate claims on communal resources. An economic system is just if, despite the inequalities of wealth, there is a safety net that provides welfare to those in "relatively grave need" (Michelman, 1969, p.15). Whilst welfare might limit the incentive effect of inequality, minimum protection is acceptable because most people would accept the principle if they had to choose their future social position behind a hypothetical veil of ignorance.

Michelman is drawing on Rawls's theory of social justice. In summary, Rawls argues that differences in wealth are acceptable if they are organised in such a way as to benefit all citizens. Arguably, this approach to justice as fairness does not interfere with the pricing function of the market. It also offers a way in which severe disadvantage can be ameliorated and just wants satisfied (Michelman, 1969, p.35).[4] A definition of just wants is outside the scope of these investigations as our objective is to clarify the basis on which just wants could be defended. Michelman's notion of minimum protection identifies those "instances in which persons have important needs or interests which they are prevented from satisfying" through no fault of their own (Michelman, 1969, p.35). In such instances, the court must examine the facts to determine whether or not such failures of satisfaction are "tolerable" in a "just society" (Michelman, 1969, p.35). The broad outlines of the tolerability test take us back to the Rawlsian notion of the veil of ignorance. The test poses the following question: would nonsatisfaction of a just want be so "grave" as not to be freely chosen by a person informed of the organisational principles of a market society, but ignorant of their social role? In distinction to equal protection doctrine, the test for minimum protection seeks to avoid any language of "de facto discrimination" against the poor whilst allowing the courts to focus on severe deprivation (Michelman, 1969, p.39).

4 The relevant cases show that the issue at stake is not discrimination but fulfilment of a just want. *Harper v Virginia State Board of Elections* 383 U.S. 663 (1966) forbids "any fee ... in exchange for admission to the vote" and gives a number of reasons why such a classification is "forbidden" (Michelman, 1969, p.24). One such reason is "judicial protection" of the rights of the poor. Likewise, *Douglas v California* 372 U. S. 353 (1963) justifies special judicial protection of indigent defendants (Michelman, 1969, p.25). Classifying the right to vote and defendants' rights as just wants gets much closer to doctrinal logic than notions of equality and inequality (Michelman, 1969, p.32).

We might say, then, that an implicit idea of social recognition underlies this approach. Recognition is linked to the general terms in which the courts in a liberal society should protect the interests of its poorest members. Michelman's voice is one of modest persuasion. Linking Rawls's theory with welfare rights certainly provides a justification of judicial intervention into social problems that might win over those less sympathetic to the activities of the welfare rights movement. Pitching the argument in terms of minimum protection, and moving away from the language of discrimination to unjustifiable deprivation, re-positions radical claims in such a way that they are acceptable to constitutional lawyers and to wider understandings of the market as a provider of opportunities. However, at the heart of this vision of fairness and recognition of the poor is a defence of a market that generates inequality. Michelman is poised like Philippe Petit on a wire between a defence of the value of the human being and a belief in the necessity of the competitive energies of the market.

It may also be the case that an account of social justice satisfies neither liberals nor conservatives.[5] For liberal critics, Michelman's key terms are too thin. Minimum protection and unjustifiable deprivation arguments effectively leave structural inequalities in place. At the same time, minimum protection is too thick for conservatives. Minimum protection seeks to justify unnecessary judicial interventions in the market.[6] Michelman took these criticisms seriously. He redefined his position as a defence of American political culture. Defending this idea meant reaffirming the values of the liberal tradition as it came under increasing political strain at the end of the 1970s.

Michelman argued that Rawls's moral philosophy could articulate a consensus position that directs attention to "our … moral capacity" or "sense of justice" (Michelman, 1973, p.964). Uniting reasonable political opinion, whether liberal or conservative, was a crude, unspoken but nevertheless prevalent popular consensus around ideas of morality. Even if jurisprudence and political science had

5 Critics on the left thought Michelman might have framed his thesis too narrowly. For Fiss, the wider failure of the law to bring together race and poverty created a "constitutional straitjacket" in which the court restrained itself and foreclosed more radical and difficult questions about economic power and discrimination (Fiss, 1976, p.161). Do Fiss's criticisms misunderstand the nature of Michelman's project? Michelman could be defended as deliberately working with conservative doctrinal categories in order to push them in a progressive direction.

6 We can briefly consider some of the conservative criticisms of Michelman's position. Welfare rights were denounced as a "regulatory apparatus designed to protect particular groups from market competition" (Winter, 1986, p.748). Taxpayers and consumers thus carried the burden of an expensive and inefficient federal infrastructure (Winter, 1986, p.749). The power of the poverty lobby obscured the fact that most would be better off through the reduction of taxes. Tax reduction could be paid for by dismantling welfare programmes. These criticisms simply misunderstood Michelman's position. Indeed, some of the more stringent criticisms seem to be not of Michelman at all but of distortions of NWRO arguments thought to be somehow present in Michelman's text.

moved away from such concerns it was still possible to argue in terms of a "moral theory" that could "impart" a sense of rigour to "the day to day, intuitive considered judgement we already have" (Michelman, 1973, p.965). The whole point of the exercise was to "strengthen our commitment to our day-to-day considered judgments" in the light of a more coherent and rigorously worked out "academic" theory (Michelman, 1973, p.965). The Rawlsian notion of "reflective equilibrium" is thus testimony to a belief in public dialogue, a faith in a general debate about social order and its values. For example, in academe one might find scholars borrowing from traditions of thought congruent to their specialisms; lawyers looking to the work of philosophers and economists reading ethics. Whether or not a dialogue informed by such values could take place in the pages of law journals was one thing; the extent to which it could speak to a society undergoing traumatic changes was another. Any discussion of welfare rights would have to lead back to a vision of the constitution rooted in a popular and principled political culture that recognised poor people as citizens.

Michelman was primarily concerned with a mode of public argumentation drawn from Rawls's notion of ideal theory. Ideal theory argues that the stability of well-ordered society rests on a broad consensus over the terms of a decent political culture. How does the argument work? Ideal theory can address a situation that is far from ideal. It can be thought of as a less demanding version of the veil of ignorance argument. Instead of this rather complex thought experiment, we are to imagine a well-informed democratic conversation. In this conversation intuitive ideas are firmed up and given more precise shape as those in the debate seek to achieve broad agreement between different positions.

The next part of our argument seeks to analyse this idea of a moral conversation. We will attempt to follow the way in which Michelman's reading of Rawls performs the very critical openness to concepts that a serious, reflective conversation requires: a kind of re-working of concepts in the light of the complexities inherent in thinking about the "real world". A particularly important assumption is that the parties to the debate agree upon the fundamental nature of self-respect as constitutive of a decent society. We will also have to revisit the contentious question of the role of the court in the defence and elaboration of welfare rights.

Let's start with the basic structure of society. Rawls defined the basic structure of society as "the way in which the major social institutions distribute fundamental rights and duties and determin[e] the division of advantages from social cooperation" (Michelman, 1973, p.968). If the notion of the basic structure is to inform a theory of welfare rights, it requires us to understand poverty in a very specific way. We have to address the "intuitive" idea that the basic structure is a social structure: different people are born into different socio-economic conditions. An individual's sense of self and expectations for his or her life are in large part determined by his or her place in the social structure. This moves away from the simplistic idea that those "on welfare" are feckless or lazy. Inequality is a structural effect. Rawls's model also suggests that inequalities are not fixed, can be addressed politically and, at least to a degree, remedied.

One final point. A general conceptualisation of welfare rights cannot be seen as providing a resolution of problems that are inseparable from the form of market society. Inescapable tensions can be refined but not resolved. One particular concern is with the relative importance of the principles of equality and liberty. Rawls offers "precepts for adjusting tension between equality and proprietary liberty". To live within the tension, one has to appreciate a kind of ongoing complexity in the management of society.

Just as reflexive equilibrium requires one to constantly adjust and reassess one's understandings and values, living in the agonistics of liberty and equality means that one's thinking proceeds by a "shifting readjustment" or an "endlessly dialectical sort of 'progress'". As Michelman points out a little later, explaining the "shifting readjustment" requires us to be "highly sensitive to contingent circumstance" (Michelman, 1973, p.972). It is as if one must remain on a "value frontier" (Michelman, 1973, p.975). We might suggest that this complexity is the intellectual and emotional cost of living well within a market society. One could, of course, simply slice through the Gordian knot by declaring that either liberty or equality was the predominant value, but this solution would be out of keeping with the decorum of democratic conversation. The pressing issue is whether or not Michelman had been able to move beyond the claims of his critics on the left and the right. The notion of reflexive equilibrium appears to be the last stand of a mannered, sophisticated constitutional theory able to defend a complex account of regulated markets and the common good. Whilst the new left might have failed to define a more equal society, the ascendant right was becoming less willing to accept compromise. Could progressive constitutionalism hold its ground?

We need to look in a little more detail at an argument that takes us from the justification of welfare rights to the important concept of self-respect, a key term that will allow the further justification of the basic terms of the fair society. The point to carry forward is that welfare rights require limitations on liberty. In particular, if welfare rights rest on taxation, then raising revenues means that a tax burden has to be justified. Rawls is not perhaps clear on this point. His lexical ordering of principles places "maximum equal civil and political rights and liberties" prior to "equality of opportunity and the difference principle" (Michelman, 1973, pp.970–971). Does this mean that the liberty to hold property effectively trumps the forms of equality linked to the second principles? Following Rawls through on these points requires us to abandon the idea that there is a predetermined lexical ordering that provides a clear argument for preferring either liberty or equality. We need to find "a mode of accommodation" between the two terms that takes us back to the "shifting readjustment" that animates Rawls's moral philosophy (Michelman, 1973, pp.975–976).

A defence of welfare rights requires "proprietary liberty" to be limited or to "give way" to equal opportunity or "occupational liberty" – a coinage by Michelman which means "freedom of choice in productive activity" (Michelman, 1973, p.973). In practical terms, a mode of accommodation might be worked out that could, for instance, justify state-funded schooling in order to ensure that people were able to take up the opportunities available to them. We cannot confuse this modification of liberty by equality with an argument for levelling. Indeed, there is a difficult relationship between liberty and equality, especially as "the Rawlsian ethic calls for inequalities to be allowed (even favoured) to a point" (Michelman, 1973, p.975).[7]

We are re-reading Rawls to find a basic value that might be acceptable to all those involved in the debate about the form that a decent society should take. This basic value is the encouragement of self-respect. Self-respect relates to a person's sense that his/her life is valuable and has over-arching meaning (Michelman, 1973, p.983). More practically, it means that one can carry out one's plan of life. Self-respect thus requires both a sense of value and the confident belief that one can act towards a goal. Lacking self-respect, we fall into depression, "apathy and cynicism" (Michelman, 1973, p.983). Michelman provides a further gloss on self-respect that shows how it applies to the degradation of the self by poverty: "[t]he discrepancy between oneself and others is made visible by the social structure and style of life of one's society" (Michelman, 1973, p.983). The collapse of self-respect can be linked to a profound sense of existential alienation: "this psychological condition is experienced as painful and humiliating. The less fortunate are therefore often forcibly reminded of their situation, sometimes leading them to an even lower estimate of themselves and their mode of living" (Michelman, 1973, p.983).[8]

7 We have to leave to one side a detailed consideration of the reasons why a compromise between equality and liberty is best achieved through a package of insurance rights. The basic form of the argument runs as follows. Insurance rights are a "specific welfare guarantee" for "certain need[s]" such as "shelter, education [and] medical care". Arguing for insurance rights takes us away from Rawls's focus on "rights to guaranteed money income" (Michelman, 1973, p.966). Explaining why Michelman reaches this conclusion is difficult. Michelman agrees to some extent with Rawls's arguments about the ways in which the difference principle might protect provision for the needs of the worst off. As it requires the position of the most disadvantaged to be taken into account, the difference principle is more effective than the rival principle of utility. Whilst utilitarian arguments justify distribution on the principle of making all people better off, the difference principle requires us to take into account the interests of those whose situation may not be improved by an average increase in the distribution of wealth. However, the problem with the difference principle is that it provides no real argument for the justification of a justiciable insurance right rather than an income right. There is a second problem with the difference principle. It is fixed on the distribution of basic social goods and does not properly address people's needs (Michelman, 1973, p.982).

8 One can sense why Michelman links this understanding of self-respect with at least some notion of welfare rights but this does create problems (Michelman, 1973, pp.983–984). The difference principle requires maximisation. How can self-respect be maximised? The difficulties that result from trying to link the difference principle to increases in income for the most disadvantaged necessitates a different approach. Note that we are not trying to derive welfare rights from the difference principle (Michelman, 1973, p.990). This directs our attention to the opportunity principle and can be focused with a consideration of the right to education. Michelman tentatively suggests

To further develop this point, we can extend the notion of self-respect to political participation and to the guarantee of minimum welfare rights. Minimum welfare rights can be linked to rights to political participation as they provide citizens with the resources to develop the capacity and ability to take part in social, civic and economic life. If the Supreme Court has recognised that "some identifiable quantum of education" may be a constitutional right, then surely it is not going too far to suggest that there should be minimum rights to preserve "life itself, health and vigor … or shelter" (Michelman, 1973, p.677)? These rights relate to "the universal, rock-bottom prerequisites of effective participation in democratic representation" (Michelman, 1973, p.677).

This takes us to a tricky problem, the role of the Supreme Court and the contentious operation of judicial review. How can Michelman deal with the problems thrown up by an interventionist judiciary? To make sense of this state of affairs, one needs to remember that for Rawls the legislative system is not a "fairness machine" (Michelman, 1973, p.993). There will always be instances of public disagreement over the justice of legislative acts or judicial rulings. Furthermore, politics cannot be thought of as an ongoing manoeuvring for position between interest groups with nothing in common. If we allow these two arguments, then we can take further promptings from Rawls's moral theory. We can see moments of tension as opportunities to work on a new consensus through principled public disagreement. At this level, each protagonist "proceeds to support his favored principles by showing how strongly their public recognition will tend to engender in the populace a sense of justice" (Michelman, 1973, p.995).

But why should judges or courts make claims to the justice of welfare rights? This theme returns us to the starting point and the question of the role of the 14th Amendment. It is worth stressing how Michelman's performance of the democratic conversation involves re-figuring concepts that are central to his own work. To focus. The sequence of argument begins with the assumption that a society may experience tensions between its economic productive capacities and basic liberties. Following the argument from self-respect, it would appear to be acceptable that certain liberties could be suspended or restricted to allow "rights to the fulfilment of everyone's basic wants on which enjoyment of these liberties depends" – especially if there is not yet a "public sense of justice" that appreciates the serious consequences for a society if basic wants are not satisfied (Michelman, 1973, p.1000).

The court's operation of judicial review should have a limited role in "realizing basic liberties", but not to the extent that the court's rulings would "flatly

that "it seems to follow that no one may be precluded from the requisite education by income shortage" (Michelman, 1973, p.989). It may also be possible to go beyond a right to education. One would need to make the link between the ability to act in the market and the very constitution of one's ability to do so. Thus, the sense of the "minimum" provided by welfare rights relates to an "adequate assurance" that "basic rights, liberties, and opportunities may be effectively enjoyed, and … self-respect maintained" (Michelman, 1973, p.991).

contradict the priority of liberty" (Michelman, 1973, p.1000). Moreover, the operation of judicial review should be limited to a period of time when it can effectively intervene in social problems. Once basic wants are satisfied, the risk is that "paradoxically" the operation of judicial review would "stunt" the development of consensus over broad principles of justice that are properly dealt with in a "participatory forum" (Michelman, 1973, p.1000). Allowing judicial review to catalyse the search for a new understanding of welfare and justice would be essential to achieving a well-ordered society.[9]

Michelman is not suggesting that judges should read Rawls and then apply his theory of justice to legitimise decision making.[10] Nor is he proposing a defence of a counter-majoritarian position where wise judges hand down rulings from on high that are justified by moral philosophy. In Rawlsian terms Michelman suggests that the courts themselves can be seen as operationalising a form of reflexive equilibrium where "intuitively appealing" principles and convictions are negotiated to achieve some kind of compromise (Michelman, 1973, p.1007). We could see it as an attempt to determine the basic form of a decent constitutional order with welfare rights at its heart.[11] This is a long way from the idea that philosopher-judges carefully deliberate the principles that

9 Michelman admits that this is an "uneasy case" for judicial review. Provided that there was a principled justification, "politically aloof courts" could override the popular legislative will (Michelman, 1973, p.1001). There are counter-positions. One might argue, for instance, that welfare rights are themselves dangerously open-ended. How can a court determine the resources which allow an individual to take part in political life? How would a court deal with the argument from welfare claimants that they could only be effective citizens if the court mandated that they should receive a "disposable income like everybody else" (Michelman, 1973, p.699)? Indeed, rather than allowing the poor to participate in political life, welfare rights actually make it more difficult as they encourage dependency rather than political engagement. Ultimately, the welfare rights argument imagines a role for the court that it simply should not play. Such points ignore the subtleties of Michelman's arguments and as such seem somewhat outside the spirit of the democratic conversation.

10 The final phase of Michelman's development of a theory of welfare rights moved from moral philosophy to a more grounded reading of the constitution. His somewhat modest "positivist" and conservative position takes its starting point from the constitution itself and eschews at least some of the arguments about the coherence of the constitution and popular morality. Michelman links Ely's approach to the interpretation of the 9th and 14th Amendments with Rawls's argument about "social primary goods". Ely finds within the constitution an over-arching value of "political participation through representation" that provides constraints on judges "supplying content" to the 5th and 14th Amendments (Ely, 1978, p.669). This is a broad principle that applies to both processes and outcomes (but is not an argument that the constitution requires "equal distribution of the benefits of government"). Such "transtextual rights" are "commanded by the constitution" and apply to both law makers and judges. A "principled" theory of transtextual rights is legitimate when the "political branch" has failed to act, but any ruling must be consistent with the general constitutional commitment to "representative democracy" (Ely, 1978, p.674).

11 Some critics remained sympathetic to Michelman's project, but unconvinced by his doctrinal analysis. See (Frelich-Appleton, 1979, p.731).

will govern the republic (Bork, 1979, p.697).[12] Michelman clearly acknowledged that there were problems in deriving a justification of welfare rights from Rawlsian principles. A practical defence of judicial decisions in favour of welfare rights must appeal to moral principles that will be more or less successful depending on their congruence with moral ideas within society at large. The more contentious a moral issue, the more likely there is to be a tension between a judicial statement of value and any popular consensus. However, whilst these experiments in Rawlsian theory provided a re-statement of welfare rights, Michelman began to feel that he had invested too heavily in a transcendental model of moral philosophy.[13] It was necessary to mediate Rawlsian thought with a more historic, even materialist form of analysis to produce a critical genealogy of American legal and political culture. Rather than the abandonment of the welfare rights project, this was its intensification.

The prophet re-armed

Suddenly, in the middle of a long exposition of James Harrington's republican theory, the voice of the author addresses the reader directly:

> Now you, true democrat, may see here hierarchy, exclusion, and alienation.
> (Michelman, 1986, p.46)

A great deal could be said about this apostrophe – its urgency, its engagement with an early modern text that speaks to our condition, and its explicit mention of alienation. Although the substance of discussion is classical humanism, the concern with direct democracy links early modern politics to the concerns of the present. The exhortation "they were kidding themselves" might apply as much to the classical theory of *isonomia* (equal rule) as it does to the experiments of the new left and the SDS.

12 Bork sought to cut the ground from under Michelman's feet by asserting that the authorities relied upon to provide the case for welfare rights are incoherent. There is simply no way to derive clear principles from contradictory cases. This is precisely why Michelman had to rely on moral philosophy to provide a proper grounding for his argument. The starting point is the idea that it is impossible to find welfare rights in the constitution. There is not "a scintilla of evidence" that the "framers and the ratifiers" of the amendments had a notion of positive rights in mind. Even if their precise thoughts cannot be reconstructed, the correct interpretation would be to understand what they "reasonably" thought they might mean. If courts proximal to the ratification of the amendments did not see them as giving a power to judges to create new rights, then it is likely that the present interpretations are way off the mark (Bork, 1979, p.679).

13 The way forward is to realise the "socially contingent character of welfare rights" and from this new theoretical position "legitimize the justiciability of welfare rights" (Liu, 2008, pp.207, 209).

How might we learn from the past? Michelman's version of radical republicanism sets out an answer.[14] The guiding idea is still the pursuit of moral philosophy in public life. For some this was a "lunatic undertaking" (Michelman, 1988, p.1495). Republicanism should be written off as it represented a rigid, historical and crudely solidaristic idea of national community based on a notion of a moral majority that a liberal should not try to defend. However, Michelman's turn to radical republican revisionism can also be seen as a bold attempt to seize and transform a central concept in American politics. The hermeneutic labour of the republican constitutionalist aims at "the renovation of political communities" (Michelman, 1988, p.1496). Republicanism is most properly "the ongoing revision of the normative histories that make political communities sources of contestable value and self-direction for their members" (Michelman, 1988, p.1495). Michelman was inspired by the desire to recover the transformatory energies of the constitution (Michelman, 1988, p.1496).[15]

Reflecting back on one of our critical questions we can see how republicanism addresses a major issue with the democratic conversation: the question of who is included and on whose terms. The earlier concern with self-respect is now worked up to provide an account of a democratic, social self embedded in historical and cultural traditions that found a "community of equals" (Michelman, 1988, p.1501). Through republican theory Michelman attempts to incorporate the

14 One target of republican thought is law and economics as it puts forward in a particularly stark and compelling form a version of Bork's old argument. Courts in a democracy should not make law as the people acting through their representatives are the sovereign law-making power. Unelected judges should not be allowed to express their preferences in place of those of the people. Law and economics dress this position up into a broader theory of democracy. Votes aggregate preferences into consensus positions. Underpinning this version of politics is the idea of the democratic polity as an arena of struggle between interest groups. The dominant parties are those that are able to create and sustain the most popular consensus positions. Without further thought, this position is "lazy and presumptuous". The law and economics argument conceals the more pressing question of the "value" of sovereignty (Michelman, 1988, p.1498).

15 Re-working the inheritance of republicanism requires Michelman to return to the theme of liberty and equality. Alongside the familiar possessive concept is a less familiar distributive understanding (Michelman, 1988, p.1320). Certainly in the first "century and a half" of the republic and in particular with the ascendancy of laissez-faire ideas of the market, "property security" was central to the way in which the constitution protected the "private sphere" (Michelman, 1988, p.1327). It was not surprising that the protection of private property became "a transcendent and constraining force" given that property had its own "long history of common-law elucidation" (Michelman, 1988, p.1328). However, this does not exhaust constitutional understandings of property. The constitution also articulates "democratic principles of political equality" that are no less part of judicial or political culture than those of possessive norms. This tradition was re-energised by progressive critique which saw as much threat to liberty in the unrestrained actions of powerful market actors as it did in tyrannical government. The question for Michelman is how to put these traditions into dialogue. Whilst suggesting that a "worthy mediation" might be "possible", he confessed that more work was necessary to determine how this could be achieved (Michelman, 1988, p.1337).

experience of the civil rights struggle and the legacy of the war on poverty into the mainstream of constitutional thinking. To understand the dynamic and range of this argument we need to go back to its basic principles: "self-government" and "government by law". These principles make for two fundamental "demands" on the organisation of the polity (Michelman, 1988, p.1501). "Social life" must be governed by norms that are collectively determined and "the people" must be protected "against abuse by arbitrary power" (Michelman, 1988, p.1501). Agonistic American politics requires the fundamental principles of the rule of law to protect one group of people from abuse by another. In the Rawlsian phase of Michelman's work this idea provided a way of articulating the notion of a political order that guaranteed representation and a role in social and public life for all citizens. The principle that rights prevent abuse of a minority by a majority is now linked to a slightly different goal. Citizens participate in the pursuit of the common good. The republic is defined publicly and collectively. The good life is not about being "left alone" to enjoy one's property. It is informed by the positive politics of mutual self-definition.

Citizenship "stands for freedom as activity" – the ongoing re-creation by the people of "the terms on which they live together" (Michelman, 1988, p.1518). The articulation of the terms of the republic's common life is constituted through public dialogue where citizens persuade each other to "hold old commitments in new ways" (Michelman, 1988, p.1501; citing Pitkin, 1981, p.279). Citizenship also requires popular political activity, the pressure that social movements can bring to bear on matters of popular concern. Michelman's account of citizenship thus pulls the focus of the argument away from "foundational authority" or "the coercive exercise of centralized majoritarian power" (Michelman, 1988, p.1531). Authority must be open to challenge. This is where the court comes in. The court confronts "the people's self-enclosing tendency to assume their own moral completion" (Michelman, 1988, p.1532). The court ensures that the republican community can sustain "the plurality" on which ongoing "transformative self-renewal depends" (Michelman, 1988, p.1532).

This is a very elegant re-working of problems that had been considered in Rawlsian moral theory. In the culture of republicanism, the justification of authority can only be based on principles that are immanent to a plural democracy. The veil of ignorance might provide a general guide for the justification of authority but it risks abstracting from the actual world of faction and political debate. In seeking a point of origin, the idea of the veil of ignorance obscures a fundamental point. Democratic justifications of authority are always *in medias res* and embedded in a specific normative context (Michelman, 1988, p.1511).

Although welfare rights seem to be a little downplayed in the later essays we can appreciate how such rights can be brought into contact with republican political theory. Rawls's notion of an overlapping moral consensus has been replaced by a notion of democratic dialogue. This is not so much the pluralist idea of the poor (or their representatives) commanding votes in debates. Democratic dialogue requires principled and inclusive discussion over the basic shape of civil life. One could imagine how the terms of minimum protection could be debated by well-informed citizens. Like the debate on race, the idea of active citizenship takes forward the sense that resources are required for all to play a meaningful role in public life. The republican state ensures that all its citizens are participants in an ongoing conversation over the very constitution of the community that holds them together.

Progressive retrenchment

We can see Edelman's work as a response to Michelman's critics and an attempt to push forward a peculiar legacy in a period increasingly hostile to liberal thinking. As with Michelman's work there is a deliberate modesty to Edelman's position. In the place of a strident claim to welfare rights, there is a more modest objective: the right to a "survival" or "subsistence" income (Edelman, 1987, p.32). A survival income is not "a call for significant redistribution", nor does it have anything to do with an argument for a "court mandated adequate level of income" (Edelman, 1987, p.32). A survival income is about subsistence. Moreover, the Supreme Court could commit to defending a survival income without over-reaching itself (Edelman, 1987, p.32).[16] How? Ackerman's notion of structural adjustment can be pressed into service. A structural adjustment takes place "when [the legislature, the executive and the judiciary] join in actions which alter the previous constitutional understanding [and] it is appropriate to view what has occurred as effectively being an amendment to the Constitution" (Edelman, 1987, p.29).[17] The key historical moment is the consensus in the Franklin D. Roosevelt era over the role of the courts and law makers in offering some measure of economic security to American citizens. It is now necessary to build on the promise of the "legislative arrangements of the 1930s" (Edelman, 1987, p.7). In making use of

16 Acknowledging some of the criticisms from conservatives, the implementation of a right to survival income would require political action but that is not to say that the court lacks a proper role in establishing and defending positive rights or "certain affirmative obligations on the part of the state to its citizens" (Edelman, 1987, p.4). The doctrinal underpinnings are twofold: substantive due process and equal protection. The former asserts that there is an "implicit" constitutional "obligation" that requires the "more equitable" sharing of resources, the latter that government "complicity" in "economic arrangements" has produced "maladministration" as a "foreseeable consequence" of government policy (Edelman, 1987, p.5). Both arguments rest on the understanding that the legislative and judicial response to the Great Depression in the late 1930s opened a new constitutional era where "[t]he Court recognized that the state has the power to take steps to protect individual citizens from economic exploitation" (Edelman, 1987, p.5). Any return to questions of the original intent of the framers of the constitution becomes a background consideration.

17 A case like *West Coast Hotel v Parrish* 300 U.S. 379 (1937), where the court "ratified" minimum pay legislation, suggests a new relationship between citizens and government. *Brown v Board of Education of Topeka* 347 U.S. 483 (1954) can also be understood in this way (although in *Brown* the court acted before the legislation of 1964 and 1965).

the structural adjustment thesis, Edelman is moving away from the representation-reinforcement approach that Bork had criticised in Michelman's work. Edelman readily admits that beyond "provision of a base survival income" the court is an inappropriate forum for the design and implementation of anti-poverty programmes (Edelman, 1987, p.8). The complexities of poverty relief must be dealt with through legislation. However, in the absence of legislation, the courts should pursue "antipoverty strategies" aided by litigators using what they can of state constitutional law to prepare the ground for a more coordinated campaign (Edelman, 1987, p.8).

What do we make of Edelman's position? As compelling as these arguments might seem, are they perhaps not still too radical for a conservative court? Edelman argues otherwise. Even a conservative Supreme Court had seen fit to show concern for the effect of state laws on the economic security of its citizens.[18] The upshot is that the Supreme Court can build on authorities to hold that "an income that does not even permit subsistence is an outcome of state-sanctioned economic arrangements that will not be tolerated" (Edelman, 1987, p.45).[19] This is a bold argument. At the level of doctrinal analysis, Edelman further clarifies the kind of position Michelman had taken, but avoids the limitations of Michelman's republicanism. Conservatives had been scathing about the irrelevance of moral philosophy for legal doctrine, arguing that if philosophers could not agree on the

18 For instance, in the early twentieth century, the Supreme Court struck down state laws that allowed for coerced labour in the Peonage cases.

19 The real difficulty is the case law. *West Coast Hotel v Parrish* 300 U.S. 379 (1937) laid down the important principle that the court would "presume the validity" of legislation that protected the "economic status" of citizens (Edelman, 1987, p.26). Edelman goes on to argue that later cases show that the court is recognising rights that "relate to family and personhood" – the very constitution of the human being threatened by poverty. It may be that the court has been cautious, preventing interference with rights, but the case law still provides justification for actual protection of rights. The education cases provide the "strongest" support (Edelman, 1987, p.33). Although one can overestimate the reach of *San Antonio Independent School District v Rodriguez* 411 U.S. 1 (1973), as the case cannot be read as an authority on a constitutional right to education, the court did affirm that "some identifiable quantum" was necessary to meet a basic need for education. It is a little unclear what this means, but arguably the case suggests that any fee levied for education cannot be set at a level which "excludes" poor people (Edelman, 1987, p.33). *Griffin v Illinois* 351 U.S. 12 (1956), on a different point (the right to a trial transcript in order to appeal), goes a little further. It is not an equal protection or "state action" point. Griffin frames the question of the reasonableness of failing to "alleviate the consequences of differences in economic circumstances" (Edelman, 1987, p.36). Further support on these themes can be gained from *United States Department of Agriculture v Moreno* 431 U.S. 528 (1973) and *New Jersey Welfare Rights Organization v Cahill* 411 U.S. 619 (1973). In these cases, the Supreme Court removed restrictions on food stamps and AFDC benefits (Edelman, 1987, p.38). The case law on medical benefits is a little more problematic, especially as the relevant authorities are bound up with issues of abortion for indigent women. One creative reading of these cases might suggest a limited right to minimal medical care provided that it is not used to secure an abortion.

correct moral response to poverty then their work was of no help to judges. The response? Show that there is, for the most part, an agreement over the moral right to a survival income (Edelman, 1987, p.19).[20] Edelman effectively demonstrates that the liberal philosophical tradition has a broad consensus around ideas of support for human needs. This move goes a long way to play off the field certain objections to philosophical arguments. Despite the strength of Edelman's position, was it too late to rekindle sympathy for welfare rights?

In the early 1990s the problematic of progressive constitutional scholarship shifted. It was as if, in response to the ascendancy of the right, liberal scholars were forced to significantly redefine their position. This chastened mood is best summed up in Sager's understanding that the search for political justice had to exist alongside "constitutional practices [that] … ignore desperate poverty and entrenched racial disadvantage" (Sager, 1993, p.435). Recalling earlier arguments, Sager stressed that it was not outlandish to assert that those who "make reasonable efforts" ought to be helped "to secure the minimum necessities of a decent life" – especially given the scale of the problem and the economic resources available. However, it was also important to acknowledge the "durab[ility]" of resistance to this project (Sager, 1993, p.411). Sager acknowledges the new conservative consensus over welfare: "aspirations" that were part of the constitutional tradition now seem extremist. The constitution was too "thin" to support welfare rights arguments. Had the curtain finally come down on progressive constitutionalism? This dark mood takes us to Balkin's notion that "we" have inherited a very particular form of predicament: the radical theorist of the constitution is in bad faith if his/her theorising does not allow that the constitution can be used for "evil" ends (Balkin, 1997, p.1716). Constitutional theorists are forced to use a language that may not accommodate their sense of justice – or rather, a sense of justice drawn from alternative American traditions (Balkin, 1997, p.1728). Can we hear very distant echoes of the voices of those lawyers who committed themselves to the poor – seeking to think, live and argue differently?

Conclusion: rule and energy

Michelman opened up a new way of talking about the constitution, marrying together doctrinal argument with moral philosophy. The theme of self-respect runs through the various phases of his work. Self-respect requires citizens to have claims on resources. This makes welfare a minimum condition of citizenship. In republicanism this idea might become a little more abstract, but it is present in the concern with the maintenance of a decent polity. Citizens can only play an active

20 The consensus can be traced across from Article 25 of the Universal Declaration of Human Rights to the various positions within contemporary rights theory. Thus, Rawls's contractarian position, with its emphasis on basic goods, or Gewirth's argument about the basic requirements of "shelter, food and clothing as a necessary condition for human action", correspond with notions that one can find in Locke and Aristotle (Edelman, 1987, pp.19–23).

role in the community if they are not crippled by poverty. Edelman brings these themes together. The notion of a basic survival income re-works welfare rights arguments. The role of the Supreme Court in preserving at least some of the inheritance of the war against poverty stresses the importance of the law in building an inclusive political community. The exclusion of the poor from the polity is a failure of democracy.

We can take from Michelman and Edelman the important reminder that legal theory must engage with formal institutions. The approach to "being with" and creative anxiety that ran through Chapters 2 and 3 needs to be modulated in order to achieve a critical understanding of fundamental legal structures. There must be some dialectical movement between the analysis of modes of inter-subjectivity and notions of rights and law. The use of moral philosophy in Michelman's and Edelman's work shows how notions of self-respect can provide a broader account of social organisation which takes moral equality seriously. Whether this borrows from Rawls or the idea of a survival income, the philosophy of the constitution is underpinned by a notion of social recognition. Although there are clearly differences between Rawls's liberalism and the traditions that frame the analysis of "being with", this does not mean that Rawlsian notions cannot be pushed in a more radical direction.[21] A similar point could be made about the moral philosophical approach to a survival income. How can this argument be developed?

Progressive constitutionalism carries forward one aspect of the struggle for welfare rights, even if it downplayed the energies that came from street protests in order to privilege sober lawyerly discourse. But what if the idea of welfare rights was too thin from the very beginning? Perhaps it is now time to set an agenda about what the courts should be doing about a political culture that has lurched too far to the right. To put the point a little differently, there is a risk of rights fetishism, or of forgetting the politics out of which rights claims emerge. Dewey and Addams returned us to the "primal" scene of creative democracy. Whether or not we want to think in terms of an "I-thou" relationship, the midnight fiction, or honourable speech, it is hard to re-frame these approaches in terms of a Rawlsian difference principle or a republican political tradition, no matter how inclusive.[22] Our times require new arguments.

It is necessary to find a point of overlap between progressive constitutionalism and the radical tradition so that points of communication and disagreement can be plotted.[23] Our argument takes us to Michelman's consideration of the Arendtian

21 See Gearey (2012).

22 Forbath has argued that one significant problem is the hostility of the republican tradition to welfare rights. Republican understandings of citizenship need to be taken in a somewhat different direction. Indeed, one ultimately has to become a critic of republicanism if one wants to push it in a progressive direction (Forbath, 2004, p.599). We will pick up on Forbath's arguments in Chapter 10.

23 Indeed, if we consider Michelman's most recent approach to poverty and constitutional rights, we arrive at a particular crossroad and a strange encounter between the "Liberal

notion of the *vita activa*. Engaging with Michelman's Arendt opens onto ideas of alienation and economy that will allow a re-engagement with the energies of critical constitutionalism. The *vita activa* describes an active, public life of civic engagement. It contrasts with what Arendt takes to be the Marxist understanding of praxis. This stresses (for Arendt wrongly) a rival idea of *homo faber*. Arendt asserts that the concept of "man as maker" cannot provide a model for a form of politics in which "everyone is visible to each other". The *vita activa* in the "modern period" must be found in a "measure" – a way of defining the public bond in an era when everything has become calculable and exchangeable – in short, a world defined by the market: a world in which people are alienated from themselves.

The problem is that the Arendtian arguments move too far from the Marxian insights of the crits. If arguments about legal forms cannot engage directly with *homo faber* – or, more specifically, the gendered, racialised division of labour in market capitalism – notions of progressive constitutionalism will risk compromise with conservative hegemony. Progressive constitutionalism must take a radical turn and bring together the figures of *homo faber* and *vita activa*. It may be that this approach can grapple with West's claim that liberalism has proven incapable of dealing with the "fundamental causes of social misery" that stem from the "maldistribution" of "wealth" (West, 1990, p.1798). The more pressing issue is the need to discover a way of holding together *homo faber* and *vita activa*. [24] We will

Constitutional Mainstream" and the "Democratic Left" – terms that map (not without remainder) onto our argument (Michelman, 2014, p.216). The gist of Michelman's argument is that these two traditions share a set of assumptions about the "moral legitimacy of coercive power" that extends beyond proceduralism and negative rights, to rights over "basic economic necessities" (Michelman, 2014, pp.215, 217). There might be disagreements over the range of positive rights, but the main point is that these two traditions of thought are bound up together.

24 Michelman's recent work seems to be moving in this (or similar) direction. His collaboration with Margaret Radin attempts to bring together pragmatism and critical legal thinking. Rather than using ideas of personality or character, Radin and Michelman deploy a notion of agency. They describe their insight into agency as an understanding of "the problematic, elusive, 'humanist' experience of subjectivity", and go on to argue that subjectivity/agency is "an historically irreversible, inexpungible, constitutive aspect of *our* experience of (human) being" (Radin and Michelman, 1990, p.1058). Note the italics, rather than the quote marks around "our". Agency is a problematic, a work in progress. Yet it is fundamental to the way in which we conceive of ourselves and understand our actions. They go on to elaborate: "[p]art of what we do, as concept-making strivers caught in forms of life, is think about the good – the better – world and ourselves acting towards it." In terms of the argument that we are developing, Radin and Michelman can be read as bringing together the concepts of *vita activa*, and *homo faber* in order to define an ongoing work on the self that is the experience of agency. This argument would certainly correspond with the idea that alienation and reification describe a kind of social death: once experience becomes reified, the self is unable to change and becomes trapped in forms of self-understanding that see things only as they are. The "better world" is very similar to the democratic collective creation of the common good that we found in Dewey's philosophy. Arendt's world alienation is thus

develop these themes in Chapter 10. For the moment, we do not want to run ahead with the argument. The first step takes us to Marx. We will be interested in how themes of self-respect can be combined with an understanding of the social reproduction of capital. The next chapter begins the long march through Marxist theory.

given a much more granular location in the everyday where men and women (and those who are neither or both) engage with the terms of their lives; terms that are as much linked to the necessities of work and the tragedy of poverty and unemployment as they are about the "active public life of politics".

Chapter 5

Reification and the consciousness of the welfare poor

Introduction

Our examination of progressive constitutionalism concluded with an agenda for further thinking. In this chapter we want to pick up on these themes and engage with contemporary accounts of social reproduction, reification and poverty.[1] The social reproduction of capital articulates work and poverty. To be unwaged, low waged or unemployed is to be unable to commodify your labour, or to commodify it in an insufficiently remunerative way. This account of social reproduction is a fundamental insight of the ClassCrit "turn to Marx". We will extend these arguments to consider Marx's understanding of the surplus population and read these themes into Piven and Cloward's writings. Picking up on the notion of a poor people's movement, we will focus on the NWRO and the CWRO. At the end of the chapter we will relate our understanding of the welfare movement to themes discussed in earlier chapters. We will be particularly concerned with the politics of social recognition that defined the activist street philosophy of the NWRO and CWRO.

1 Grasping the social reproduction of capital requires an understanding of what Marx called the "articulation of production" (*Gliederung*) or an "economic form" that is composed of combinations (*Verbindung*) of elements. These elements coordinate the means and relations of production (Marx, 1973, p.17). In *Capital III*, Marx referred to this structure as "the entire formation of the economic community" (*Gestaltung*) (Marx, 1954, p.770). Production relations (or relations between people and the means of production) are based on culturally and socially contingent constructions of gender and race (and, of course, other factors which we cannot presently consider). Social relations are independent from the mode of production itself but can become structured by the mode of production. These relationships have to studied in very specific ways. As Hall has pointed out, one should not transpose one pattern on another: the "racism within plantation slave societies in the mercantilist phase of world capitalist development has a place and function, means and mechanisms of its specific effectivity, which are only superficially explained by translating it out from these specific historical contexts into totally different ones" (Hall, 1986, p.337). As explained in this chapter, we want to determine how race and gender map onto forms of work and worklessness. This will allow a critical purchase on ideas of reification and alienation. To follow Hall's argument, our approach is limited to an engagement with the historical period set out in this book.

Bringing it all back home: intersectionality and reification

To understand the emergence of a concern with social reproduction and reification in critical legal thinking we need to engage with the reception of Marx in the work of scholars associated with a later wave of CRT. Marxist thinking was largely absent from foundational debates on racial identity. These themes were touched upon in Chapter 3, where we read the work of scholars on double or unhappy consciousness and argued that this moment represented a failed opportunity to develop the relevant conceptual language. We broke off our discussion around the theme of ethics and will continue to delay any further analysis of ethics as we need to deal with a prior point. Why is the turn to Marx important?

The beginnings of an answer can be found in Richard Delgado's work. Delgado has argued that the critical tradition neglected "material factors such as profits and the labor market" in the analysis of "racial hierarchy" and gender hierarchy (Mutua, 2008, p.889).[2] To carry forward a critical account of race and gender we need to define such "material factors" and examine their importance to constructions of race, gender and class. Our investigations will be particularly concerned with the ClassCrits – a grouping of CRT and LatCrit thinkers who, in Grahn-Farley's words, "trea[t]" race and class as two distinct and, at the same time, interdependent concepts" (Grahn-Farley, 2008, p.935). The ClassCrits appropriated Marx in a subtle and sophisticated way. To this end it is worth bearing in mind McCluskey's positing of ClassCrit thinking. It is necessary to counter a kind of right-wing argument that presents "conflicts amongst cultures" as somehow "essential" and "prepolitical" as well as resisting those on the left who see an engagement with race, gender or sexual orientation as a distraction from a proper analysis of class conflict (McCluskey, 2007, pp.1295–1296). We could label this intersectional thinking – provided that we understand this contested term as a way of engaging with the coming together of class, race and gender from a very particular perspective:

> [A]t [the] intersection: theoretical reflections start in and through a silhouette of life, after the fact, with all the countless, priceless, motionless layers of time folded, compressed … and the various corners of the world suddenly brought to light, to the center stage. This seems how a life, instantly, becomes an

2 See the debate around the feminisation of poverty. Mutua argues that the concept should be "retired" in favour of methods that get at the "multidimensional nature of poverty" and can be used to "promote[s] anti-essentialist, anti-subordination principles and practices", which, in turn, may enable "coalition" building (Mutua, 2001, p.1182). Mutua's argument should be read alongside those of Park and Broad. Broad argues that the concept of the feminisation of poverty must be "expanded" beyond the work of both feminists and scholars of transgender issues to date so that it can comprehend "racialized" and "sexualized forms of subornation" (Broad, 2001, pp.1145, 1159). Park makes a similar point in relation to poor immigrant families (Park, 2001, p.1164).

> afterlife, serial constellations of Nachträglichkeit (belatedness or deferred effects), as one seeks to "find an order in the drama of time."
>
> (Lee, 2012, p.468)

How do we read this strange voice? Our guiding principle is that intersectional analysis is a thinking of complexity, "layers" and "compressions". It is therefore entirely opposed to any approach, Marxist or otherwise, that seeks to reduce phenomena to the effects of an economic base or any other prior structuring instance. The intersectional voice is also aware that it is speaking after the fact as a latecomer, discovering life in vague figures and shadowy representations. We will argue below that this kind of thinking picks up on a theme within the philosophy of alienation: the reification of consciousness. We will go into much more detail below, but there are other key themes that we can carry forward from Lee's argument.

How can a "silhouette of life" be "brought back to center stage" so that one can "find an order in the drama of life"? These are potent metaphors. They play with notions of acting and agency. If we are actors in a drama, how do we come to consciousness of the staged nature of our lives? To continue the metaphor, if the drama is ongoing, when we become conscious of the role we are playing we must realise that we are latecomers. Players in a scene that started a while ago. Lee then shifts the metaphor. It might be said that "[o]ne needs to stand back in order to reflect" (Lee, 2012, p.468). Does this mean that one needs to stand back from the drama to appreciate its proper nature? Already we are encountering the intricacies of intersectional thought. As we know from our earlier analysis of double consciousness, simply standing back and reflecting may not be enough. How do we know that our reflections do not simply repeat the assumptions that we are attempting to critically appraise? The latecomer knows that s/he must think through inherited forms of consciousness. In other words, what the passage above captures is a very specific moment in recent critical theory.

Lee captures the condition of the unhappy soul who is seeking a way forward through an engagement with the puzzling legacy of the past. Unhappy souls try to find themselves in the struggle with the meaning of history's riddle. This is the split double subject who is anxious precisely because s/he knows that s/he is not how s/he has been cast. Anxiety relates to the very problem of being fixed by, strangely, a "silhouette of life". We thus come across a nuanced way of thinking about reification. Intersectional thinking resits the argument that this is abstract philosophy. It is an engagement with life itself. To be precise, the ClassCrits – as intersectional thinkers – have sought to develop understandings of how social structures of class *and* race *and* gender come together with market relationships to determine forms of being. The double-ness or triple-ness, the folded nature of these lived categories of being, is such that they constitute, at one and the same time, the point at which being is fixed and, as we will see, the possibility that this fixing or reification can be *thought through* and critically assessed.

Critical assessment has to begin with the material conditions which define the form of one's being. The determination of being must be thought of in terms of complexity. Critical purchase on determinations of being must also engage with the material circumstances of the thinker. What then are material circumstances? Summarising the dynamic of this kind of thinking Mutua wrote that the ClassCrits "see the economy as a historical intergenerational human organization that includes reproduction and production" (Mutua, 2008, p.869). Mutua is focusing on how social relationships create and sustain hierarchies that are definitional of identity. Our sense of ourselves comes out of the material world in which we are located. But how do we *understand* the way in which identities are reproduced and we are led to play certain roles?

We can return to the notion of a form or a silhouette, a reflection of life that has somehow been internalised and fixed, and repeat the question that we asked in Chapter 3: what is the precise nature of this process of internalisation? To pick up on Lee's analysis, we would also have to examine how this process of fixing itself becomes invisible so that the silhouette passes itself off as real. The desire to comprehend a process that (in Selma James's metaphor) parcels out roles to people is not just the task of the academic or the philosopher. In case this seems a somewhat abstract consideration we want to stress that this approach will allow us to read the writings of anti-poverty militants with the sensitivity they deserve. To return to the surface we need to go deeper. We need to examine "how our own situations are organized and determined by social processes that extend outside the scope of the everyday world" (Smith, 1987, p.152). How do we grasp this process of reproduction from within?[3]

This is the point at which we can make a more extended reference to the theory of reification. As explained in Chapter 1, our working thesis on reification linked the term to a specific aspect of alienation: the way in which social and economic processes are misunderstood and/or made invisible with the effect that the self is frozen or "thingified". We are concerned with reification in this chapter because it directs our attention to the way in which historical, cultural and economic norms

3 Stressing the specific historical and cultural circumstances in which race is constructed means moving away from the pointless debates about how racial difference might be somehow biologically grounded or already present in human nature: "racial or ethnic characteristics" only become "socially pertinent" in specific, concrete situations (Hall, 1986, p.338). Racism gives symbolic meaning to the "differences between men" – differences that are to do, in part, with the structure of labour (Du Bois, 1899, p.4). Clearly these are fluid relationships. Race is a relational phenomenon understandable by reference to "the positioning of different social groups in relation to one another with respect to the elementary structures of society" (Hall, 1986, p.338). These positionings are complex and differentiated: "they are practices which secure the hegemony of a dominant group over a series of subordinate ones, in such a way as to dominate the whole social formation in a form favourable to the long-term development of the economic productive base" (Hall, 1986, p.338). There is not some mysterious force that makes capitalism racist; rather, there are particular forces operating at particular historical junctures that make for an "overdetermination" of economic relations with racism.

are bound up with the social reproduction of capital. These norms are internalised by social actors. We will see that reification directs our analysis to the way in which a feeling of worthlessness becomes what one "is". However, this is to run ahead with our argument. We need to focus on the way in which reification or the fixing of identities and the social reproduction of capital can be linked together.

We can demonstrate this point by referring back to Selma James's classic reading of Marx. James refers to the "hierarchy of labour powers" (Delgado was perhaps echoing this expression). The structuring of labour power by the market requires that certain labourers carry out certain functions and that this parcelling out of function is by reference to a labourer's "natural and their acquired capabilities" (Marx, 1954, p.349). James notes that "these acquired capabilities are taken to be our nature and fix our functions for life, and fix also the quality of our mutual relations" (James, 1973, p.6). James's approach is entirely congruent with intersectional thinking, an understanding of the folding of economic function and social relations. James also shows how the acquisition of economic functions is concealed. They are parcelled out by the market itself. Those determined by market functions then identify so strongly with their role that it appears to be their nature. Our capacity for kinds of remunerative and un-remunerative labour thus appears to be natural when it is in fact an effect of economic and social organisation. These supposedly natural capacities then go on to define how different kinds of people relate to each other. They are simultaneously race, gender and class relations. James presents a number of examples: "planting cane or tea is not a job for white people and changing nappies is not a job for men" (James, 1973, p.6).

James is thinking about the organisation of markets around waged and unwaged work. To recall the theme from Chapter 1, we come back to Marx's thinking on commodification. In the hands of James (and other scholars) this term is given a broad meaning. Commodification of labour does not just mean that labour provided in market terms is bought and sold like any other commodity. It means that in order to properly explain the buying and selling of labour we must look at those forms of labour that are uncommodified. Uncommodified labour, work done for the most part by women rather than men, can be seen as the affective work of caring for children and sustaining family life (Law, 1983, p.1251). We could extend this point and argue that there are other forms of commodified work that exist alongside formally commodified work. From an historical perspective slavery could be described in such terms. Suffice to say that we can immediately appreciate the relevance of intersectional analysis in thinking about commodification. Quite simply, we cannot explain the commodification of labour unless we look beyond traditional class relationships based on the mass employment of male labourers in industry.

So, the class terms in which labour is commodified are inseparably linked with gender and race. For instance, low-waged work has conventionally been the preserve of marginalised social groups whose conditions of labour have excluded those forms of protection and solidarity enjoyed by more organised and privileged workers. Even within forms of low-waged work, there are differentiations on the basis of gender with particularly precarious forms of employment reserved for women. There is one other point. In the context of the welfare state, benefits are provided in an uncommodified form. State agencies fix benefits levels rather than the labour market. Even though benefits take an uncommodified form, the general context is still one of commodified wage labour. This very distinction between commodified and uncommodified labour must be carefully policed by the state with strict conditions for receipt of benefits and the various forms of supervision, discipline and control. Building on Piven and Cloward's argument, welfare can be seen as a "surrogate" form of control that operates alongside the market and is particularly relevant when markets appear to break down (Piven and Cloward, 1972, pp.7–8). Precisely because "normally dominant" patterns have been disrupted, welfare bureaucracy creates alternative forms of discipline to hold in place the broader market order. We lack the space to trace these historical, social and economic structures in detail but the main point is that these structures of social life affect the ways in which people think of themselves.

So, reified consciousness has to be seen as the way race, class and gender are linked to understandings of self. This is the key point in the classical analysis of reification. One suffers from reification at the moment one takes one's market position as a personal destiny (or even perhaps as a matter of bad luck). Whilst there are undoubtedly many modes in which one blames oneself for what one has become, the task is not to trace their various manifestations. Our main concern is to grasp how one understands these defining structures. This theme from Marx returns to our argument above.

Marx uses the metaphor of an observer gazing at "motion" of "the heavenly bodies" to describe the difficulties of seeing "social production" clearly. Just as an observer of the stars from earth can gain a sense of their movements in space, one can gain an understanding of the systemic effects of social production from within one's location in the structure itself. Of course, we need to make a distinction between Marx's own theory and the writings of poverty activists. We will not necessarily find the application of Marx's ideas in the latter but we will attempt to use a broadly Marxist framework to articulate themes that run through the literature on welfare activism. This concern will be developed in the last section of this chapter. For the moment we need to remain with Marx. Most specifically, we have to look clearly at "the influence of the growth of capital on the lot of the labouring class". We also need to see that social production in capitalism is "a movement of alternate expansion and contraction" (Marx, 1954, p.593). Perhaps this seeing should more properly be called a coming to see. We will argue below that it is not so much the achievement of the lonely thinker as an experience of collective political agency.

The construction of worklessness and poverty

Thus far we have linked reification to the social reproduction of capital and examined the idea that we can critically recognise the way in which our being and consciousness are shaped by economic and social processes. But how does the economic determination of being relate to both the reproduction of capital and the reproduction of poverty? Just as class, race and gender determine patterns of employment, we must acknowledge that they play a significant role in the reproduction of patterns of deprivation and exclusion. What, then, is the nature of those forces that parcel out not just work but worklessness as well?[4] Once we have clarified these themes we can return to our fundamental question: how does worklessness relate to the reification of the consciousness of the poor?

It is interesting that these themes, at least in outline, can be found in *Capital.* A reading of the relevant chapters shows that the theme of reification runs through the analysis of the surplus population and capital accumulation. Marx may not have had a sophisticated analysis of race or gender, but provided we allow that the social reproduction of capital covers those social relationships that structure both the labour force and the surplus population (including those who fall into poverty), we can find the basic form of an account of work and worklessness in *Capital.*

To understand the relationship between work and worklessness we need to examine the interface between technology and mass employment in a national economy. Certain fields of industry or agriculture require large labour forces.[5]

4 We need to refer briefly to Marx's understanding of poverty. Pauperisation and the social reproduction of capital are inseparable concerns. In other words, the emergence of a class of wage labourers is fundamentally linked to a "sub-class" consisting of those who will be unable to commoditise their labour. Although this is something of a generalisation, it does not suggest that Marx's approach to poverty was simplistic. As with the analysis of class and gender in this chapter, the guiding theme is the need to examine complexity. This takes us to the second component of Marx's work, the critique of the understanding of poverty in political economy. One of the central themes is the rejection of Malthus's thesis that population would rise until it outstripped the resources capable of its support. Malthus's premise was that families increased as wages rose: a family with a large number of working children would have a greater income than one with a smaller number. The Poor Law also encouraged the poor to breed. The remedies were obvious. Abolishing the Poor Law and limiting the number of children born in working-class families would stabilise the supply of labour and reduce poverty. Malthus did not understand the real pressures at work. The working class were made "supernumerary" not through their propensity to breed but by the very operation of the market. Marx sketched out a series of interacting factors that would tend to the creation of a "supernumerary" working population. The most significant factors were the "unlimited prolongation of the working day", the use of machinery in production and distribution, and the increasing employment of women and children. Alongside effects linked to the contraction of markets abroad and the cessation of hostilities in foreign wars, the system of production inevitably threw people out of work. Thus, Marx writes: "[i]t was … far more convenient, and much more in conformity with the interests of the ruling classes … to explain this 'over-population' by the eternal laws of Nature, rather than by the historical laws of capitalist production" (Marx, 1954, p.581).

5 Marx writes that the reproduction of labour power "must incessantly re-incorporate itself with capital" for the expansion of the latter. We arrive at something of a vicious circle: the "reproduction of labour power forms, in fact, an essential element of the reproduction of capital itself". From this notion of reproduction, we can return to the

However, technological innovation lowers the demand for labour. Mechanisation throws people out of work. At the same time, mechanisation produces opportunities for employment in other branches of industry as "capital continues growing for a time on its given technical basis" requiring "additional labour power" (Marx, 1954, p.590). What some economists call the "flexibility" of labour is for Marx the notion of the surplus population of workers, where surplus has to be understood by reference to the "labouring population['s]" relationship to capital accumulation conceived as "social capital in its totality" or as the "attraction and repulsion" of labour by capital within a national economy linked to global trade cycles. This is the key point in the analysis. As labour enables the accumulation of capital it also produces the "means by which it itself is made relatively superfluous" (Marx, 1954, p.591). It is as if capital "forms a disposable industrial reserve army that belongs to capital quite as absolutely as if the latter had bred it at its own cost". This has nothing to do with "actual increase in population" (it is not a natural law). The creation of disposable labour has everything to do with "the changing needs of the self-expansion of capital, a mass of human material always ready for exploitation" (Marx, 1954, p.592).[6]

A surplus population is not an unfortunate side effect of the system, it is an effect of the system's normal functioning.[7] If one studies Marx's analysis in

idea that the accumulation of capital relates to a process of expansion and contraction. A point is reached in the "general basis of a capitalistic system" when "in the course of accumulation" the "productivity of social labour becomes the most powerful lever" (Marx, 1954, p.582). This is the case with the development of machinery in production but also the division, combination and concentration of labour that goes hand in hand with technological development, competition in the market (as each capitalist vies to make his/her business as profitable as possible), and cycles of trade that – depending on the rhythms of the market – allow some businesses to expand and condemn others to cóntract or fail completely. Various branches of industry also have a relationship of attraction and repulsion. The combination of these factors leads to a number of effects: the centralisation and concentration of capital in the hands of those capitalists who are either luckier, cleverer or more ruthless than their competitors, the switching of individual capitalists between more and less profitable lines of business, and the fluctuating demand for labour power.

6 As Lebowitz has pointed out, Marx's critique of political economy began with a rejection of the rigidities of economic thinking that classified man as either capitalist or worker (Lebowitz, 2003, p.141). This is associated with Hegel's thinking of a "determinate being" as grounded or concretised by a "manifold of determinations" – each of which appears "permanent and persistent" (Lebowitz, 2003, p.142). It is therefore the case that each determination can be posited as a ground, and the others perceived as non-essential. Lebowitz argues that this theme is retained by Marx. It may be that he "assumed in Capital that individuals … were only bearers of … class relations" or the "personification" of "economic categories". In reality human beings must be conceived as concretised in "all human relations and functions … in whatever form they may appear" (Lebowitz, 2003, p.142).

7 The existence of a "reserve army of labour" keeps the costs of labour down or incentivises those with jobs to work harder.

Capital, it becomes clear that a number of factors need to be taken into account. However, we also need to examine the various forms that the welfare state has taken in the period after *Capital*. It is also necessary to think much more clearly about the role of the welfare state in the differentiation of the surplus population and take into account the role that race, gender and class play in determining who suffers from the effects of unemployment and low-waged work.[8] If we want to study reification in the consciousness of the welfare poor, we need a clear grasp of these themes.

We can look to the work of Piven and Cloward to clarify our thinking. Their focus is on the profound "economic convulsion[s]" that determined the context of poverty and worklessness in the America of the 1960s (Piven and Cloward, 1972, p.200).[9] Piven and Cloward show how mechanisation in southern agriculture dramatically impacted on patterns of employment in the years after 1945. Gathering pace over the next couple of decades, mechanisation allowed a dramatic increase in the size of farms whilst at the same time leading to a fall in demand for unskilled black labour. By "becoming economically obsolete [poor people]

8 The reproduction of labour is based on a complex differentiation of gender and race. It does not take place so much behind our backs as through the colour and gender of bodies. If we were to sketch out a "grid" of possible experiences, it would be constructed around the nodes of black male/black female/white male/white female, then differentiated further (crudely) around other understandings of ethnicity and further differentiated by understandings of class. Our grid would then have to take into account the temporalities of these positions: how they are lived in both personal and historical time.

9 In order to understand what happened in the post-war years, and particularly the intersection between worklessness, welfare and race, we need to briefly sketch the foundations of America's "quasi-welfare state" in the years between 1933–1938, the period of the New Deal (Katz, 1996, p.236). The response of the federal government to the Great Depression was fundamental in supporting capitalism during a moment of crisis. Government intervention laid down the structures of welfare and relief that enabled the economy to recover. The latter period of the New Deal saw legislation on social insurance and public welfare. The Social Security Act 1935 divided responsibilities for welfare between federal funding of work relief and social insurance, state control of general assistance, and partnership between states and central government over public assistance for persons such as widows and children. The 1935 Act was also structured on a marked distinction between social insurance based on contributions and means-tested public assistance under the Aid to Families with Dependent Children programme (Davies, 1993, p.18). Social Security operated within an existing cultural pattern of racism and exclusion that determined that state aid went largely to white workers. Many states, particular those in the South, resisted the implementation of the Social Security Act and AFDC. To some extent the outbreak of World War II and the sudden demand for manpower meant that it was not necessary to address the deep-seated problems that lay behind the tensions in the New Deal. The fundamental issue was that "relief practices enforce[ed] low wage labour" (Piven and Cloward, 1972, p.124). Low-waged labour was itself embedded in a pattern of work structured around race and gender to "ensur[e] a pool of marginal workers" (Piven and Cloward, 1972, p.126).

became objects of indifference" (Piven and Cloward, 1972, p.210).[10] The dire situation in the South led to the unprecedented migration of black agricultural workers to northern cities.[11] Two thirds of the rural population abandoned the country for the city. Northern cities may not have been characterised by the "near feudal" structures of coercion and control that existed in the South, but persistent discrimination prevented migrant labour from making use of the traditional opportunities offered by urban employment.[12] Although the ghettos nurtured

10 Prior to mechanisation a social and economic system had developed where poor tenant farmers, resident on the land of planters, would work long and hard in the summer in order to bring in the cotton harvest. Such was the demand for labour that women and children would also be employed (but on lower wages to the men). In the winter months the tenant farmers would attempt to survive on what they had been able to save but invariably ended up in debt to the planters. This system effectively ensured a pliant workforce, even though it meant that there were some social obligations from planter to tenant farmer that enabled the latter to cope in the months without pay. With mechanisation the demand for mass labour dropped off suddenly. The use of crop-dusting planes, mechanised cotton pickers, combine harvesters and cotton gins can be compared to the effects of earlier technological innovations in the industry of the 1800s. The average social labour required for the harvesting of cotton fell. Skilled operatives were needed to service the machinery but most families found it very difficult to survive. Alongside the contraction of the demand for labour and the increase in the size of farms, tenant farmers began to lose what little land they held at the permission of the planters as more and more land was brought into cultivation. Minimum-wage legislation did not help. Easy to avoid, most planters saw it as a spur to invest more in machinery than in the labour force: "[t]he poverty of tenant farmers had always been severe. Now that they had become economically superfluous, their poverty became desperate" (Piven and Cloward, 1972, p.205). Although the AFDC was in place in the later years of the 1940s, a variety of factors meant that welfare rolls did not rise. Piven and Cloward show how gender and race were fundamental. Many southern states had enacted limits on welfare entitlement that restricted or even completely excluded black women from eligibility. Restrictions related to sexual morality could also be deployed to deprive families of benefits. Evidence heard by the Mississippi State Advisory Committee also pointed to the widespread existence of sharp practices within welfare administration designed to deliberately reduce benefits, restrict information on eligibility or intimidate women into not making claims. There were also ways of avoiding the implementation of the Food Stamps Act 1964 which gave poor families access to nutritious food through the operation of a rival scheme based on the distribution of surplus food: "cornmeal, flour, and lard" (Piven and Cloward, 1972, p.208).

11 Opportunities in defence industries during the war years created jobs and encouraged the migration of around 6 million people from south to north. The end of the war brought unemployment at the very same moment that mechanisation was beginning to impact on southern agriculture.

12 New patterns of underemployment developed. Mechanisation had destroyed many low-skilled jobs. Social problems caused by lack of work were exacerbated by the concentration of black migrants into ghettos. Lacking political and social power, those condemned to ghetto life had to put up with slum housing, rotting infrastructure and persistent crime. The failure to sustain conventional patterns of employment put further strains on black families, leading to increasing divorce, abandonment and single-parent families. Concerns about social breakdown became reflected in popular fear of

discontent, social deprivation was not in itself enough to account for the rise of militancy. Equally significant was the breakdown of deference that was an achievement of the civil rights movement. A new wave of political activism found a leadership amongst the nascent black middle classes and strategic opportunities for organising in the war on poverty (Piven and Cloward, 1972, p.223).[13] Despite the failure of the Poor People's Campaign, the politics of race and poverty had become a significant element in the social ferment of the late 1960s.

Reification and resistance

How can we explain the NWRO in terms of the thesis developed above? We want to argue that it is possible to see the NWRO as organised around resistance to reification. What seems at first to be a "politics of consumption" is a subtle critique of reified consciousness in the social circumstances of the commodification of labour (Kornbluh, 2007). Whilst litigation was central to the movement's ideology and strategy, these strategies were linked to understandings of the reifying effects of the dependency on markets. We will show how law and rights talk provided critical terms to articulate the reification of self that poverty and welfare dependency produced. After a brief description of the movement's history, organisation and ideology, we will address the ways in which the NWRO confronted social alienation and the reification of consciousness.

The NWRO had an ideology clearly articulated around a number of key ideas and claims. The overarching concern of the movement was a desire to establish "welfare or an adequate standard of living as a citizenship right and a human right". In the words of George Wiley, "the way to do something about poverty is to give the people the money they need to meet the basic necessities of life at least at a minimum level for health, decency and dignity" (Kornbluh, 2007, p.68). We can appreciate the influence of Martin Luther King's thinking on economic justice in such sentiments; the NWRO clearly fits into a tradition that sees social rights as

crime and disorder, "white flight" of businesses and families to the suburbs, vandalism, juvenile delinquency and – in the summers between 1964 and 1968 – wide-scale rioting.

13 The sudden and dramatic rise in numbers on relief, 58% in the three years between 1965 and 1968, came in the context of this disorder. Even in the South, numbers claiming welfare went up 43% (Piven and Cloward, 1972, p.245). How can this be explained? One reason is that it was easier and cheaper to allow the welfare rolls to increase than it was to put together substantive intervention to prevent poverty. Earlier in the period, there had been limited attempts to combat discrimination, such as the Executive Order against discriminatory employment practices in 1941 and a Commission on Civil Rights in 1947. There had also been the ruling in *Brown v Board of Education* 347 U.S. 483 (1954) and the Civil Rights Act of 1957. However, most urban blacks remained discriminated against in employment and disenfranchised from local politics. For instance, urban renewal schemes dedicated to slum clearance were used to clear land for business and investment rather than for the regeneration of the inner cities.

both compatible with and implied by civil rights (Jackson, 2007). This line of thinking can also be traced outside the American context to T.H. Marshall's ideas on citizenship. Kornbluh and others have presented these arguments as a "politics of consumption" but we want to push this argument in a slightly different direction.

The NWRO's politics of consumption were developed against the prevailing terms of commodified wage labour. Indeed, moving beyond the social citizenship tradition, the "right to live" was rooted neither in waged work nor childcare. The right to live was an incident of citizenship and required by ideas of equality within an advanced democracy. The movement understood that the labour market was unable to provide decently remunerative jobs. Workfare schemes also failed to offer a route into permanent employment. If the market was unable to provide families with a wage, then a decent welfare system should go beyond rent and food to cover those consumer goods that were taken as necessary to a decent standard of living.

The NWRO articulated a very particular political consciousness. It addressed the welfare state as an agency that served to discipline a certain portion of the population. This operation of welfare was well attested to by both activists and claimants. Forms of classification were themselves "dehumanising". As one report suggested: "[a] system which requires such a finely computed budget allowance as 48 bobby pins per year for a woman, 12 haircuts for a man if he is employed and 9 if not, must result in abuse of human values and rights" (Brager and Purcell, 1967, p.297). The welfare poor were the subjects of schemas of classification and control that defined their needs and then subjected them to scrutiny. Those who became dependent on the state surrendered their autonomy and agency. Consider Mary Spurlock, a welfare activist, who published an article in the NWRO newsletter with the following acrostic on the word welfare: "Wanting, Envy, Losing, Fear, Anger, Revenge, Emptiness."

Spurlock's definition of welfare demonstrates the crippling of the self occasioned by welfare dependency. Other documents suggest that this was not an isolated condition. As the Moreland Commission Report on Public Welfare in the State of New York pointed out:

> Welfare policies tend to cast the recipient in the role of the propertyless, shiftless pauper. This implies he is incompetent and inadequate to meet the demands of competitive life. He is then regarded as if he had little or no feelings, aspirations or normal sensibilities. This process of proving and maintaining eligibility in combination with the literal adherence to regulations and procedures tends to produce a self-perpetuating system of dependency and dehumanization.
>
> (Brager and Purcell, 1967, p.78)

It is hardly surprising that the writings of anti-poverty activists contain themes that also run through the philosophy of reification. The frustrations of dealing with bureaucracy ran from "baffling" and "incomprehensible" confrontations with the Welfare Department to more intense forms of "harass[ment,] intimidat[ion]" and disenfranchise[ment]" (Sheehan, 1976, p. viii). One report noted that any complaint against unfair treatment was automatically disqualified: "[t]he validity of any criticism is denied on the grounds that low-income people do not understand the complexity of the conditions that they are protesting." This theme was picked up by an MFY report that stressed the disregard paid to the recipients of welfare services: "[w]hen residents of the lower class community attempt as individuals to redress their grievances with public agencies, they are often defeated before they start" (MFY, 1964, p.68).

In the face of bureaucratic inflexibility, NWRO strategies that insisted on due process and respect can be seen as an assertion of the dignity of welfare claimants. There were other ways of resisting. If welfare bureaucracy denies a viable way of being, the logical extension of this position is to commit suicide. A contemporary report cites an unnamed claimant:

> [O]ne of these days, I'll go up to the top of the Brooklyn Bridge, yell "Here I go", and then jump off. And you know what? Nobody will know! Nobody will care. Nobody will miss me. Maybe the welfare would be happy because they wouldn't have to give me money anymore.
>
> (MFY, 1964, p.73)

These poignant words show how the isolation and desperation of the poor was compounded by their treatment by welfare agencies. The language of a relative surplus population may get at structural positioning but it does not allow us to articulate the withering of the self. To become or to be considered surplus or wageless is to suffer from "depression, self-hatred and pessimism … a flight from life" (Campbell, 1984, p.209). We might even say that poverty is non-being or occasions a "total existential crisis" (Campbell, 1984, p.24). The poor man is a "phantom man" (Wallace, 1965, p. ix). To be poor is to be cancelled out.

You can remain rancorous or begin to see through to the real causes of your frustrations. In struggling against these forces of anomie, NWRO activists came across a major theme in the analysis of alienation and reification. To take a prompting from the classical analysis of alienation and reification, the human response to rationalisation and bureaucracy is the "affirmation of everyday life and its demands" (Löwith, 1982, p.76). To become a member of the NWRO was to take part in a movement that offered its members a different understanding of themselves. Movement activists knew that one had to begin organising in subtle ways:

> Start not with groups who seek to produce great change, but rather … create groups which satisfy various needs within the framework of life as it is now lived in these areas … as the formation of a cooking class … or a sewing

> class … [Then] the people we attempt to recruit [for the action of organisation] will already have had experience in group life.
>
> (MFY, 1964, p.76)

Politics begins at home. Building a movement began with experiences of being with others that might become ways of urging participation in a wider, public life.[14] We could perhaps contrast this vision of organising with that of bureaucratic definition of needs. The human needs the movement understood were those of company and social intercourse; the language of dignity and rights were ways of articulating and defending those forms of sociability that came from cooking or sewing together. A politics of conviviality.

We can read these themes into the CWRO. A pivotal figure in its organisation was Alicia Escalante. Escalante was active in the formation of the East Lost Angeles Welfare Rights Organization (ELAWRO) in 1967. The organisation faced similar problems to the NWRO: racist bureaucracy, stigmatisation and discrimination (Bermúdez, 2014, p.96). The catalyst for the formation of the organisation were cuts in the medical programme initiated by Governor Reagan in 1966, and the group were successful in preventing the initiation of the Medi-Cal reforms. Escalante came into contact with leading members of the NWRO, and inspired by figures like Johnnie Tillmon, ELAWRO was incorporated into the NWRO. The link was, however, short lived. Escalante felt that the NWRO never properly understood the problems faced by Spanish-speaking welfare mothers. Despite this split, both groups cooperated in campaigning against an amendment to the Social Security Act that placed conditionalities on receipt of benefits. Although ultimately unsuccessful, ELAWRO, now called the CWRO, continued to play an ongoing role in community organising, and, indeed, in the development of Chicana feminism.

Writing in a Chicana feminist journal, *Encuentro Femenil*, Escalante outlined her life as a militant. The authority of her writing comes from being there, experiencing the life of a welfare recipient. Escalante thus knows what being on welfare can do to people. Hardly surprisingly, these thoughts resonate with those of NWRO activists. It is only the depth of the "hurt" that can inspire a person to "fight" – to "gain back everything" that had been "lost" (Bermúdez, 2014, p.101). Fighting back re-asserts lost dignity: a sense of one's self as "a woman, an individual … a human being" (Bermúdez, 2014, p.101). The moment of self-realisation comes amidst the routines of the everyday. Recounting her first protest meeting, Escalante notes that it took place only after she had "sent the kids off to school and packed their lunches". The slow process of self-becoming is signified

14 This is exemplified in NWRO activities in Nevada: the occupation of Caesar's Palace Casino, and the creation by Ruby Duncan and others of Operation Life – a community organisation that in fact outlasted the NWRO and provided resources to deprived neighbourhoods of Las Vegas (Orleck, 2005). It is worth noting that Sparer was involved in Operation Life, and saw it as an exemplary community organisation (Law, 1984, p.427).

with deprecating "I liked what I saw them doing, so I thought I would become part of the NWRO" (Bermúdez, 2014, p.101).

Re-fashioning the self as an activist brings new knowledge. Insights into what has been hidden from those who do not question why things are the way that they are. Outlining the CWRO position against conditionalities, Escalante wrote:

> Forced labour is the means by which the welfare system helps to manipulate the labour market to the advantage of only the employers, the owners of industry, business and finance ... Forced labour does not create jobs ... On the contrary, is has the effect ... of driving wages down by increasing the competition of already scarce jobs. In short, the purpose of forced labour is to undercut the bargaining power of labour. And of course, it does not even begin to resolve the welfare mess or the problem of mass unemployment and poverty.
>
> (Bermúdez, 2014, p.105)

Escalante's argument provides a subtle appreciation of the inter-linkages that exist between social and economic phenomena. Forced labour (calling conditionalities what they are) serves to expand the pool of the industrial reserve army with welfare recipients. Escalante makes the essential link between welfare and a particular organisation of labour, a further exemplification of themes that run through Piven and Cloward's work. This writing testifies to an engaged and critical sensibility, able to see through the claims of apologists for welfare reform.

Beneath the shadow of the freeway

Contemporary scholarship on the NWRO has made much of the rhetoric and writing of the women at the core of the movement (Triece, 2013). In establishing the distinctive ways in which the NWRO articulated itself we can usefully make reference to their writings on the peculiar dynamics of movement sociality. The milieu in which NWRO activists operated can be gleaned in D.H. Melhem's poem dedicated to the eastern regional director of the organisation, Jeanette Washington. The poem can be read as an investigation of the anger caused by alienation and reification. A single, unpunctuated sentence describes Washington in unsentimental terms, but at the same time performs the sociability, the care for others, that was the NWRO's animus (Melhem, 2005, p.77). Washington was herself a poet. In "The Good Life", she writes of NWRO practices of conviviality (Kornbluh, 2007, p.39). Her poetry is composed of fragments of protest songs, from Guthrie's "Hard Travellin'" to "We Shall Overcome". Varying the rhythms of her lines, she evokes the activities that bring the good life into being. Washington's poem suggests that, whatever else the good life might be, this most Aristotelian of terms is realised when people come together.

Poetry can provide other insights. Consider the short poem "Allí por la calle San Luis" (over there on San Luis Street). Like Lorna Dee Cervantes's famous poem, from which the title to this subsection is taken, Tafolla's poem is a scene of work. However, whilst Cervantes's piece is a domestic scene set around a "fire-place in a backyard" where a daughter talks to her grandmother, Tafolla's piece is work in public view. Carmen Tafolla shows how work is placed in both social and psychic economies. The scene evoked in the title is an "elsewhere" – "over there" – to the side of the street, not the business of the main thoroughfare, but a stall selling cheap food; and an ancient ritual is enacted between two women:

> West side – corn tortillas for a penny each
>
> Made by an aged woman
>
> and her mother.
>
> Cooked on the homeblack of a flat stove,
>
> Flipped to slap the birth awake,
>
> Wrapped by corn hands.
>
> Toasted morning light and dancing history –
>
> earth gives birth to corn gives birth to man
>
> gives birth to earth.
>
> Corn tortillas – penny each.
>
> No tax.
>
> (Fisher, 1980, p.411)

The aged woman and her mother are focused on the task in hand; a mundane task, that is nevertheless a focus of experience, indeed, long experience if an "aged woman" is working with her mother. But this is also a pathetic scene: why is it necessary for two aged women to be selling tortillas on the street for a penny each? The hard work of poor people. The "homeblack" of the stove is a description that evokes the domestic, but here what is normally private and intimate (the kitchen) is in full view. The poem then modulates into a different idea of work, childbirth. The hands that are cooking are hands that have been involved in the birth of children. Women's work is the "dance" of history – this stately and noble metaphor sitting oddly against the sidewalk scene, and a kind of informal economy ("no tax"): generations going on, whilst the cycles of economy repeat themselves. The lyric "toasted morning light" suggest a register of perception quite different from the world of market exchanges of Calle San Luis.

Tafolla's poem, then, is one of work – the kind of work that her ancestors did: a "long line of maids, nursemaids, and servantpeople". In writing, one asserts a kind of agency, and a form of memory, which, whilst it pays tribute to the past, also signifies that the present is different. The work of this poem, the form it provides for memory, thus contrasts with the forgotten, low-status labour of the two women sat by the side of the road. These themes are pulled together, and connected more explicitly to political activism, in the following passages from Johnnie Tillmon:

> I'm a woman. I'm a black woman. I'm a poor woman. I'm a fat woman. I'm a middle-aged woman. And I'm on welfare. In this country, if you're any one of those things you count less as a human being. If you're all those things, you don't count at all. Except as a statistic.
>
> (Tillmon, 1972, no page numbers)

Tillmon's piece begins with a statement of identity. At one level it is a list of attributes, some of them pejorative. But it works within a critical statement of what this identity means. The attributes described in the opening paragraph are used to destroy personhood, to turn a human being into a role, a stereotype or a frozen version of themselves. Tillmon is cleverly and subtly engaging with resisting reification, a resistance that is communicated at the level of the text by a grain of voice. Note, if nothing else, the deliberate punctuation in the first line, and the way in which the second paragraph is contrasted with the third:

> I am 45 years old. I have raised six children. There are millions of statistics like me. Some on welfare. Some not. And some, really poor, who don't even know they're entitled to welfare. Not all of them are black. Not at all. In fact, the majority – about two-thirds – of all the poor families in the country are white.
>
> (Tillmon, 1972, no page numbers)

A specific impression of a life, a biography interrupted by the way in which the reifying qualities of welfare turn the unique into the general. The voice of experience continues talking. The social reality of poverty is not just a matter of race because the poor are black and white:

> Survival. That's why we had to go on welfare. And that's why we can't get off welfare now. Not us women. Not until we do something about liberating poor women in this country.
>
> Because up until now we've been raised to expect to work, all our lives, for nothing. Because we are the worst educated, the least-skilled, and the lowest-paid people there are. Because we have to be almost totally responsible for our children. Because we are regarded by everybody as dependents [sic]. That's why we are on welfare. And that's why we stay on it.
>
> (Tillmon, 1972, no page numbers)

Tillmon unpicks the terms of the welfare system. Precisely because the work that women do is unwaged and because social and economic patterns define women as suitable for this work it remains of low social status. Staying on welfare is not a personal choice but the structural effect of a system of social and economic reproduction. Welfare serves a structural function, perpetuating a system that preserves low wages and unwaged work. However, note the way that the term liberation appears. Just as the Cahns spoke of dissent as the voice of the poor, liberation is the marker of humanity. Tillmon announces a theme that we have already come across in Escalante: one has to become an activist to survive; to create the self and its values: "[f]or those of you mothers who think I may not be a good mother because I am a militant, on the contrary my children are very well taken care of in every respect" (Bermúdez, 2014, p.101). Self-recognition becomes a politics that creates a new awareness of a communal self. The movement comes out of meetings, talking, organising; it is a correspondence of interests, a performance of its own agency. There is a colour line and a poverty line:

> Either it breaks you, and you start hating yourself, or you break it.
>
> (Tillmon, 1972, no page numbers)

The legacy of the welfare rights struggle

How can these themes be framed? Can one speak of movement theory? Are we shifting to a register that is somehow inappropriate for an account of the NWRO or the CWRO? To misquote Löwith, it might be that any theory is "powerless" when confronted with the "naked existence" of a hostile, alienating reality and comes "under [its] domination". Had the movement succeeded, it may have made "social policy less segregated and stigmatising" than it had been, and may even have provided "the basis for the kind of social solidarity" that had eluded American policy makers (Kornbluh, 2007, p.187). The welfare rights movement's arguments on citizenship might have provided the basic structure for "equality across lines of race and class" (Kornbluh, 2007, p.184). Can we therefore point to an inheritance from the activism of poor men and women, an inheritance that might indeed allow us to understand what it means to be a poverty activist, or a poverty lawyer in contemporary times?

In the arguments above, we linked the working through of reification to the notion of social recognition. We argued that reification and recognition are important terms in the critical engagement with alienation. If one reads Johnnie Tillmon, or Mary Spurlock, or if one reflects on the organising acumen of women like Beulah Sanders or Alicia Escalante, one arrives at the idea that these women did create themselves through their actions. Tillmon, for instance, knew exactly what was vital in organising against poverty: "[e]ither it breaks you, and you start hating yourself, or you break it." Arguably, we have identified the terms of an activist street philosophy that has at its core "the problems of the subject of action" – whether this articulates itself in terms of a struggle for La Raza, civil rights or poor people (Lukács, 1968, p.145). The subject of action is a we – a we that recognises itself as a political agent and whose agency is expressed in action. Notions of rights and dignity that the welfare movement deployed have to be understood as operating in this very peculiar context. The legal strategies, the test cases, the marches, sit-ins, occupations and meetings were all part of a continuum. We cannot make the mistake of misreading this theme as an argument about marching or litigating as both were clearly important strategies.

We do not mean to suggest that we see the welfare rights movement as the subject of history (or as the realisation of some primal form of recognition). Both these tendencies in the theory of alienation and reification make claims that are hard to defend. Our position is much more modest. In forms of welfare militancy and organisation we can find creative thought and action that enabled those involved to think of themselves differently. Agency is linked to this assertion of worth. This goes back to the "uses" of Marx and intersectionality that we discussed in the opening sections of this chapter. Marx's critique of the market is based on the very possibility of seeing through, of understanding reality. Intersectional thinking is very much part of this tradition. The root of the problem is misrecognition, or quite literally failing to see things for what they are. You risk simply living through the categories that the market and its culture have imposed upon you: white man or black woman; rich man, poor man. In whatever way you are embodied, a non-critical acceptance of these terms freezes the self into rigid forms. How is it possible to live modes of identity without repeating oppressive social norms? The following passage defines the response:

> When the poor wage their own war against poverty, they win a new image of themselves. Private lives have been transformed by the organised achievement of social goals.
>
> (MFY, 1964, p.70)

This is the moment that brings into being the critical thinker and activist. Note the emphasis on agency in these lines: the poor "wage their own war" on poverty. In this active engagement they gain "a new image of themselves" – "private lives" are "transformed". The significance of the theme of agency is clear and it points to one final question: what is the role of the lawyer in the struggle?

Contemporary accounts point to the inevitable tensions that developed in the movement between working-class activists, movement lawyers and their middle-class allies. We want to point to a different working out of the problems and potential of this alliance between lawyers and militants. If NWRO activism can be understood as the creation of authentic terms of agency, how can poverty lawyers understand their own engagement? Perhaps the emphasis is less on doctrine and test cases, and more on the lawyer's own conceptualisation and understanding of his or her role. This leads to further pressing issues. In the next chapter, we will argue that the legacy of the NWRO is bound up with questions lawyers posed to themselves about their own ethics, and an anxious sense of vocation.

Conclusion

In this chapter, we have used the work of the ClassCrits to bring together elements of Marx's thinking with intersectional analysis. This has allowed us to grasp the relationships between work, worklessness and the social reproduction of capital. We have linked these themes to alienation and reification in order to study the way in which social norms are internalised. We have used these themes to read our way through accounts of the militancy of the NWRO and the CWRO. The welfare movement's politics of consumption were rooted in an appreciation of the commodified nature of work and the discipline of the welfare state. Militant thinking countered these experiences of exploitation and bureaucracy with an assertion of the inherent human dignity of all citizens. We argued that the welfare movement produced a sophisticated philosophy of communal self-creation. The final section of the chapter elaborated this form of critical thinking. It offered a way of understanding how radical lawyers might grasp their engagement in social struggles. These themes will be investigated in the next chapter.

Chapter 6

I must make something of myself

Conscience, anxiety and "being with" the poor

Introduction

Why should a lawyer work alongside the poor?

In this chapter we turn to poets and unconventional practitioners of law to provide insights into the anxious conscience of the radical lawyer. The chapter opens with a brief analysis of William Stringfellow's thinking. We will be interested in Stringfellow's approach to Marx. Whilst not unsympathetic to Marx, Stringfellow pressed into service a distinct set of concepts for describing the work of the poverty lawyer. We will argue that Stringfellow's writings can be read as an ethics of poverty law that builds on but extends beyond his Christian faith. Stringfellow's idea of an "existential situation" opens onto a practice of poverty law as "being with" the poor (Stringfellow, 2005, p.54). The constitutive anxiety of the poverty is a visceral response to the social degradation of other human beings.

The chapter will develop as follows. The first section will trace the similarities between Stringfellow's thinking and our analysis of commodification in the previous chapter. Stringfellow's concept of the powers of darkness can be understood as a way of grasping the alienating and reifying effects of capitalist markets on human being. The next section engages with key terms for our reading of Stringfellow: conscience, freedom and being with the poor. We will use these concepts to make ideas central to Stringfellow's faith more generally available for an ethics of poverty law. The concluding sections read these ideas into Stringfellow's writings and elaborate the important links between conscience and anxiety. The final section shows how our thinking moves beyond Stringfellow's faith and into a general understanding of the constitutive anxiety of the poverty lawyer.

The powers of darkness

What do we make of Stringfellow? Any interpretation of his writings must address his radical Christianity. Consider the following statement:

> ... there is no Christian jurisprudence. There is not a particular philosophy of law which has special integrity in the Gospel. Nor is there a way really to make

> the positive law or the ethics of law, the purpose of law which men offer as a measure for positive legislation, compatible with the Gospel.
>
> (Stringfellow, 1957, p.96)

The Gospel does not offer a philosophy of law. There is simply no way to make law coordinate with the Gospel. It would follow that, as a Christian, Stringfellow's praxis is entirely excessive to law and justified from the point of view of something quite irreducible to human standards. At the same time, Stringfellow must show how the divine command or call can be heard in this world. What are the terms of this praxis? To clarify. This chapter does not seek to suggest that there is an account of the social reproduction of capital in Stringfellow's work. Nor are we in search of any particular engagement with the ideology of the movement. The focus of the argument is the way that Stringfellow and Marx touch in compelling ways on matters of alienation and reification. Alienation and reification are for Stringfellow "the powers of darkness". Commodification and the effects on human life of the powers of darkness are not the same thing. However, there is a relationship between these terms. Most importantly for an outline of Stringfellow's radical praxis, this relationship raises the question of how one thinks and acts when confronted with the alienating and reifying effects of the powers of darkness.

The powers of darkness are "the fundamental institution of society: specifically, "property" and "money" (Stringfellow, 1957, p.34).[1] To engage with "the powers" as a Christian means moving beyond the limited terms that would oppose spirituality to materiality. One would also have to reject the easy conclusion that money is "the root of all evil" (Stringfellow, 1957, p.36). How can one talk publicly about what property and money mean when these over-simplistic reactions limit creative thinking? On one hand, a poor man might object to any lecture on money and poverty from a "young, white, Anglo-Saxon, Episcopalian, Harvard attorney", whilst on the other, a "banker" would "disqualify" the views of anyone who had little money himself. A productive critical engagement on money and property would need to bring together theology and economics. It is important to remember, though, that Stringfellow is focused upon "the truth of the fall" as much as "economic doctrine" or "precise empirical statement[s]: sin as much as profit, conscience as much as class" (Stringfellow, 1957, p.42).

From a Christian perspective "money" is a "fallen … institutio[n] of the world". Money "has lost its essential integrity as an institution", which means that "it exists in a state of distortion as to its true meaning and function" and has become "both symbol and fact of the alienation" that "exists between and among

1 As Wink argues, "[i]n short, the powers comprise all of social, political and corporate reality, in both visible and invisible manifestations" (Wink, 1992, p.26). Wink sees Heinrich Schlier's *Principalities and Powers in the New Testament* (1961) and Hendrikus Berkhof's *Christ and the Powers* (1962) as the beginnings of modern scholarship. However, Wink notes that whilst these texts opened up possibilities of a "Christian social ethic", the work of these pioneers was limited to a "dogmatic context" (Wink, 1992, p.25). Stringfellow's thinking clearly suggests a new perspective on this position.

all men [...]" Having money is not "a sin", but as a fallen institution, the potential for sin is inherent and inseparable from money (Stringfellow, 1957, p.36). Money as value is meaningless. Indeed, just as the poor are made invisible, money makes invisible the reality of systemic injustice: "[i]n this world men live at each other's expense, and the affluence of the few is proximately related to, and supported by, the poverty of the many" (Stringfellow, 1957, p.41). The sinful or alienated nature of money is found in the way in which money is itself "the value and worth of other things" and that the worth "of men" can be "measured in monetary terms". The poor are not outside this circuit of money: "the idea that money has integral value is popular among the poor and is – ironically – the incentive for much of their own exploitation" (Stringfellow, 1957, p.39). In summing up, we almost come back to Marx's language of fetishism: "[w]here money is an idol, to be poor is a sin" (Stringfellow, 1957, pp.39, 40).

We can trace certain parallels between this language of sin and Marx's thinking on alienation and reification. The metaphors are particularly interesting. Money conceals its own lack of substance as it is the nature of the powers of darkness to conceal themselves. Just as commodities hide the labour that goes into their creation, money obscures real human worth. However, whilst the theology of the powers runs in parallel with certain of Marx's ideas, Stringfellow was not a Marxist. The fetishisation of money has a fundamentally religious meaning. Money "enshrines" itself in the "place of God himself" (Stringfellow, 1957, p.40). We are still within the purview of an account of reification as idolatry or the sin of "embrac[ing] a person or thing" rather than God "as the source and rationalization of the moral significance of ... life in the world". It follows that how one got one's money is largely irrelevant and cannot be considered as "evidence of virtue". On these themes, the Gospel is outrageous. Man is "not saved by any work of his own" – least of all thrift and hard work. Moreover, there is no sound position from which to proclaim the innocence of the poor and the "malice" of the rich. Indeed, even in economic terms, there is no way of showing that in "every transaction" a "direct one to one cause and effect relationship" can be traced between "the lot of the poor" and those who benefit from economic success. Speaking in theological terms, we have to appreciate that "all human and institutional relationships are profoundly distorted and so entangled". No one is innocent (Stringfellow, 1957, p.42).

Stringfellow is putting forward a notion of praxis: "[a] Christian does what he must do as a Christian" (Stringfellow and Towne, 1971, p.2). Christian praxis rejects all simplistic accounts of morality and what Stringfellow takes to be Marx's position: that the poor are poor because the rich are rich. There is no causational relationship between wealth and poverty. Money and property are "powers of darkness" because they conceal God. Moral significance is found in the search for God and in the truth of the Gospel – excessive to any human meaning. Whilst Stringfellow roots the meaning of these terms in his own life and faith, they are of more general application. To understand this position another important theme must be sketched out (a proper engagement is postponed until the next chapter).

If no one is innocent, then it is impossible to say with certainly that one is acting ethically. This is a very peculiar way of thinking about ethics. It would appear that ethics can only be found in a kind of not knowing or the broken nature of any claim to be acting ethically. We will argue that the suspension of ethics relates to an anxiety which is not an entirely negative disposition.

Steps beyond: conscience and vocation

To develop our position, it is important to grasp an understanding of conscience. We normally think of conscience as a kind of inner tribunal where we debate significant matters with ourselves.[2] We need to move beyond this sense of the word. The idea of the call or the idea of a vocation as a calling, requires the person who feels called to engage in serious self-inquiry that is "more than individualistic insight". It must be rooted in a "social context" and the "discipline of human experience" (Stringfellow, 1966, p.98). In the Gospel, the guide for a radical examination of one's being in the world is a sense of "the new or restored maturity of a human life in Christ" (Stringfellow, 1966, p.99). Thus, answering the call demands "a personal and public transfiguration". The apostolic church symbolised this transfiguration in baptism. Baptism is the entrance into "the common life of all human beings in community" (Stringfellow, 1966, p.99). The experience of transformation is thus irredeemably political: "radically – even cosmically – political" (Stringfellow, 1966, p.99).

Once baptised, one takes on a new relationship with others and with the world. Conscience is this "discernment" of new life in "any matter whatever" (Stringfellow, 1966, p.100). As such it is a "charismatic gift" as it comes from God or the "militant" presence of the holy spirit. The operation of conscience cannot be confused with senses of personal rightness or consensus. Conscience expresses itself in a praxis that "disdain[s] all mundane or conventional prudential calculations" (Stringfellow, 1966, p.100). Later in the chapter, we will link the practice of conscience with living the common life. In common life, one comes across the

2 We are after something more primordial. From this perspective, the call is "strictly nothing" or it remains "obscure and indefinite" (Heidegger, 1962, p.318). The call is not information about anything in the world, about events or people. It is not a "soliloquy" of a putting of the self "on trial" (Heidegger, 1962, p.318). The call is a "calling forth" of the self to "its ownmost *potentiality*-for-Being-its-Self" (Heidegger, 1962, p.318). The call may even come against our "expectation" and "will" (Heidegger, 1962, p.320). That the call comes from "me" and "beyond me" leads to the assumption that it comes from God. It may very well do. There is certainly something recondite and secret about the call, even though one might proclaim it publicly. Hearing the call opens one to resolute action on the basis of nothing other than an affirmation of what one already is, a nullity or a not-ness that must act and assume responsibility for itself. Not-ness, in terms of our analysis, relates to the very possibility that you can grasp yourself and understand yourself in a resolute way. To hear the call of conscience is to become resolute and to assume the responsibility for the not-ness that one is.

poor in their poverty. The poor offer their own suffering as a form of Christian sacrifice.[3] For a person of conscience, this sacrifice is a provocation to be alongside them and to do what one can to work against the powers of darkness.

To the extent that Stringfellow engaged in jurisprudence, it is driven by a critique of the "moral decadence" of law that has "virtually abandoned the poor" by failing to "counsel them in their complaints, [refusing] to represent them in their causes of action" and "neglect[ing] their rights as citizens". Most importantly, the law is "almost totally indifferent to their entrapment in poverty" (Stringfellow, 1966, p.18). The profession remains blind to the problem, "muttering" negatively about "socialised law" even though "American jurisprudence" remains committed to the principle that "even the least in society are entitled to counsel and to equality before the law" (Stringfellow, 1966, p.23). Stringfellow denounces the form of legal education that trains up a cadre of lawyers to act for the "great corporate powers, the government and the prosperous". Law schools prepare their students to "serve property rights, even to the neglect of human rights" (Stringfellow, 1966, p.24). An instructive example is the concern that law students should study "accounting" rather than be required to uphold "the ethical assumptions of American society" (Stringfellow, 1966, pp.23–24). However, this is not just about law schools. The failure of lawyers and educators to engage with social problems "jeopardises the whole of society, not just the poor", as it means that "entitlement to legal representation" is "by virtue of class, or wealth or race or sex or other status" (Stringfellow, 1966, p.24). If access to justice is not a reality it becomes a "fantasy", even for those who can "purchase" the services of an attorney. In such circumstances, the rule of law is a profoundly "compromised" ideal.

So, Stringfellow relates "moral complacency" to the invisibility of the poor. American society has been careful to keep "the poor out of sight". Because the poor are absent, "the mind is not appalled by conditions the eyes have not seen; the conscience is not moved by what the nostrils have not inhaled" (Stringfellow, 1966, p.25). Thus "concealment" and "ghettoisation" are synonyms. Urban

3 Stringfellow's analysis of this peculiar situation could perhaps be read through Derrida's thinking in *The Gift of Death* (2005). In his reading of Heidegger, Derrida stresses that "responsibility" is grounded in "an experience of singularity" and this experience necessitates an engagement with death. The thesis can be reconstructed as follows. If I cannot take the other's death from him/her, but I can die in his/her place, my death is the "irreplaceability" that I must understand if I am to comprehend myself. Responsibility is thus founded on what no one can take from me or do for me (Derrida, 1996, p.44). In Heideggerian terms, this is the meaning of authenticity. Realising the reality of my own death allows me to comprehend the possibilities of my life. One has to take one's own death upon one's self: "therein resides freedom and responsibility" (Derrida, 1996, p.44). Do we not therefore come upon a paradox? Death, which creates the possibility of sacrifice, or giving one's self completely for the other, is the one thing that cannot be exchanged or traded or "transferred". Death thus gives us an insight into the "sameness of the self". Singularity, as the being for death of this particular individual, is the "clearing" for the call of conscience and the "site" where "the information" is heard (Derrida, 1996, p.46).

renewal did not address the problems of the ghettos. Such was the case in "central Minneapolis" when the "old downtown negro ghetto" was "relocated", or in Buffalo when the construction of a "new thruway" to carry white commuters in and out of the city made it seem as if the "blight" of the "downtown area" had simply disappeared. The ghetto continued in existence beneath the flyovers and bypasses where traffic thunders over "the roofs of the tenements" (Stringfellow, 1966, p.25). Precisely because the poor are removed or made invisible there is no real "human contact" with them. The poor become characters in a "charade, crude stereotypes which make sense as a way of rationalising the lives of broken down figures that one sees in the city" (Stringfellow, 1966, p.25). Thus, the public assume that one is "poor by choice" and not through "circumstances" that are beyond one's control. Of course, if poverty is an effect of "moral decadence", to not be poor is a token of one's "moral superiority" (Stringfellow, 1966, p.26). Against this sloppy thinking, Stringfellow opposes his own experience: "I have yet to meet a man who elected to be poor, and I have never met an affluent man whose estate could be truthfully accounted for as his own individual accomplishment" (Stringfellow, 1966, p.26).

So, the voice of conscience is not a form of moral reasoning that engages in "hypothetical speculations" working out imaginary courses of action and the moral scruples that they might raise. Moral reasoning might be able to "reduce the trauma of decision making" but the common life, being with the poor, confronts one with an ongoing ethical dilemma: why should the poor suffer in my place (Stringfellow, 1966, p.102)? Stringfellow responds to this question by asserting that one must make one's self "wholly vulnerable to God's judgement" (Stringfellow, 1966, p.102). To hear the call of conscience is to commit oneself to this obedience. There is no reason why one should. One is radically free in the world. One does not have to be with and suffer with the poor. We can thus refer to conscience as a response to a call or a demand that one accepts in one's own freedom. Once committed, conscience is also keeping in mind, a resoluteness or a commitment to a way of living and thinking. Resoluteness can be understood as a fundamental element of praxis if we remember Stringfellow's and Towne's assertion that one lives one's Christian commitment. As such, it is a life lived in common with others and through this "being with" seizing hold of oneself and asking "how do I live?" We can see that Stringfellow's notion of conscience gives a very specific orientation to the lawyer's engagement with the world. To answer the call is to take on the meaning of one's vocation. Is this idea of conscience specific to Stringfellow's Christianity? This is not the case. It is a question of how one chooses to read Stringfellow and in particular how one might decide to read Stringfellow alongside Buber's notion of the face to face.[4] In reading Buber and

4 Jewula notes that in studies of the phenomenon of the caller and the called there are certain similarities between Heidegger's and Buber's understanding of conscience. Jewula is concerned with the silence of the call that says nothing. This, to be precise, has nothing to do with objects in the world. But silence is a mode of discourse, as

Stringfellow together, we can get at the relationship between theological ideas and a radical theory of experience. We need to re-work certain themes around anxiety, freedom and our common life, our "being with" each other.

At home with the poor

We will examine Stringfellow's autobiography. Like any writer worth reading, Stringfellow confronts the reader with the uncanny. *My People is the Enemy* is already an arresting title. It has biblical echoes; "my people", though, remains something of a mystery. The easiest way of understanding the title is to read "my people" as the poor and the sense would continue the idea that the poor are the enemy to the non-poor – the good citizens of America. But who is this author to speak for the poor? Not just to speak for them, but to announce that they are "his" people? Read alongside the subtitle, *An Autobiographical Polemic*, this set of arguments and associations takes on more definite biblical allusions. In the sense that Christ will "bring a sword" the autobiography will cause conflict or *polemos*, something that is confirmed by the epigram from John 1:7 that speaks of one who is "coming with the clouds" so that "everyone will see him" and "wail on approach of him". Read properly, the title seems to suggest that Stringfellow's writing will lay bare the experiences of a particular soul who identifies with the poor to the degree that his identity becomes theirs. The eschatology of John 1:7 may be misread in this context. This is less to do with the end of the world, and more to do with the beginning of the world and a particular calling.

My People is the Enemy is a record of experience. The text and its experimental aspects urge the reader to take the book seriously as an engagement with how a man has lived his life. What can be learnt from experience depends on whether or not you are radically open to the reality of poverty. This has nothing to do with being "analytical", with the "statistics of poverty", the "coincidence of poverty with racism", the "causes" of poverty or the "resolution" of poverty (Stringfellow, 2005, p.3). There are no policy prescriptions or models of lawyering. It is a witnessing and a testimony to "the time I lived and worked in Harlem" (Stringfellow, 2005, p.3). Witnessing Harlem is not speaking for "the Negroes" or the "Puerto

"only he who has something to say can keep silent". It is precisely this silence that takes *Dasein* out of the world of "the they" and allows a "rich disclosedness of itself" (Jewula, 2013, p.329). Whilst Buber does not describe the call as silence, he does refuse to give it a general content. Each call is unique to the circumstances in which an individual is called. The response is also unique. For Buber, the uniqueness of the response relates to conscience and the courage through which an individual hears the call of the thou, affirms it, and acts on it (Jewula, 2013, p.329). The call in *Being and Time* also relates to resoluteness and conscience. For Jewula this means that *Dasein* is neither separated from the world nor lost in it, but through resoluteness or conscience takes up a proper relationship to people and things. Resoluteness shows the "there" (*da*) of *Dasein* as the situation in which *Dasein* is always involved with the quotidian world (Jewula, 2013, p.331).

Ricans" of the tenements. They can speak for themselves. It is to talk about one's own life and work.

We will see that the very form of the text is authentic to the way in which experience is presented and "theorised". This is related to Stringfellow's own assertions that he is neither a theologian nor a philosopher. The immediate problem is life. Any references to theology and philosophy are embedded in this context. However, it would be a mistake to see this as a form of anti-intellectualism. Consider the structure of the text. It is roughly organised into five sections that describe the resolution to become a poverty lawyer. The book moves from initiation, through acceptance, involvement and premonition to epiphany. Thus, any insight is part of a process of living through that takes both writer and reader from the "depths of estrangement" to the ethical determination of "the way to live" (Stringfellow, 2005, pp.121, 142). We will see that this organisation of the book corresponds with a questioning of the meaning of one's ideas, choices and decisions within experience that is inherently meaningful (even if the world is not).

How does "initiation" begin? Poverty announces itself through the smell of waste: "the stairway smelled of piss" – an impression immediately qualified: "the smells inside the tenement" were "somewhat more ambiguous" – an ambiguity that is differentiated into "a suffocating mixture of rotting food, rancid mattresses, dead rodents, dirt, and the stale odors of human life" (Stringfellow, 2005, p.2). Human life is decay, waste. People are known by "what they have left behind", the fragments of lives which are no more than junk, the traces of a family jammed into an apartment "25x12 feet". What is left behind are the stark reminders that people lived just to survive. The apartment contains no more than fusty bunk beds and an "ugly convertible sofa" – this "home" is no more than a cockroach-infested flophouse. The passage, as a whole, moves towards the idea that despite the filth this is a home for human beings. Already, the word is being subjected to a certain strain. Home, the place from which others are excluded, is where one is with all the others. Something of a riddle:

> This was to be my home.
>
> I wondered for a moment, why.
>
> Then I remembered that this is the sort of place in which most people live, in most of the world, for most of the time. This or something worse.
>
> Then I was home.
>
> (Stringfellow, 2005, p.2)

Home exists in the estrangement and negation of home. A home that is not a home. Home is, first of all, the home of others. All those others who had occupied the tenement before Stringfellow. Pondering the question of the others who have come before him leads to the final strophe of this opening sequence. This apartment is also a symbol of all the others for whom "this or something worse" was home. The final twist is this epiphany that brings the narrator home. But how? In one sense he is unlike the others on whom he is meditating. He has chosen to come to "Number 18, 342 East 100th Street Manhattan" to be with the poor (Stringfellow, 2005, p.2). After all, he is a Harvard-educated lawyer. Those who are forced to live in cockroach-infested tenements, or something worse, are in an entirely different situation. Is Stringfellow setting up some bogus identification between "them" and him? Or, is there an entirely different meaning that leaves this notion of home radically open? To be at home, in the sense that Stringfellow wants to elaborate, is precisely to ask this question of others. To be at home is to be estranged from oneself in asking the question of oneself that necessitates addressing all the others: to be at home is to be uncomfortable.

This is how Stringfellow's resolute commitment expresses itself. The book begins with this biographical fragment and then effectively works backwards to provide an answer to the question as to why Stringfellow made the decision that takes him to the tenement in Harlem. We could read this as the authentic claim to the meaning of one's life, the coincidence of a past, a present and a future. The biographical structure of the book presupposes that life is not simply a set of events experienced in time. There is a pattern or even a secret to inner life that can be brought to light and used to explain the decisions that one has made. This is linked to the idea of freedom – more precisely the "extraordinary freedom" – of the Christian (Stringfellow, 2005, p.32). We can begin to understand the meaning of Stringfellow's decision. We need to see how his biography is bound up with this peculiar understanding of freedom as "integrity" and ultimately the question of what it means to be with the poor (Stringfellow, 2005, p.25).

Stringfellow gives us a very good sense of the way in which freedom requires us to assert ourselves against received wisdom and rituals. The freedom of the Christian is not at all conventional. This is made clear in the section of the book entitled "Acceptance", which we can read as a particular appropriation of the meaning of being in the world, of living with others. From a more conventional idea of freedom, practising law in Harlem was what Stringfellow was free to do. It was a choice that presented itself. He was free to choose between a number of options: working with a "large Boston firm", returning home to "join an established firm" or "open[ing] my own practice" in Northampton (Stringfellow, 2005, p.35). The decision to practise law in Harlem involved weighing a number of factors: the chance to be involved with "people, not institutions" and contact with his friends and clergy who were already based in the inner city. But, above all, to practise law in Harlem was to be engaged as both a lawyer and a Christian with a mission, with a living of faith that performed the "secret" of God's spirit in the world. Suffice to say that practising in Harlem was considered by some to be an eccentric decision.

It would appear that Stringfellow used his freedom to become poor (or at least poorer than other graduates of Harvard Law School). We can link this expression of freedom with the concept of resoluteness that we mentioned in the brief analysis of conscience above. In determining his future course of action or in thinking about what determined it, Stringfellow meditates on his own upbringing in a poor family during the depression (Stringfellow, 1964, p.36). Although his family had been poor, the experience of poverty did not determine their life chances. Being poor did not stand in the way of getting an education, scholarships or other opportunities for work; indeed, as a child, Stringfellow confesses that he "was not really aware that we were poor" (Stringfellow, 1964, p.36). The white experience of poverty contrasts with the "confining and dehumanising … poverty of the black ghettos" (Stringfellow, 1964, p.37). How are various meanings of freedom and poverty bound up in this account? We might say that there is a material poverty that does not prevent either social mobility or a kind of spiritual or resolute freedom. There is also a difference between white and black experiences of poverty. Whilst the former can still exercise their freedom, the latter are defined and controlled by a more extensive and damaging poverty, a poverty that is a "renunciation" of freedom or a kind of "psychological" wound (Stringfellow, 1964, p.37). Freedom, then, suggests something neither entirely an inner spirit nor material circumstance. One cannot simply, through force of "personality", will one's self free. Moreover, poor material circumstances would limit or even foreclose the call to commit to Christian life (Stringfellow, 1964, p.47).

The allegory of the shoes

Freedom, in a conventional sense, is freedom of movement. As a lawyer Stringfellow moves freely – ignoring boundaries between race and class and the physical boundaries of the city. He moves between the ghettos of the inner city and the penthouses and wealth of the outer city (Stringfellow, 1964, p.7). Stringfellow mixes with his poor clients, academics, clergy and theologians. He spends his time between the street, the law office, the courts and the seminary. His freedom is not granted but earned. The path of experience leads from initiation to acceptance. But what is accepted? First of all, it is explained in terms of race. Stringfellow describes himself as a "white Anglo-Saxon" amongst "Negroes and Puerto Ricans" (Stringfellow, 1964, p.3). Whilst one may be free to move in and out of the ghetto, this counts for very little unless there is a more significant connection with the people of the abyss.

Stringfellow offers an allegory of "symbol" of his "experience" in this regard (Stringfellow, 1964, p.24). He bumps into a friend one day and they fall into conversation. The man notices Stringfellow's shined shoes. Stringfellow confesses that he polishes his shoes every morning (Stringfellow, 1964, p.24). The shined shoes mean that Stringfellow "had remained [himself] and had not contrived to change, just because [he] had moved into a different environment". The lesson that Stringfellow took from his friend was that "in order that my life and work [should have] integrity I had to remain whoever I had become as a person before coming there" (Stringfellow, 1964, p.25). Most importantly, this knowledge allows those whom he encounters to "be free to be themselves" (Stringfellow, 1964, p.25). The allegory of the shoes focuses our concerns with integrity, acceptance and freedom. This could easily be misunderstood as a trite homily. What is the centre that allows the self to remain authentically open to other people? It is not really about the shoes. Indeed, Stringfellow points out that shining his shoes was a "custom" in which he had been "indoctrinated" when he was in the army (Stringfellow, 1964, p.24). The polished shoes stand for something else. Reflecting on his time in the military, Stringfellow points out:

> … where I happen to be and what I happen to be doing does not determine the issue of who I am as a human being, or how my own person may be expressed and fulfilled. I learned the meaning of this vocation in the Army. It was an emancipating discovery, for then it became possible to go anywhere and do any kind of work – in full knowledge of my own identity and integrity.
> (Stringfellow, 1964, p.25)

This passage provides a good exemplification of what was said above about how one has no power over being but lives it in an ongoing way. One's resoluteness is a projection of the fact that one has to come to be in the way that one is. For Stringfellow, as for our general analysis above, this is inseparable from ideas of conscience and commitment. Rather strangely it is located in experiences in the army rather than the Church. "Who I am" appears to come out of this vocation. A moment's reflection on the etymological roots of vocation takes us to the idea of being called. What is this call? The call is heard in and through one's being in the world. One's understanding of oneself as a human being, one's most profound sense of self is a response to the call. Somewhat abstract. What do we mean? Does this take us to some notion of the strong but flexible self? The power of a strong soul to include customs or practices on its own terms? Perhaps we could say that it is, in part, the courage to stand by a decision and to acknowledge that one's freedom is based on some quality of the self. In hearing the call, the self opens to its own resoluteness in grasping the possibilities of its own being.

Is this something of an evasion? One might imagine that this narrative of poverty law would show how the self had been profoundly changed by its experiences amongst the poor and had somehow become more true to itself. This is not so. The self is not swamped by the "they" to become diminished. Experience is cumulative. Experience builds on itself and its own openness to the world. We can trace this theme in Stringfellow's writing to the idea of an ethics, or what one brings to one's practice as a lawyer.

How does Stringfellow become "open" to those in poverty? Poverty is, first of all, a set of zones or boundaries which create the ghettos within the inner city. Poverty is set apart from the usual life of the city. Its reality is described in terms of density of population, people reduced to a "mass" that fills up space. But poverty is not just density "plus" those factors to which poverty research draws our attention: "dilapidated housing … infestation of vermin … unemployment" – "poverty" is lived and has an "existential" dimension. Poverty is experienced in the "life of each person" (Stringfellow, 1964, pp.5–7). Poverty is the singular experiences of poor people. It is an "essentially personal burden" that covers all aspects of one's life, "the relentless daily attrition of contending with the most primitive concerns of human existence". Nevertheless, we can speak of certain generalities. As modern research suggests, time works differently for the poor who suffer the "enormous burden of waiting". The poor, massed together in rotting tenements, are deprived of the privacy that the non-poor take for granted. Lacking privacy, the poor also lack the essential solitude that is required for the development of an inner life, "the secret and private life of [one's] own" that everyone needs (Stringfellow, 1964, p.6). Deprived of privacy or space at home, the streets become the place where life is lived. Stringfellow notes the vibrancy with "jukeboxes in the candy stores" (Stringfellow, 1964, p.8). It goes without saying, though, that the street is also a "precarious, primitive society" – crime, gang fights and police harassment. The police are "something like an occupation army" (Stringfellow, 1964, p.8). In a theme that becomes essential to Stringfellow's thinking, "[p]overty is vulnerability to death in its crudest forms" (Stringfellow, 1964, p.6). This depiction of poverty cuts against the anonymous reality captured in the figures and graphs of social science.

The truth dawns slowly. A lawyer's education has to be unlearned to get at the secret. At law school one might have intimations that the legal system could itself be a power of darkness. To the extent that law takes seriously the common dignity of those human beings that it represents, it has to represent "outcasts" – those who have been "socially discriminated against" (Stringfellow, 1964, p.38). But jurisprudential concepts of dignity have to be set against Christian understanding. To show concern for the outcast and the despised is to be involved with "the intercession" of Christ in the world. Acting from the spirit of Christian compassion bears witness to the failures of the legal system. If this is what the poverty lawyer learns, how can s/he bring this experience to the law?

The course of action that Stringfellow settles upon is simply to be present in the ghetto and to be there for as long as possible. Not to make overtures to people or to seek out clients but simply to become known. For two months after moving to East Harlem no one spoke to him. They merely watched. Stringfellow helped out a boy called Monk with certain legal problems, and on Monk's word, made contact with other young people on the street: "the street became as much of an office as I ever had in Harlem" (Stringfellow, 1964, p.42). Over time, Stringfellow becomes aware of different people, different clients and the particular problems that they face. The fundamental orientation to this work, though, is not a high-sounding sense of charity or humanitarian concern. The poverty lawyer has to understand the "vulnerability of daily life" (Stringfellow, 1964, p.44). If the face-to-face means anything in Stringfellow's work it is this sharing of existence, a trust that is gained only through exposure to the people with whom one works. Simple in some ways. Completely demanding in reality.

The exposure to the life of the poor provides insights into the irrelevance or failure of law that are not gained in any other way. Narcotics legislation, for instance, criminalises those whose addiction destroys their personality. Addiction should be treated as a problem requiring a therapeutic solution (Stringfellow, 1964, p.47). The poverty lawyer encounters clients who would prefer to be arrested or stay in prison because prison conditions are so much better than those outside. The lawyer becomes familiar with certain dodges. Rent control legislation, meant to protect the poor in their property, allows a landlord to raise the rent after each change of tenancy (Stringfellow, 1964, p.73). This plays into the hands of the owners of slum tenements as the influx of people into the ghettos means that tenancies change rapidly. Profits can be increased further by never making repairs or doing so slowly and begrudgingly. The poverty lawyer also begins to realise that the legal system itself enacts a ritual of justice. Overcrowded prisons, underfunded courts and legal services mean that most cases are dealt with in a perfunctory manner. Stringfellow mentions one instance where he agonised over his client's case only to find it dealt with rapidly in a 20-second conference and resolved with a plea bargain. Above all, the lawyer experiences the daily reality of racism and police harassment. The way in which black and Puerto Rican people are victimised, assaulted, hassled, arrested and imprisoned by white police. Law in the ghetto is primarily known through the police (Stringfellow, 1964, p.54). The failure of the legal system is at least one factor in the sense of rising tension in New York, and Stringfellow's premonition of coming race riots.

The legacy of the civil liberties struggle in the South suggests that the resolution to problems of race in the North are essentially legal: legislation provides the mechanisms to prohibit discrimination and protect the dignity of all American citizens. Stringfellow makes a simple point. Anyone advocating a legal solution to the profound problem of racism simply does not understand the depths of hatred that "the negro" shows for the white man. A completely justifiable hatred. Racism is, for Stringfellow, the complete alienation of man from man and the coming violent conflagration can only be prevented if white privilege is "surrendered". White people must "die" to their privilege "by suffering the hostility and rejection of Negroes" and "by risking their lives and the future of this society in the hands of Negroes" (Stringfellow, 1964, p.129).

Being with the poor

Stringfellow's experiences in the ghetto enable him to see the law in a different way. This takes us back to the earlier analysis of the common life lived with others. Stringfellow's own analysis of this theme begins with a peculiar understanding of the suffering of the poor in place of those who are not poor. We might say that the relationship sketched out by Stringfellow is a form of "being with" the poor. For the most part we are not with the poor. The city is divided up in such a way as to keep them at arm's length. However, the non-poor need to remember the suffering of the poor "for their own sake" (Stringfellow, 1964, p.28). The poor are, most immediately, the victims of "slum landlords, [...] scab employer[s] ... corruptible cops" and the "whole array of parasites whose own power or profit ... depends upon the continuation of poverty" (Stringfellow, 1964, p.29). In a more theological sense the poor are "intercessory for the rich", poised as they are so precariously and close to the power of death. The suffering of the poor "substitutes" for that of the non-poor. In this proximity to death, men realise their radical "estrangement" from each other and from the "rest of creation" (Stringfellow, 1964, pp.29–30). The poor immunise the non-poor from a general suffering. They take the power of death upon themselves through their condition. In other words, the poor substitute themselves for the rich in the piety of their suffering. At the same time, though, no one can stand in for the singularity of the other person, "no man may deliver his brother [from death], nor may a man deliver himself" (Stringfellow, 1964, p.31). Alienation of man from man is rooted in this singular exposure to death of which the poor are both the reality and the symbol. Their "awful vulnerability" is the common human condition.

One might not be able to stand in for the poor but one can stand alongside them. The figure of Christ is the token of this resolute commitment. Christ's example can be thought about in the language that we developed above.[5] Stringfellow's Christian ethics of poverty are a response to poverty and the power of death. The piety of the poor immunises them from the well-meaning entreaties and interventions of those who seek to give charity or somehow speak for them. At the same time one must stand with them precisely because they are more proximate to the power of death, and learn from their "intense humility" (Stringfellow, 1964, p.31). Although this might read like another homily on the dignity of suffering, it is much more strange and has nothing to do with "spiritual values" nor "splendid abstractions about God" (Stringfellow, 1964, p.32). There are examples: the child who gave Stringfellow his coat because he could see that he was freezing: a gift that was a "sacrament" (Stringfellow, 1964, p.43). The immeasurable gift that the poor give the non-poor is the very figure of Christ who "offers His life for all, even though none are worthy of His life" (Stringfellow, 1964, p.31).

Faith in Christ is the courage to face "the stark relentless activity of death in all the works of men" (Stringfellow, 1964, pp.31–32). Christ mediates between suffering man and God, offering himself as a sacrifice, a stand-in. The figures of Christ and the poor thus intersect. To be with the poor is in this mystical sense to be with the spirit of Christ in a common life. Once one knows this truth one is properly free: to be poor and to "work" with the poor (Stringfellow, 1964, p.32). To be responsive to the call is to be part of the world, or working the riddle of the

5 On these points Stringfellow is very close to certain themes in liberation theology. For instance, Gutiérrez argues that faith in Christ is an understanding of conscience and the call. Faith runs ahead of itself in that it is the courage to face ongoing hardship and suffering. Christ calls to the "nullity" of man, a call through which theology is lived and practised as a "critical reflection on the word of God" (Gutiérrez, 1973, p. xxxiii). One responds in Christ to the "cry" of the poor (Gutiérrez, 1973, p. xxxxvii/xxxxviii). The cry of the poor reveals the "active presence of the Spirit" heard in the opposition to the denigration of human beings, but also in the requirement for ongoing "personal transformation" (Gutiérrez, 1973, p. xxxxvii).

meaning of a world in which the poor suffer. To experience "being with" the poor is to be confronted by values that seem perverse but which demonstrate an exuberant care for others, a care that sets itself against the power of death.

Admiring the houses of the very poor

Stringfellow's writing describes an acute engagement with a world of social suffering. This final sequence of our argument works from Stringfellow's thinking to a more general structure of an ethics of poverty law. This is a tentative development of themes that will be fleshed out in subsequent chapters. What we want to carry forward is the notion of ethics, anxiety and conscience as an inseparable complex of ideas and experiences. One is radically free. If one has the gift of faith, one responds to the demand of conscience and works out what one's radical freedom to respond might mean in the context of one's faith. But what if one does not have faith? Anxiety might be the mark of conscience engaged with social degradation but lacking faith. In this context, freedom has a specific signification where the self, in its anxiety, is confronted with its own possibilities of being. In anxious freedom a peculiar quality of the self appears. Freedom in the context of anxiety relates to the question of whether or not one can act and think resolutely. One needs to think and act resolutely to take on one's alienation.[6]

The lawyer appalled by the fate of others finds him- or herself in a peculiar orientation to the world.

Consider the following lines:

When I was younger
it was plain to me
I must make something of myself.
Older now
I walk back streets
admiring the houses
of the very poor:
roof out of line with sides
the yards cluttered
with old chicken wire, ashes,

6 In the technical analysis of conscience in *Being and Time* the call is addressed to the "self" which is then lifted out of its lost-ness or alienation and "brought to itself by the call" (Heidegger, 1962, p.317). There is also a depersonalised quality to the call. This depersonalisation is central to grasping the real significance of the call and the self coming to the self.

furniture gone wrong;

the fences and outhouses

built of barrel staves

and parts of boxes, all,

if I am fortunate,

smeared a bluish green

that properly weathered

pleases me best of all colors.

No one

will believe this

of vast import to the nation.
(Williams, 1976, p.25)

Who speaks in this poem, and what do they tell us?

We might say that this is a poem about a question of the meaning of certain objects or things that are invested with human significance. These objects or things are stand-ins for a certain class of person: the poor. The poem dramatises a particular feature of discourses on the poor: the poor are absent. In this poem we only know them from their ramshackle houses. The poet, or indeed the poet's older self who appears to be the narrator of the poem, seems something of a dilettante. If you remember one of the voices that opened this book, it was of someone who desired the opposite of Williams's narrator. The unnamed author of the SDS pamphlet wanted to be with the poor. The things described in the pamphlet evoked a world of presences, the human warmth of an all-night bar, for example. Williams's narrator is content to be a *flanneur*, a wanderer through the poorer quarters (not an unromantic image), enjoying his leisure and noting the colours with a painter's eye.

It is worth noting the versification. The poem appears notably unpoetic. On first reading it seems to be no more than chopped-up prose. Why, for instance, do the lines end when they do? There are ghostly rhymes and the rhythm is at best irregular. Although the language appears to be everyday – nothing special or particularly poetic – the unusual line endings force the reader to read differently. Everyday language is rendered strange. Slowly an artistry appears. The form of the poem only comes with thought and with several readings. Does the irregular construction of the poem perform the irregular construction of the houses of "the very poor"? If so, is this a poor poem? Poor in what way? In that it is a poem that performs the very disconnect of writing poetry about the poor? Of turning someone else's misfortune into an aesthetic object? Note the expression, "if I am fortunate, / smeared a bluish green / that properly weathered / pleases me best of all colors". One might say: here is a man with a peculiar and refined sensibility who sees beauty in everyday objects; however, he has no conscience. What he does not appear to notice is that the houses of the very poor are to him merely something of a spectacle for his sophisticated reflection and amusement. Meditating on this point takes us towards the rather peculiar atmosphere or mood evoked by this poem – one of a kind of disconnectedness from the lives of others whilst one is, as it were, amongst them.

In other words, the narrator is poor in his ethical response. However, we might pause for a moment. Does the poem save itself by confronting us with this point? The very distance that we have from others which allows us to pontificate on their misfortune, indeed to reify them, to see them as objects, is a poverty of the human spirit. In some senses, then, the ethical poverty with which this poem confronts us is even more acute: the poet sees objects instead of people and reads people as represented by their objects. It is, then, a poem about reification. The alienated narrator is dead to himself and to the world of others. By confronting us with this alienated consciousness, the poem forces us to examine our own.

Is this right? The poem confronts the reader with a social and individual drama. The narrator begins by telling the reader that he should have made something of himself. Perhaps this is the voice of the self-made man. The figure of self-reliance, responsibility and hard work. However, as one reads, the poem suggests that the narrator may not have made something of himself. Indeed, he appears to waste his time writing poems about poor people. The line "older now …" suggests a modification of a youthful attitude; but what has replaced the bold opening statement? A reflexivity? A standing back? There is at least the suggestion that "admiring the houses / of the very poor" is more worthwhile than youthful beliefs in becoming someone. Does the poem recommend this self-reflexive questioning? Whether or not we are concerned with lawyers or poets, the poem dramatises the moment of reflection, perhaps even the moment out of time, when one examines the pattern of one's life.

But note the last lines of the poem. Last lines are significant, as we would hope to find in them the moral of the tale. But instead we have this gnomic and apparently unhelpful statement. The reader wants to ask "what is of such importance to the nation?" But the terms of the question are quite peculiar. Why, for instance, does the nation suddenly appear? What has this scene got to do with the nation? A private meditation on aesthetic taste becomes something of a public statement. But about what? The poem has set up a number of possible answers (and indeed a strange resonance with the ruling in *Goldberg v Kelly* [7] which spoke of the nation's basic commitment). It is of importance to the nation because the imperative to "make something" of oneself is what makes us a proper, mature citizen, contributing to the welfare of the nation. Or does one contribute to the welfare of the nation by asking the question of one's self? The good citizen engages in critical self-reflection. Whether or not one makes something of one's

7 *Goldberg v Kelly*, 397 U.S. 254 (1970).

self can be the difference between fortune and misfortune, wealth and something less than wealth. Lurking behind this question is thus the question of our life with others and the distance from others that makes this question of import to the nation. The poem will not tell us the answer. It confronts us with the task of working out the meaning of the question for ourselves.

What, then, is of import to the nation is the recondite nature of the question that hides itself from us. Williams's poem enacts a very peculiar tension. We could say that it is the drama of the alienated consciousness that knows it is alienated and seeks the passage through its own alienation. This poem uses a jump cut to link together two frames: that of the younger self and the reflexive older self. These two times are run together. The poem suggests that the only way in which we can reflect or ask the question of ourselves is in resolute reflection in a moment out of the time of the everyday (where there is no real time for reflection). Rather than the onward, forward motion of instants, this is a slow time, or a folding of time when past time becomes present to the reflecting mind in order that a question of the self can be posed. In other words, in folded time, the self might change, might become something, realise its own possibilities. The question of the self cannot be posed outside of this moment in and outside of time.

The poem performs this possible moment of vision. If the narrator of the poem reflects on the peculiar details of his life and projects his questions about himself onto these details, then the "import to the nation" is the question of how this projection can take place in a wider sense. For the lawyer it must involve questioning the practice of law. The structure of the question can be established by thinking about the way that one lives, and the anxiety that one acts ethically.

So, Williams's poem is important because it brings together anxiety with the general structure of the question that we ask ourselves. We struggle with the issue "what will I become?" Whilst this may be an inner drama, it does not remove us from the world. We are always and already in a world of concerns. Moreover, this question is not necessarily one of wealth or material success. One is anxious over the possibilities of one's situation. We believe that this is what Stringfellow means by the "existential situation" of the poverty lawyer or his assertion that "life in the law" is "a vocation" not "a career" (Stringfellow, 1964, p.170). As difficult as it is, we need to keep this in mind if we are to understand the being of the radical lawyer.

Conclusion

We have been reading William Stringfellow's thinking as an exemplification of a resoluteness that leads to an ethics of practice rooted in a common life. For Stringfellow praxis is an engagement with grace in the here and now. An ethics of practice accepts that the law is a tool. The critical question is the spirit which one brings to the law. We can appreciate that for Stringfellow this is a radical Christianity – a particularly striking way in which a resolute determination of the value of action informs a profoundly creative ethical anxiety. We are hopefully now in the position to see how an ethics derived from Stringfellow's work allows us to think more broadly about the vocation of poverty law. To stress, this is not to argue that ethics needs to be faith based. The problem which we will address has been strikingly put by Louis Wolcher: "[m]aintaining confidence in the ground of our actions – indeed, in our entire way of life – is what lets some of us sleep at night" (Wolcher, 2010, p.387). So, our next task is to see whether this understanding of an ethics of anxiety can be read into one of the most important recent engagements with the practice of poverty lawyering: the new poverty law scholarship.

Chapter 7

Theory in the key of life

The anxiety of the poverty lawyer

Introduction

Whilst there was no engagement with William Stringfellow in the new poverty law scholarship, the concern with the anxious ethics of lawyering runs through the writings of its practitioners. The radicalism of the 1960s and early 1970s casts a long shadow. How was it possible to resist the alienating reality of a professional relationship that produced "mass ... justice for poor people" (Tremblay, 1992, p.949)? Our focus is on three different models of poverty law: Alfieri's subtle thinking of counter-hegemonic practices as an "ethic of resistance" (Alfieri, 1991, p.622), White's humanist lawyering and Lopez's rebellious vision of problem solving. Despite the differences between the various approaches there is much that unites them. However, the characterisation of this form of scholarship as postmodern is not that helpful.[1] It is more accurate to see poverty scholarship as carrying forward into new times the themes discussed in the last chapter. White's description of her work could apply equally to Lopez and Alfieri: the poverty lawyer seeks "neither to escape nor to repress the paradox inherent" in his/her role (White, 1990, p.863). In other words, poverty lawyers practise with an

1 Whilst the term postmodernism has its uses, it is not clear how helpful it is in defining the work of the new poverty scholars. There is certainly the sense in which ideas drawn from the canon of postmodern thinkers have provided an important influence on the work of Alfieri, White and Lopez. However, Alfieri is well aware of what he calls the problems of post-structuralist notions of "discourse and history" (Alfieri, 1993, p.2570). Despite their disagreements, Alfieri and White might actually be in agreement about the role of continental thinking. White makes a passing reference to reading "Foucault and Derrida" when working as a legal aid lawyer but declares herself free of "postmodernist paralysis" (White, 2002, p.1923). She is on nodding terms with Foucault's ideas of discourse (White, 1987, p.1990). Her criticisms of Alfieri, broadly congruent with feminist suspicions of Foucault, accuse him of ignoring real violence in focusing on interpretative violence (White, 1990, pp.857–858). Whilst probably a little unfair, such comments do not suggest any particularly extended reading of Foucault. Broadly similar points could be made about Lopez's work. Although Lopez lists Foucault as an influence it would be wrong to see any real Foucauldian input into the development of rebellious lawyering or lawyering as problem solving.

ongoing anxiety. The anxiety of the poverty lawyer is ultimately an expression of "being" with the poor.

Field notes on anxiety

Anxiety has a number of valences that are variations on the theme of being with the other person. To build on the last chapter, anxiety is a way in which encounters between lawyers and their poor clients are lived. What makes the lawyer anxious is not just the social differences that define the professional relationship but a concern with whether or not this gulf can be crossed. Confronted with the "face-to-face" situation in which lawyer and client encounter each other, even the well-meaning lawyer might take refuge in the various rituals and power games that serve to distract from the visceral nature of acting for a poor client. Anxiety is the prevalent mood of a certain realisation. The lawyer-client relationship is as much a problem as the reasons that have caused the client to consult a lawyer in the first place.

The experience of law by those in poverty is one of profound anxiety occasioned by the claustrophobic sense of being defined by rules that are inaccessible, of being left waiting, uninformed and stigmatised. Precisely because one is subject to the rules of the welfare system, one's needs are subject to the decisions of bureaucrats over which one has very little control (Sarat, 1990, p.345). Welfare rules are perceived as a kind of ominous presence – "pervasive and obtrusive" extending into the most intimate spaces of life (Sarat, 1990, p.344). The rules that determine eligibility or levels of benefits are labyrinthine and appear to operate in the interest of the system and its personnel. Phone calls go unanswered, letters receive no reply and information on decisions is almost impossible to find. Legal services lawyers or welfare workers are perceived in the same way: collaborators in a system that serves its own ends. The very idea of having a hearing is absurd. In reality a hearing is a ritualistic way in which one is allowed to speak and left "unheard" (Sarat, 1990, p.360).

It is not just the objects of the welfare system who feel anxious and intimidated. The anxiety of the poverty lawyer is occasioned by the responsibility of speaking for another. The poverty lawyer questions whether s/he has the strength required to take on another's pain. In a certain mood this peculiar form of self-questioning is the mark of authentic life and can be linked to the poverty lawyer's engagement with ethics. Ethics comes from the fraught anxieties of the authentic self's existence in a world of social degradation. Thus to understand the ethics of the new poverty law scholarship, it is important to study the ways in which its practitioners conceptualise the lawyer-client relationship. Framing an ethics for poverty law raises the very question of the resources that one can use to authentically grasp one's work as a lawyer.

Alfieri provides an insightful articulation of the anxiety of the poverty lawyer. He grasps the dialectic of the lawyer-client relationship. His theorisation of poverty law deploys many of the ideas that we analysed in the previous chapters.

Alfieri produces an account of a reflective, critical consciousness rooted in counter-hegemonic practices.[2] How, though, does this thinking open onto a broader, more problematic understanding of the poverty lawyer's own self-understanding?

Alfieri's thinking provides an ongoing meditation on a particular problem. How do the terms that we use to think about our relationships with others both enable and constrain us? The first target is "class power" (Alfieri, 1987, p.688). Class as a designator of social being limits and opens certain ways of thinking and acting that impact on the relationship between lawyer and client. We can map the notion of hegemony onto the constraints of class. Counter-hegemonic thinking endeavours to encourage the political engagement of poor people. The fundamental problem is that in working in a counter-hegemonic way, the lawyer may be imposing patterns of thought and action on his/her client. Even radical thinking carries the risk of reproducing forms of hierarchy and domination. The ideology of professionalism can never quite escape from hegemonic social forms that compromise the possibilities of radical lawyering.

Navigating this tension requires us to analyse the "language of lawyer domination and control" (Alfieri, 1987, p.692). Like Sparer, Alfieri goes back to Martin Buber. One can surely appreciate the relevance of Buber to an account of counter-hegemony. Alfieri's reading picks up on the paradigmatic scene of poverty law, the encounter between the lawyer and the client. Buber's "open mutual world of relation" requires "the affirmation of the other in a lived relation" (Alfieri, 1987, p.696). The transformational encounter cannot be turned into a formula. To pick up on our earlier arguments, it has to be seen as an opening of the self to the other person. In the dynamic of such a relationship, the lawyer must confront not only his or her own prejudices but the experiences of the other person who is before him/her. The lawyer cannot hide behind technical languages. Dialogue must generate its own vocabulary. This may mean learning from clients or helping them to confront the world view that has served to make them isolated and passive. It is an exercise in allowing or encouraging the client to become an active participant. If the hegemonic ideas of lawyer as professional expert and client as passive victim can be worked through, a "mutual unfolding" may take place (Alfieri, 1987, p.697).

At the same time, learning from the client cannot involve simply accepting the client's view of the world. The notion of dialogue needs to be supplemented with

2 The two major traditions of poverty lawyering can be described as direct service and law reform. In the former, legal services are provided directly to the poor whilst in the latter legal professionals focus their energies on securing legislative change. Critics argue that the direct service tradition carries with it the risk of turning poor people into isolated and passive clients of lawyers, no matter how well intentioned and committed lawyers are to the struggle against poverty. Whilst winning a case may have positive effects, the direct service tradition does not help build the political agency of poor people. The law reform tradition may score notable successes but it takes attention away from systemic injustices.

practices of critical reflexivity. Critical reflexivity engages with ways of thinking, habits "conscious and unconscious" that have become "formations of power" that create social roles and courses of action which define and limit what can be done (Alfieri, 1987, p.663). How can critical space be opened in the lawyer-client relationship? Critical, reflexive dialogues must be initiated that enable some purchase on the problems that poor clients and their advocates face. For instance, arguments about levels of benefits or even minimum income must "break the spell that the labour market casts" (Alfieri, 1987, p.671). To the degree that the poor become a class for themselves, to the extent that they can articulate a communal programme and take coordinated action towards its ends, hegemony can be challenged. However, in order to link together the language of class and that of critical reflexivity, Alfieri has to theorise the problematic space of interiority that reflexivity presupposes. He builds his argument by reference to E.P. Thompson, a major figure in the history of the new left (in its British rather than American manifestation). Most importantly for Alfieri, Thompson's idea of class works at the level of "experience and consciousness" and opens up the possibility of "making and remaking human relationships" (Alfieri, 1987, p.666).

Thinking class in this way allows a somewhat more concrete impression of how the struggle for interiority is fought out in terms of "practical consciousness" engaged with the "wholeness" of the "lived social process" (Alfieri, 1987, pp.680–681). This approach to class moves beyond a simplistic reductionism. Furthermore, it gives us a strong sense of the way in which social values are embedded so that hegemonic social relations appear unquestionable: simply "the way things are". As we have seen, this experience of self and the world is bound up with the way in which the dominant order reproduces itself at the level of "subjective meanings" (Alfieri, 1987, p.681). Agency comes out of the realisation that one is not entirely defined by hegemonic terms. The idea of agency can be scaled up to define the concept of the poor as a class for themselves. The hope is that as a class the poor can become reflexive, can conceive of themselves as both individuals and something more: "an historical class engaged in a daily active process of making and remaking human relationships" (Alfieri, 1987, p.666).

These are useful ideas. We can find in this argument the classical delineation of resistance to alienation and false consciousness. Entirely in keeping with arguments that we have explored in previous chapters, class appears as a "node" around which contradictory practices can be articulated provided that they can be understood from the perspective of shared experiences. Shared experiences provide a point of reference for different people and frame individual and communal recognition. In Alfieri's later work the notion of shared, communal experience becomes the underpinning of the idea of client autonomy (Alfieri, 1991, p.622). Alfieri makes a great deal of the overlap between Foucault and Habermas in plumbing the "administrative density" of the world of welfare. He finds in the latter practices of civility and reflexivity that can be used to characterise counter-hegemonic communications between lawyer and client.[3] The focus tightens on those forms of language and ritual that confirm and cement lawyerly dominance. Narrative becomes the fundamental analytical tool that carries forward the Buberian insight that authentic communication can happen and that reified roles can be worked through. Ultimately, some form of redemptive transformation can take place. From this perspective, narrative is the recounting of personal experience, and with it comes the promise that an authentic response to the other's experience can open up new possibilities in the relationship. Can this promise be honoured?

A notion of reflexive communication can certainly indicate how the redemptive possibilities of the lawyer-client relationship rest on a dialectical encounter where lawyer and client change each other. The dialogue between lawyer and client "bear[s] witness" to the frustrations of the struggle against poverty and "empower [s]" the client by making his/her experiences public. At its best, "learning from the client's narrative" is an insight into the world of another where the normative meanings of the struggle for dignity and self-identity get erased by lawyerly, administrative and other expert discourses. If lawyer and client can come together a qualified solidarity replaces the isolation of both parties. This form of being together offers a more nuanced understanding of poverty law than the earlier call to class solidarity. But there is still something blocking an authentic relationship: the structure of the legal profession itself. Just as the lawyer always has prejudices and pre-understandings that colour his/her view of the client's experience, the

3 Habermas asserts that the post-war "welfare state compromise" is a profound contradiction. Instead of making for solidarity it has led to the "breakdown" of "consensual mechanisms" and "coordinate[d political] action" though "bureaucratisation" and "monetarisation" (Habermas, 1989, pp.349–362). The crisis of the welfare state cannot be understood in terms of class or the old categories of Marxist thought. Welfare operates within a context where the worker is no longer simply paid the minimum for survival. The worker has to be paid enough to consume. These changes go hand in hand with a "humanisation of work" and formal legal rules that shield the lifeworld from the worst excesses of capitalism (Habermas, 1989, p.349). Habermas is also concerned with the development of resistance to "administrative density". He argues that there is a need for new relationships between "autonomous, self-organised public spheres on the one hand and domains of action regulated by money and administrative power on the other" (Habermas, 1989, p.296). Habermas urges a "democratic generalisation" of interest across the various public spheres. Concerned persons and social movements must take the place of political parties that have been compromised by their co-option into networks of money and power. The fundamental problem is that resistance to such co-opted political forms and the growth of administrative power must go beyond mere "spontaneous" gestures of "refusal". The answer, at least at an intellectual level, is to change the way in which advocates of welfare think of the welfare state. The approach to the welfare state has to become "reflective" (Habermas, 1989, p.296). Welfare advocates must address how the capitalist state is "restrained" and controlled. Arguments about levels of benefits, or even minimum income might "break the spell that the labour market casts on the life history of all those capable of working", but are "not revolutionary enough". Revolutionary energy must thus come out of the reflectivity which will create new understandings of political agency.

historic structures of the profession are loaded with "foundational allegiances to certain ways of knowing, thinking and speaking" that constitute a "lawyer positioned construction of ideology" (Alfieri, 1993, pp.2570, 2574). How does the professional position of the lawyer compromise authentic understanding?

Consider the "triage" of welfare clients on legal aid. The lawyer must choose from those crowding the office on a Monday morning who will be represented and who will not. The triage of welfare clients is a "gatekeeping function" – a primordial ritual that enacts the decision-making power of the professional (Alfieri, 1993, p.2574). We might say that this issue raises afresh the same concerns with exclusion and power, the stalled encounter between lawyer and client, the explicit and implicit ways in which poverty lawyers are bound up with the hegemony of law and the legal system. The decision to represent a client is justified as an expression of lawyer's discretion, which is guided by the rules and ethics of the profession. How secure are the decisions on triage that lawyers make? The modernist ideologies of "liberal legalism" serve to justify decisions by reference to assumptions about the nature of expertise, the well-being of the client and notions of the public good. If these are questionable, then it appears that the decisions a lawyer must make are no more than operations of "contextual discretion" (Alfieri, 1993, p.2639).

This takes us towards the issue of ethics. Scholarly accounts of poverty law attempt to stabilise and articulate the norms that inform lawyerly discretion and define the best way of linking together theory and practice to bring "coherence and insight" into the diverse tasks of the lawyer (Alfieri, 1996, p.201). However, Alfieri is not convinced by the available models. They serve to "limit [...] the advocacy process to a bounded set of discursive practices" that effectively conceal the fundamental problem from a lawyer faced with a decision that has to be made (Alfieri, 1991, p.627). This is an acute dilemma. The lawyer remains tormented. Alfieri admits as much, referring to his approach to ethics as "neither resolved nor final" but "ongoing and uncertain" (Alfieri, 1993, p.2611). There is the desire to work with uncertainty and to hang on to the possibility that law somehow retains an authentic political engagement with the experience of poverty. Thus contextual discretion confronts the poverty lawyer with a genuine agonistics of decision making: a decision must be made, and may be coherent with professional ethics, but, at the same time, it may simply conceal triage – a pragmatic need to control limited resources rather than anything more principled. Within the context of embedded bureaucracy, with its rituals of distancing and disempowering clients, the lawyer keeps in place the structural reasons for the abuse of claimants and perpetuates an unjust situation.

We arrive at the idea of the poverty lawyer as an existential hero. Although Alfieri is aware that the modernist trope of exile runs through theories of poverty law, the figure of the absurdist, existential hero is a little different. The poverty lawyer as existential hero is engaged in a Sisyphean situation, attempting to resist alienation through an alienated practice. As Alfieri notes, advocacy itself has become a processing of people, "a formulaic and mechanical convention devised to process individual cases on a mass scale" (Alfieri, 1993, p.685). Thus, the trauma of the ethical decision maker, condemned to make decisions that may go against deeply held principles. The agony and contradiction of the practice is a token of a human being who will not allow reified forms to conceal the terror of the world. The ethical lawyer remains wedged between "the dual commitment to ethical precept and particularized context" (Alfieri, 1996, p.205). In Buber's terms, the existentialist lawyer is opened to real speech because s/he will not hide behind inauthentic ethical norms that conceal the struggle in the world and the play of meanings that are inseparable from our "being with others" (Alfieri, 1991, p.646).

How is this agony "emancipatory" rather than a "technical form ... of ethical judgment" (Alfieri, 1993, p.2662)? Proper ethical thinking must resist any easy "resolution" (Alfieri, 1993, p.2573). It may be the case that this putting on hold of certainty is the key to a sensibility that can unfreeze, at least for a moment, the certainties in which institutional modes of thought and practice have become paralysed. At this limit, it may be possible for the poverty lawyer to help create "a strong individual and collective sense of dignity or personhood" that enables human authenticity, moral agency, and rational volition (Alfieri, 2014, p.1132). We might say, then, that this thinking of ethics provides the ambiguous and difficult space where an institutional structure exists in tension with "intrinsic personal and professional value commitments to race, dignity, identity, and role" (Alfieri, 2014, p.1131).

Humanist lawyering

Whilst not accepting Alfieri's definition of the modernist lawyer as hero, and critical of his approach to theory, White's vision of practice, like Alfieri's, is written in the tradition of those who "put their ass on the line".[4] White labels her work a "humanist" or "three dimensional vision of poverty law" (White, 1990a, p.3). Three-dimensional poverty law extends beyond the "technical" concerns of doctrinal poverty law (such as the assertion of the right to be heard in proceedings) to the forging of new critical tools that can be used to get at the subtle (and not too subtle) construction of modes of domination and subordination.[5] The inheritance of the movement is clear in the following statement:

4 It is also intriguing that one of Michelman's metaphors recurs in White's work. The islands of protection from the storms of economy that Michelman had hoped to find in welfare rights become for White, in more troubled times, the failure of welfare rights and lawyers themselves to save those "stranded by the economy" (White, 1990a, p.41).

5 White's early work drew on experiences of lawyers and community activists in South Africa to create a model of "three dimensional lawyering" (White, 1987). The first dimension covers those practices of legal assistance or expert discourses deployed in securing legal change. The second dimension is engaged with working alongside the community to devise legal and political strategies to protect interests and resist government power. The third dimension is described as "political theatre" (White, 1987, p.8). Political theatre links formal litigation to "speak outs" where those involved can find their own voices. Three-dimensional lawyering is thus a way of bringing people

> [W]e should attend to, and engage with, the poor people's movements around us. Only as we become committed to those projects – in all of their human complexity – will our lawyering support, rather than subvert, our claimed goal of "empowerment" of the poor.
>
> (White, 1990, pp.872–873)

Times have changed since the heady days of the 1960s and 1970s. There is no "large grassroots organization of poor people" and the ascendant right has declared war on welfare (White, 1987, p.542). This is not a cause for despair. New times require creative labour and a re-examination of the practices of poverty law. In particular, the "[a]mbitious images of litigation as empowerment" may need to be critically reviewed (White, 1987, p.538). One needs to look outside the courtroom and the "narrowly instrumental goals" of litigation (White, 1987, p.538). Reflecting on *Goldberg v Kelly* 397 U.S. 254, White suggests poverty lawyers must learn that "the prime social agents" of the struggle against poverty must be "those groups who have been the objects of systemic social and political subordination" (White, 1990, p.887). This view is a refraction of certain movement themes. The lawyer is still avowedly an advocate for the poor but the point of litigation is to encourage poor clients to "become more politically effective in their own lives", learning the confidence, tactics and skill that enable them to become activists rather than mere "supplicants" to their lawyers (White, 1987, p.540).

However, the fundamental issue is that poor clients see the law as alien and alienating. The rituals of the courtroom and the practices of advocates themselves leave people feeling "isolated" and dependent on a power they do not understand (White, 1987, p.433). The lawyer is in a dilemma. Aware that s/he must "translate" his/her clients' problems into legal language, the lawyer is also concerned that "immer[sion]" in "chaotic stories of suffering" may not be the best way of preparing a case. The reality of the client's situation is thus filtered out in the presentation of a legal argument. This "compounds the alienation that poor clients already feel towards the legal process" (White, 1987, p.545). How can this tension be navigated? There is a pragmatic solution. Whilst the lawyer must speak the language of law this does not mean that "organization" outside the "formal boundaries" cannot take place (White, 1987, p.545). The practical solution to alienation is to create "parallel spaces" for political action alongside litigation (White, 1987, p.545). The lawyer shuttles between the courts and political organisation, hopefully achieving synergies between law, community organising and other forms of political action.

We can consider one intriguing example. Reflecting on litigation for poor people in Los Angeles in the 1980s, White draws the reader's attention to a theatre group (the Los Angeles Poverty Department) who worked alongside local law centres and law firms engaged in litigation over homelessness. The theatre

together in a common cause, encouraging innovative ways of pushing for legal change, popular empowerment and public engagement.

group ran workshops and performed on street corners. Working within the traditions of agitprop and the theatre of the oppressed, the street theatre of the Los Angeles Poverty Department drew attention to the plight of the poor and furthered new ways of understanding and presenting the experiences of the homeless. Most importantly, homeless actors were given the "power to define social reality for a moment". The group's creation of the play, their acting and stagecraft serve to both "engage" and "disorientate" their audiences (White, 1987, p.548). Drama is a statement of agency and humanity, "a radical, even threatening assertion that, in spite of their pain, or rather through it, [actors] create the terms of their own lives" (White, 1987, p.560). There are a number of interesting themes. The "speak out", the very idea that a form of language and performance can be created that gives performers momentary control of the world, says a great deal about the power of language both to alienate and to offer a way of countering alienation. Indeed, actors testified that their experiences in the theatre company gave them a new sense of "self-esteem" and allowed them to "make sense of the world" – even "saved" their lives (White, 1987, pp.561–562).

It is as if, at least at this point in her work, White encountered something of a split between the formal limits of the law and the possibilities of those parallel spaces where something might happen. The experience of experimental theatre is such that we need to look beyond the "horizon" of "procedural justice" and "formal equality" to the "real world" (White, 1990a, p.3). New modes of "participation" need to be generated by people themselves and cannot be handed down by lawyers or anyone else. Echoing, but re-working the ruling in *Goldberg*, White argues that the "nation's basic commitment" is to both "innovation" and "substantive equality" (White, 1990a, p.3). Like Alfieri, White is anxious that the practices of law profoundly limit the spaces in which these goals could be developed.

In later works White started to make use of feminist post-colonial scholarship. The focus on language in this work parallels Alfieri's experiments with hermeneutics. Power (and the resistance to power) runs through "the web of subterranean speech norms and coerced speech practices that accompany race, gender, and class domination" (White, 1990a, p.4). We are embodied language users. The way we talk, the words that we use position us in certain ways. Those in command of legal analysis and modes of administrative power can "undermine the capacity of many persons in our society to use the procedural rituals that are formally available to them" (White, 1990a, p.4). The procedures that we would otherwise use to institutionalise norms of decent treatment "disable *all* citizens – especially those from subordinated social groups – from meaningful participation in their own political lives" (White, 1990a, p.4).

The lawyer is implicated. These themes are intensified and developed in the story of Mrs G, a welfare claimant dependent on AFDC payments. Mrs G got into difficulties when she received an insurance pay-out. The story of Mrs G revolves around the various rituals of subordination that impact upon her attempt to resolve an alleged overpayment of her benefits. Beneath the surface of procedures that are formally equal, the story shows how three bureaucratic logics – intimidation, humiliation and objectification – serve to limit Mrs G's options. Whilst these logics are specifically those of welfare administration they are based on broader social and political scripts that have been internalised by clients. As a poor black woman resident in the rural South, Mrs G had been subjected to a long history of subordination. As an object of the welfare state she is positioned in discourses that define her needs and the level of benefits to which she is entitled. She explains to her attorney that she lives in fear of being accused of cheating. Her lawyer is implicated in these systemic logics, as well as the more mundane but equally positioning problem of having insufficient time to devote to her case. Mrs G is thus also caught up in the machinations of her lawyer who is attempting to game the system, to use strategies that, whilst they may produce the desired result, present Mrs G as a victim. Mrs G asserts her autonomy in departing from the strategy advised by her lawyer and puts to the court her own view of her case.

The case further elaborates an account of alienation. Mrs G's feeling that rules have "boxed" her in is evidence of the way in which the "public regulation of social life" has reduced human activities to the norms of bureaucracy. The "expanding bureaucratization of modem life" comes into tension with those "face to face networks and practices that as human actors, we rely upon to make sense of our social experience" (White, 1990a, pp.40–41). In "capitalist or patriarchal societies" bureaucracy "becomes a specific vehicle of gender and class subordination" (White, 1990a, pp.40–41). White draws a moral lesson from Mrs G. Reflecting upon the case, White argues that being open to a client and her experiences "involves a willingness to let what one hears from the other disrupt one's own perspective and revise one's commitments" (White, 1994, p.17). As the argument develops, it brings in a slightly new set of concerns around the language of the good and well-being. The key concern is that an autonomous person must be able to "aim at the good". This is to say that one needs to be able to make choices between equally compelling and valuable ends. Genuine choice requires self-knowledge, an active engagement with the choices that one has been offered. A person who "drifts through life unawares is not leading an autonomous life" (White, 1994, p.382).

How does the lawyer respond to these issues? Answering this question brings White to an ethics of lawyering. The following statement is instructive: "I have increasingly realized that the path toward bridging – and also respecting – the distance from the people with whom I work is a path that leads me to question myself – my values and visions and indeed my personhood – in deeper and deeper ways" (White, 1994, p.17). White is talking about professional ethics, but also something much deeper – a way of being, or a way of being a lawyer where one is engaged with the needs of others to a degree that one can step out of or away from one's own sense of self.[6]

6 Indeed, it is perhaps at this level, and particularly in White's work, that we come across themes reminiscent of those in Derrida's and Foucault's work. When talking of the

It is hardly surprising that some of the most insightful mediations on poverty law come from those occasions when established poverty lawyers seek to encourage others to follow their path. For White, the "supposedly self-regarding question" of seeking fulfilling work takes us to a harder question: how can lawyers work with their clients towards "that elusive horizon we call justice" (White, 1993, p.2). We arrive back at the scene of ethics and the question of the self's relationship to the other. Whilst White is not committed to a dialectic model of the play of consciousness, such an approach might not be too inaccurate to describe her understanding of the work that brings the self alongside others. The "elusive horizon" of justice echoes the traumas of Alfieri's Sisyphean lawyer (White, 1993, p.4). The nagging question of elusive justice compels the lawyer to question her life, to confront the choices that she has made. Although White is some distance from Stringfellow we can perhaps find a similar anxiety informing her work. Responding to the needs of others, practising as a poverty lawyer, requires a sense of vocation (White, 1993, p.4). Vocation might not be understood as a call from elsewhere, but White's thinking closes the distance from Stringfellow in the affirmation that one's actions in the world are definitional of the self.

Rules for radicals

As an introduction to Lopez's work we can consider the following short passage which frames the scene of his personal contact with poverty law and lawyers in "East L.A.":[7]

influence of postmodernism, White returns to CLS and deconstruction as offering the "ground breaking kinds of questions that can keep [poverty theory] going" (White, 2002, p.1923). Whilst White does not build this point in any great detail, we could take forward at least some idea of the "aporia of responsibility" from our engagement with William Stringfellow. In Derrida's formulation, the aporia of ethics means that "one always risks not managing to accede to the concept of responsibility in the process of *forming* it" (Derrida, 1996, p.61). We might say that "responsibility" cannot be derived from a general concept and must be a demanding and alarming provocation. Perhaps there is something of this thinking in White's notion of "situated piece work". However, to the degree that piece work relies on dialogic consensus it is incompatible with the idea that ethics can only ever be expressed in a "language that is foreign to what the community can already hear or understand only too well" (Derrida, 1996, p.74). The difficult idea is that ethics – or at least Derrida's notion of ethics – exists outside any comforting framework. It is perhaps possible to see how this resonates with Stringfellow's thinking. Clearly there is no model for an ethics of poverty law.

7 Lopez's ethics, like those examined above, are double and complex, reflecting his own mode of life. Living as a migrant community, the Chicanos, like other immigrants, had to learn how to mediate their identity with that of the dominant culture. The relationship between the formal and the informal is not straightforward. One does not replace or become more dominant than the other. One can celebrate the festival of Cinco de Mayo and the Fourth of July (Lopez, 1987, pp.162–163). Different cultural identities exist alongside each other, often in ironic ways. Irony is "dissimulation" and

> In my limited experience, these lawyers too rarely worked with us – with individual clients, with families, with extended networks of diverse people, organizations, coalitions, and communities. They often appeared unable or unwilling to imagine how our knowledge of the problems we faced and the strategies we already employed might mesh well, enhance, or even potentially revolutionize what they did as professionals.
>
> (Lopez, 2009, p.24)

There are parallels with Alinsky's *Rules for Radicals* in Lopez's work. Alinsky's text was central to a generation of activists working as community organisers. We can perhaps read Lopez's notion of problem solving as a re-working of Alinsky with special reference to poverty law. Lopez identifies with a tradition of poverty law committed to "fundamental social change" and rooted in orientations to practice and a shift away from black letter law to a different thematic: problem solving. What is problem solving? Our way into this idea is via the celebrated distinction that Lopez makes between rebellious and regnant lawyering. Rebellious lawyering can be defined in different ways but it makes use of "an alternative vision of community problem solving" (Lopez, 2004, p.60). Later this alternative vision is described as the "intermingling" of "obedience and rebellion" in struggles over "how we live" (Lopez, 2009, p.15). Lopez's idea of problem solving gestures to a theory of the good life and how we "thrive" – challenging the "dominant notions" of public and private "organisation" (Lopez, 2009, p.15). As a practice it is dedicated to taking on "transparently inadequate institutions" and encouraging innovation (Lopez, 2004, pp.67–68).

This idea of practice is developed with a distinction between formal and informal ways of problem solving. The informal human capacity for problem solving has been overwritten by "expert" forms of discourse; a sealed world of specialist, "top-down" solutions. Institutions staffed by experts and bureaucrats create patterns of behaviour that effectively organise communal desires into conventional forms. The rebellious vision takes shape against the hegemony of experts. It looks to the way that "ordinary folks" deal with everyday "hassles". People have an inherent ability to solve problems through "stock stories". Rooted in personal and communal practices, stories enable us to understand the complexities of the world and to act in ways that make the world meaningful. Problem solving and

is related to the Greek term "to speak". Thus, there are ways of speaking that identify the speaker as an immigrant and a foreigner, but also ways of dissimulating or allowing different meanings to exists alongside each other. Lopez's understanding of problem solving is rooted in this sense of practical intelligence and mediation of identities (Lopez, 1987, pp.164–165). The immigrant lives a double life, neither outsider nor insider, neither entirely comfortable with the political and cultural traditions of Anglophone America but unable to accommodate the norms of the dominant culture. Once we read the notion of rebellious lawyering in the context of these passages we get a much clearer sense of the complexity of the idea.

storytelling express desires to "move the world" in a particular direction, an endeavour that requires us to persuade others to act in circumstances of "complexity, difference and vulnerability" (Lopez, 2004, p.69).

Lopez's idea of problem solving shares certain important features with Alfieri's and White's accounts of poverty lawyering. We can appreciate how Lopez is engaged with alienated consciousness. Problem solving is a way of resisting the objectification of professional discourse. Lopez's argument (rather like White's) is that we don't need to use the language of counter-hegemony. Resistance is already lived. How can lawyers, in the way they think and act, learn from these forms of life? Answering this question takes us to the knot of anxiety in Lopez's vision.[8]

An extended meditation on a peculiar problem: how can the professional relationship between lawyer and client become a means of transformation and social change? We will look at "Seven Weeks in the Life of a Rebellious Collaboration". An experimental piece of writing, this essay reads rather like a short story or a script.[9] Lawyer and client are agonising over whether or not to commence a civil action for deprivation of rights. The authorial voice intervenes to offer comments on the dynamics of the interaction between two characters: the lawyer Martha Fisher, and her client Jesse Cruz. The conclusion is in the form of a memo from Martha Fisher to a colleague in her law office. The text is reminiscent of one of B. S. Johnson's novels. The author himself appears towards the end of the essay to berate the characters:

8 Whilst one can appreciate the pragmatics of problem solving, certain issues remain unresolved. One particularly pressing question is the extent to which the problem-solving model can get at the increasingly subtle forms of corporate decision making and modalities of governance that may already have included within themselves the rebellious vision. Presumably Lopez's writings are not meant to help powerful decision makers become more powerful. Perhaps Lopez is not trying to suggest that these two traditions of thinking and problem solving are always separate. To refer back to the previous notes, there are perhaps complex patterns of accommodation and double-ness that run through the model of problem solving. Regnant problem solving could open itself to the rebellious vision or indeed the rebellious vision could collapse into a set of rehearsed procedures. The problem, then, is reminiscent of the argument that radical ideas become "pods" (the metaphor is from *The Invasion of the Body Snatchers*, 1956) that concerned Gabel and Kennedy in "Roll Over Beethoven". Admittedly, the emphasis is different. The rigidification of once-vital ways of problem solving is perhaps immanent to all forms of social life. It is also worth stressing that there are marked echoes of Dewey in Lopez's thinking. Problem solving carries forward Dewey's ideas about the importance of communal or democratic ways in which issues can be addressed through open forms of debate and decision making.

9 Lopez is playing with the form of poverty law writing. Whilst grounded in theory, it would seem inauthentic to have an overly theoretical or even academic approach to problem solving. Lopez's experiment in writing is best achieved in "Seven Weeks in the Life of a Rebellious Collaboration". The title already suggests something different from a law journal article. The reader encounters an essay outside the conventions of legal scholarship.

> Part of me thus wants to shout: "Open your eyes, Jesse – even wider still. Don't be fooled by the seductively simple promise of "equal right under law." [...] But ... another part of me feels like I've already done too much "shouting," too much taking over ... All of this bothers me a lot. I'm a little discouraged, maybe even a little depressed, over how I've handled some matters. And I know I'm in for a lot of soul searching ... I only hope I don't allow myself or encourage anybody else to waste a chance to fight in a way we'd all be proud of ...
>
> (Lopez, 1989, pp.1712–1713)

This, one might think, is authentic anxiety. The conclusion enacts the emotional and existential context of a "rebellious collaboration" (not just between the characters but between the characters and the author of the piece). An essay has become a narrative in which a final voice enacts the experience of self-doubt, frustration and the desire to continue the struggle. The lawyer-client relationship and the profound problems of human interaction that it throws up cannot be sanitised, nor even perhaps theorised, unless the account engages with this inherent complexity. Client and lawyer must face "the enigma of their relationship head on" (Lopez, 1989, pp.1712–1713). Both need to be sensitive to, without uncritically acquiescing in, their respective needs and concerns. Both depend on the other to make some sense of how their overlapping knowledge and skills might inform plausible courses of action.

Without citing Buber, Lopez describes the relationship between client and lawyer as an "enigma" within whose mystery the relationship has to be worked out. The collaboration between Fisher and Cruz does not present some stereotypical image of oppressive lawyers and passive clients. Whilst there are tensions in their interactions, they are not fatal to their ability to cooperate with and learn from each other. Note also that they challenge each other and "put a part of themselves on the line". The essay is authentic as it compels the reader to examine the dynamic of the relationship into which s/he enters.

The anxious dialectical process of problem solving thus offers us another vision of how one might escape from the alienating and reified practices of law. Like the other writers we have read in this chapter, Lopez returns to the scene of legal education to elaborate this idea. Lopez's realisation is that "legal education has incredibly little to do with lawyering" (Lopez, 2009, p.20). Lawyering is an activity in the world where one works with others. Legal education is an educational ritual that protects the mystery of the law. A mystery at once beguiling and estranging. That the law school is an experience in alienation is suggested by the comparison of lawyers to clergy who preserve an "enigmatic aura" around their own power. The secret of legal education is something of a pact between teacher and student:

> If you are willing to put to the side who and what you are, including how you think and feel, you can perhaps enter the ranks of those who can operate

> comfortably within and even command what otherwise cannot be fully described and yet informs so much of those very systems that together rule our lives.
>
> (Lopez, 2009, p.22)

Law schools conceal the fact that law's rituals (and legal knowledge) are based on "everyday problem solving" (Lopez, 2009, p.23). Problem solving becomes the figure of a link between these two worlds, a way of thinking, rooted in modes of life that do not estrange the thinker from thinking, and, unlike legal reasoning, is not "fundamentally different from and superior to how people who hail from places like East L.A. think" (Lopez, 2009, p.22). Lopez compares his elite legal education unfavourably to the efforts of "volunteer East L.A. coaches" who "taught him" what "point guards and halfbacks and shortstops do" (Lopez, 2009, p.22). The stress is on the word *do*. Learning to play football provides a scene of self-creation that rivals the arcane rituals of the law school. Football coaches provide a hands-on way of learning through doing. On the field, one comes to know how to "cooperat[e] and compet [e]" with others (Lopez, 2009, p.22). It seems fitting for a book that includes a Kerouacian evocation of the vitality of the streets to move to this equally beat scene where the tyro is inducted into the world of men. Sport, and learning to play sport, are metaphors for living in a world in which one creates one's self.

Lopez's theme, then, is one of the messiness of the "real world" – "the inevitable intermingling and mutually defining character of obedience and rebellion, of lay and professional problem solving, of the way we work and the way we live" (Lopez, 2009, p.15). His work defines a kind of counter-time, a mundane utopianism where one should treat "each moment as a potential opportunity to [act as if an imagined] world [was] already in place" (Lopez, 2009, p.15). Lopez's vision involves a commitment to work, even if one finds work estranging, because it is through work as "a vocation" that one comes to oneself through "collabora[tion] with others" (Lopez, 2009, pp.27–28). The ethic of collaborative working leads beyond narrow expertise and "bounded rationality". Through working together, we might escape the organisation of the social world around "[n]umbing variations on Henry Ford's assembly line" (Lopez, 2009, p.32). Problem solving is a way of imagining "how we might live together in a fully robust democracy" (Lopez, 2009, p.32). As ethic and vocation, problem solving requires a certain honest view of the self. This is precisely the difficulty that lies at the heart of Lopez's discourse. We are all implicated in "maintaining the status quo" (Lopez, 2009, p.33). We deny our complicity, "immuniz[ing]" ourselves by blaming a mysterious "them" in order to "emotionally distance ourselves" from the very problem of our bad faith (Lopez, 2009, p.33). Too easily we all become hollow beings, automatons, sleepwalkers.

Conclusion

Poverty law has at its centre the problematic of the self's anxious relationship with others. Poverty law is an ongoing process, a way of living a sensibility or following a vocation. We cannot leave our argument on this point. We have read about the various ways in which the influence of movement lawyering fed into the new poverty law scholarship. Any ongoing examination of poverty law and particularly of the sensibility of the poverty lawyer must take place against the backdrop of a tradition which carries forward the experiences of the recent past. In the next chapter, we will pick up on this central concern.

Chapter 8

A long way to nowhere

Remembering the movement

> The role of progressive lawyers not only is to engage in crucial defensive practices – a liberal practice within the court system – but also to preserve, recast, and build on the traces and residues of past conflicts.
>
> (West, 1990, p.1802)

> It's time for all Americans to get off welfare and get back to work. You're going to love it.
>
> (President Donald J. Trump, Speech to Conservative Political Action Conference, February 2017)

Introduction

Poverty law is clearly not the preserve of "a handful of oddball lawyers" (McThenia, 1995, p.17). How do we carry forward the memory of a history that we forget at our peril? The point of this chapter is to make the memory of the movement a "useable past" for our difficult times. The long retreat from the war on poverty characterises the period that runs from Richard Nixon's administration, through Ronald Reagan and George H.W. Bush to Bill Clinton's third way and the presidency of George W. Bush. It is perhaps too difficult to properly assess Barack Obama's presidency, and certainly too soon to offer any meaningful analysis of President Donald Trump. However, we will show that the crisis of 2008 triggered a return to, and reinvention of, "classic" themes in poverty law and a certain renaissance in critical legal thinking. It may even be that the growing resistance to Trump produces something truly significant.

The first part of this chapter will pick up on earlier arguments. We need to concern ourselves with the direct aftermath of the failure of the NWRO and go back to a time before the new poverty scholarship. Themes from Chapter 2 will also return. CLS will be presented as carrying forward a critique of the movement, and we will trace these ideas into "second wave" critical legal thinking. Against the conventional position, the argument will stress an essential, if problematic continuity in critical thinking. This continuity can be traced further back to new left ideas about experience and authentic action. Returning attention to the new poverty law scholarship, we will argue that it carried forward both positive and negative inheritances from welfare activism but arguably failed to produce a convincing account of itself. Towards the end of the chapter we will show that a new mood has come into poverty law in the years following the banking crisis of 2008. With the rise of LatCrit a political and intellectual movement has appeared that is committed to working out a praxis of democratic and ethical lawyering. LatCrit provides a new frame for contemporary poverty law.

Hard times

In the late 1970s and early 1908s, poverty law descended into crisis as it became subject to "hostile and unrelenting political pressures" (Feldman, 1995, p.1531). These pressures came from the intersection of various factors: the failure of the movement, political shifts that redesigned welfare services,[1] the reorganisation of the Office of Economic Opportunity (OEO)[2] and the Reagan "revolution".[3]

1 As the start of the 1970s, welfare activists and poverty lawyers found themselves in changing political circumstances. The failure of Nixon's Family Assistance Plan (FAP) was significant. The FAP's demise "marked the end of the most ambitious effort for welfare reform" since the New Deal (Patterson, 1981, p.190). Nixon's increasingly conservative rhetoric denounced the "new despotism" of "entitlements" as making for "the demise of the virtues of self-reliance and individual responsibility" (Nixon, 1992, p.290). The sense of the unravelling of the New Deal continued during Jimmy Carter's period in office. The incumbent president certainly appeared to have the sense that radical reform was necessary, promising in the early days of his administration that it was time for a "complete overhaul" that would "abolish [the] existing welfare system". The proposed Program for Better Jobs and Income (PBJI) was intended to "break the welfare cycle" and "transform" the way in which federal government dealt "with the income needs of the poor". However, despite various amendments, the PBJI failed to receive congressional approval.

2 Legal services had been brought under the OEO in 1964. Legal services lawyers were involved in litigation of class actions, law-reform activities and supporting the general efforts of other departments and agencies involved in the war on poverty (Bellow, 1980). Legal services programmes were reorganised in 1973. The Legal Services Corporation Act 1973 set up a non-profit corporation to administer the body's government funding. During Nixon's period in office, the OEO had run into serious political opposition. Vice President Agnew branded OEO lawyers "ideological vigilantes" who had become "social engineers on a grand scale" (Agnew, 1972, p.930).

3 The assault on welfare moved on two fronts: tackling poverty programmes and limiting the coverage and cost of social insurance. The social and economic problems of the late 1970s were presented as the failures of a weak, vacillating liberalism that had mismanaged the economy and sponsored a vast network of state-funded programmes that had destroyed the work ethic (Midgely, 1992, pp.13–28). Hostile to the Legal Services Corporation (LSC) as governor of California, Reagan began cuts to its financing and placed restrictions on the kind of cases that could be funded. He castigated the student radicals, feminist and welfare rights activists who had undermined family life and hard work, leading to family breakdown, welfare culture and disrespect for authority. In 1986, after becoming president, Reagan spoke of the "tragedy of welfare" and warned

Poverty law was not finished but it was forced to adapt itself to new circumstances.[4] Poverty lawyers themselves had few illusions about the difficulties and frustrations of their work (Wexler, 1970). There was a retreat from the radicalism of the earlier era as a profound "scepticism" emerged about the possibility of using "law as a vehicle for social change" (Cummings, 2001, p.451). Those still committed to the cause of poverty lawyering realised that it was necessary to shift focus from litigation and test cases to assisting in helping the activism of poor people (Wexler, 1970; Bellow, 1977). Although there were differences of understanding about relevant strategies, a central theme runs through the various debates about the future of poverty law: an acute awareness of the legacies of the movement and an urgent need to re-assess the politics of the new left.

At stake was the transmission of a spirit, a way of doing things that was partly to do with the movement, the new left and feminism but was not restricted to these articulations. Radicals returned obsessively to a key question: how was authentic action possible? We can examine some representative pieces. Gabel and Kennedy's celebrated dialogue "Roll over Beethoven" is a text of transition. Read properly, "Roll Over Beethoven" is an attempt to work out what had become of a generous spirit that had hardened into a set of attitudes and slogans. The democratic energy of the SDS had become the revolutionary fury of the Weathermen, Port Huron the ruins of 18 West 11th Street. The fundamental theme is the desire not to repeat the past, and to learn its painful lessons. In different ways the interlocutors return to the problem of sustaining an alternative vision of society. How can it be imagined? If it is something like a form of authentic social solidarity, and if we

that there was a danger that the welfare programmes had created "a permanent culture of poverty". Invoking themes drawn from the lexicon of the culture of poverty, Reagan went on to talk about "a second and separate America, an America of lost dreams and stunted lives". Blame was placed squarely on "misguided welfare programs instituted in the name of compassion". In this version of history, the war on poverty represents a watershed. An "opportunity society" in which poverty was declining but was destroyed by government programmes. The pantheon of "ruined" lives included the welfare mother who receives more from public assistance than by working, the family unit broken apart because it pays not to have "the father present", and the pregnant "teenage girl" who can get an apartment and medical care provided she does not marry the father or her child (Ronald Reagan Radio Address to the Nation on Welfare Reform, 15 February 1986, at www.presidency.ucsb.edu/ws/?pid=36875). President Reagan set out to place further restrictions on the LSC's funding and freedom of action. The Supreme Court also began to move away from its earlier sympathy for welfare rights (Cummings, 2001). For instance, in *Dandridge v Williams* 397 U.S. 471 (1970) the court refused to link benefit levels to family size. In Loffredo's words, the Supreme Court "encouraged political discourse … to degenerate into a virtual free-fire zone with respect to the rights and lives of poor people" (Loffredo, 1993, p.1285).

4 Conservative thinking on welfare borrowed from Mead's ideas. Mead denounced the dependency culture that destroyed any proper experience of civil being. Those dependent on the state had surrendered their autonomy and agency. They were a mere burden on the community that supports them. Rather than generous government benefits, welfare should provide the minimum standard of survival (Mead, 1992).

allow that this vision can only be evoked rather than described, then we can understand exactly why the dialogue form is so fitting for this engagement. It is a conversation over the meaning of an inheritance, an attempt to celebrate the free movement of thought with all its twists and turns. What does it mean to be a radical now that the 1960s have gone? How do you achieve the balance between the seeming failure of a period of radical social action and the hard times of the present?

Sparer identified this peculiar constitution of CLS. He wrote that "[c]ritical legal theory is concerned with radical social change at a time when even liberal social movements appear to be at a standstill" (Sparer, 1984, p.554). The cynical rejection of political vision exists in tension with a more affirmative strain focused upon "social critique" informed by theory and practice (Sparer, 1984, p.519). These concerns tie together the various expressions of critical thinking that appeared between the mid-1980s and early 1990s. Whilst the received account of a "split" between feminists, crits and race theorists is broadly correct, over-emphasising the differences between tendencies obscures a debate that ran through all these forms of progressive thought. For the feminists, it was necessary to grasp the complexity of a way of thinking that could "affirm human values [and] assist in the development of collective identity" (Schneider, 1986, p.598). No wonder that "the richly textured experience of law" comes out of "social movement practice" (Schneider, 1986, p.592). Dialectical thinking offers itself as a way of navigating the tensions between creativity and the political forms in and through which this creativity must express itself. Asserting a feminist belief in reflection on personal experience is part of a "political vision and [the] struggle for change" (Schneider, 1986, p.590). The problem is that grand theory forgets this truth. The whole dynamic of this thinking, like that of Gabel and Kennedy, is to resist easy solutions and slogans. Dialectics is important because it is "dynamic and complex" and based on "the concrete, daily and 'trivial' experiences of individuals" (Schneider, 1986, p.603). Feminist dialectics engages with "the social dimension of individual experience and the individual dimension of social experience" (Schneider, 1986, p.603). Dialectics relates theory to practice and practice to theory to produce a mature way of thinking, engaged with the "possibilities and limits, visions and defeats" of progressive thought and action (Schneider, 1986, p.604).

The foundational texts of CRT engaged with exactly the same requirement for rooted theory. Calmore's celebrated use of Archie Shepp's music is exemplary. Shepp's playing evokes a form of creativity that was "broad" and "novel" and "able to bridge conflicting perceptions of the world" (Calmore, 1992, p.2134). Most importantly, it expresses something "authentic" to black culture experience (Calmore, 1992, pp.2134, 2140). In the face of "isolation, insulation, and marginality" the only possible "constructive respons[e]" comes from a "racially distinctive, experiential perspective and cultural orientation" (Calmore, 1992, p.2134). If critical theory was both an extension and a break with CLS it would have to perform this radical openness to "conflicting perceptions" – not least the "gap" between "egalitarian" ideas and the ongoing reality of poverty and racism (Calmore, 1992, p.2134). Shepp's music is significant as a model for critical thought because it does not "imitate white or dominant scholarship's canons, methods, and analyses", and brings its own "distinctly stylized dimensions to legal scholarship" (Calmore, 1992, p.2147). Style communicates substance. We can obtain a clear sense of this theme if we turn from Calmore to another foundational text of CRT.

Cook's re-working of Martin Luther King's notion of the beloved community shows how the race crits were drawing on the past to respond to the demands of the present. Cook returns to King's writing to answer some pressing questions that lurk within critical legal thinking: what would a transformed social world look like? How can one imagine "reconstruction" (Cook, 1990, p.991)? CLS scholars evaded this question as they were ignorant of a tradition of black Christian thought and action. Rooted in the experiences of people and their practices over generations, the black Christian tradition's notion of beloved community gives a meaningful response to the question that killed CLS. Reconstruction has to come out of a tradition in which community was always practised. King's theology of the beloved community, a term adopted by the SDS, is an understanding of the social and emotional relationships that underlay civil rights organising. The beloved community is not, however, something frozen in the past. Like the feminist notion of dialectics and the crits' own ongoing conversation, theory and practice are mutually informing. King was moving towards an appreciation of economic justice and democratic socialism, embedded in traditions of black faith-based activism. The critical moment is precisely this sifting of a tradition to see what clues it offers for an understanding of the present. As Calmore put it: "[w]e must recognize that America's cultural identity, values and meanings cannot be separated from its past and present social relations of domination and power" (Calmore, 1992, p.2132).

The mid-1980s and early 1990s saw an intensification in critical examinations of the legacy of 1960s radicalism. In pursuing this theme, it is important to connect the general debate over the nature of critical theory or critical legal thinking to the ongoing re-workings of poverty law. Radical lawyers felt that they had to retain a critical distance from their own activities and assess both the failures of the past and the possibilities for action in the future. One practitioner admitted that there was no sign of a "law engineered revolution" on the horizon but counselled against despair (Bellow, 1980, p.345).[5] It was necessary to examine the profound limitations of both the legal system and the strategies of the welfare rights movement. Tushnet picked up on these themes, commenting that welfare litigation "arguably diminished the power of welfare recipients, firstly by deflecting them into a fruitless struggle against a bureaucracy that readily swallowed the Court-prescribed dose of due process … and secondly by bolstering the idea that fairness

5 Other commentators stressed the limited advances made in cases like *Goldberg v Kelly*, 397 U.S. 254. See Simon (1990).

was not far away in the American welfare states" (Tushnet, 1980, p.709). The activities of the NWRO had entrenched the power of the very system that they were struggling against.[6]

This led to another particularly "gloomy" conclusion. The welfare rights movement failed because the poor could not be organised and there was no clearly "identifiable opponent" from which "concessions could be won" (Abel, 1985, p.497). Representing poor clients against the "lumpen bourgeoisie" may have been a noble act but the efforts of well-meaning attorneys do not build a "collective organisation" out of which a sustainable long-term movement could emerge and sustain itself. Legal aid, for all the limited good it might achieve, was "like other welfare programs, [...] essential to the maintenance of capitalism" (Abel, 1985, p.592). It may even be that legal aid distracts from the real terms of the problem. Poverty lawyers should have started with the fundamental problem: "poverty, oppression, discrimination, or alienation" (Abel, 1985, p.598).

The assault on welfare bureaucracy had been met by a redesign of the system. Whilst this responded to the impact of welfare litigation, it did so in a way that had not been anticipated by the poverty lawyers. One particularly marked effect was a shift in power and influence away from those who had a social work background to a reliance on new forms of management practice, computerisation and the proletarianisation of welfare casework. These changes in welfare administration show how the agenda was slowly shifting away from welfare practices inherited from the New Deal and to new forms of accountability and "quality control" (Simon, 1990, p.1206). "Productivity enforcement" in welfare administration was driven by the need to reduce welfare budgets, exploit new forms of technology and streamline bureaucracy (Abel, 1985, p.1218). It would appear, in summary, that whilst the "oppressive and punitive moralism" of the old system had been rooted out, the experience of public assistance was still one of "bewilderment and opacity" for most clients (Abel, 1985, p.212). Even those working for welfare bureaucracies felt "alienat[ed]" and subordination to new hierarchies of management (Abel, 1985, p.212). Most radicals tended to agree that merely attempting to operate within the terms of the welfare state ended up solidifying existing

6 The second major strategic shortcoming of the welfare rights movement was its failure to link arguments about welfare to "minimally decent work" (Simon, 1990, p.1513). Poverty lawyers tended to concentrate on resisting what they saw as coercive work requirements for welfare claimants rather than develop an engagement with training and meaningful work. Poverty activists thus remained within the conventional paradigm of welfare thinking rather than seeking to influence a broader agenda about the kind of jobs and training that might offer ways out of poverty. Focusing solely on welfare also had the damaging effect of further marginalising the poor and cutting them off from other members of the working class who, whilst not reliant on public assistance, might have shared concerns about wages, work and conditions of employment. Finally, privileging welfare benefits as core objectives limited the constituency to which the movement could appeal. This strategy made it difficult to organise those who were only on benefits for a limited period of time or those who moved between public assistance and poorly paid work.

power relationships without "changing the objective circumstances of domination that make it difficult for equity and solidarity to flourish" (Abel, 1985, p.212).

This changes everything

The period of the presidency of George H.W. Bush saw the development of new conservative thinking on welfare. Bush's inaugural address spoke of the importance of "high moral principle" – and the need to "free" citizens from "the demoralization that rules the slums". The "old way" was to use "public money" to end the problem of welfare. What was more important was the "will to act", and – most centrally – "the goodness and the courage of the American people". The will to act would express itself through voluntarism: a "new" and "hands on" activism that "gets the job done". Then, the famous metaphor. The army of volunteers and community organisations is likened to "a thousand points of light" spread "like stars throughout the Nation, doing good".[7] These themes were honed into a very particular vision of a small-state approach to welfare. President Bush was careful to contrast his version of the "good society" with Lyndon B. Johnson's Great Society. Johnson's "federali[sed] virtue" robbed the people of their "moral sensitivity" and wrongly asserted that "only government" could "help people in need".

Although the language of voluntarism certainly had appeal to conservative sentiments, it was also a strategic necessity. Reagan's fiscal policies had led to a significant deficit. There was little room for any further spending on social programmes or welfare. We will see that Bush's compassionate conservatism returns in a different key presently, for it would be fair to say that fundamental reform of the welfare state was to be a feature of Clinton's presidency rather than an emanation of compassionate conservatism.[8] Indeed, the new scholarship on poverty law was to be marked by the traumas and challenges of third-way politics.[9] The Personal Responsibility and Work Opportunity Reconciliation Act

7 See http://avalon.law.yale.edu/20th_century/bush.asp.

8 By 1996 there were 36 million people living below the poverty line (Amott, 1994, p.166).

9 Clinton was a self-proclaimed New Democrat, seeking a workable compromise between different shades of political opinion (Berman, 2001, p.101). Clinton's liberalism spoke to "economic populism" and the "culture and values of mainstream America". It tapped into a public desire to defend aspects of the welfare state from the Republicans (Amott, 1994, p.177). A bold approach to welfare reform had been a feature of Clinton's election campaign. In a book that served as a manifesto, Clinton pledged to "make work pay". Future reforms would limit benefits to a defined period after which the claimant would either have to take a job or take part in community service. After all, welfare was a "second change, not a way of life" (Amott, 1994, p.172). Clinton's focus was on the working poor and the notion of time-limited benefits was presented in the context of increased funding for education, training and childcare. It was also taken up as a major policy initiative that would deal with the problems of the AFDC.

(PRWORA) became law in August 1996 and brought in a number of sweeping changes. A system based on cash benefits was replaced with one "that provides most assistance through social service programs supporting work activity" (Allard, 2007, p.305). A time limit, set at a maximum of five years, was put in place for individuals claiming benefits. This provision effectively terminated an open-ended right to receive cash benefits from the state. Certain states used powers under the Act to make eligibility periods even shorter. The PRWORA also mandated that those in receipt of benefits had a two-year period to find work at the penalty of losing their entitlement completely.[10]

How was it possible to hang onto the energies evoked by movement lawyers and the NWRO? The early 1990s had been a period of retrenchment in the theory of poverty law. The critique of rights that had animated critical legal thinking in the 1980s was opening onto a different moment: "an ideological struggle over the constitution and re-constitution of the meaning of lawyer's practices" (Buchanan and Trubek, 1992, pp.691–692). There was a developing consensus around ways of working that made use of feminist insights as well as those derived from CRT. For Trubek, the "problematic" was that of pluralism. There was "no single body of practice or cases to describe"; there was no one way of accounting for poverty (Trubek, 1994, p.995). A healthy disregard for the "model of the heroic poverty lawyer litigator" was also required. Trubek agreed with White and others. Any theory of poverty law had to be rooted in specific practices. Generalisations were misleading and unhelpful. Poverty lawyers had to address themselves to "non-bureaucratic solutions and new attorney-client interactions" (Trubek, 1994, p.995).

The new poverty law scholarship was certainly pluralistic, innovative and committed to continuing poverty law in difficult times. The cost was a failure of confidence that expressed itself as a reluctance to think beyond local solutions to immediate problems. Some critics have suggested that the embrace of postmodern theory, in particular a focus on discourse and narrative, provided no real advance in understanding. Surely Piven and Cloward would have agreed that poverty was "a multi-faceted phenomenon that cannot be reduced to any single analysis or approached from just one point of view" (Trubek, 1994, p.986). The new poverty scholarship left the impression that the only way to understand poverty law was to examine its various practices against a background of theoretical plurality. For instance, White's criticisms of Alfieri, and her championing of a situated theoretical practice stressed the pragmatic at the expense of broader claims that might have orientated the movement to a shared political position.

10 Exceptions were made for single parents looking after small children. The AFDC was replaced with Temporary Assistance for Needy Families (TANF). TANF gave block grants to states and powers to set up and run schemes subject only to overarching federal guidelines. Regulations relating to food stamps were also tightened considerably. The federal government retained control of these programmes, unlike those under TANF.

Blasi (1994) and Handler (1992) took particular exception to the use of postmodern theory and the micro-analysis of power relationships between lawyers and clients on which it focused. The concern with narrative also deprived poverty law scholarship of different ways of using theory to get at more structural concerns. Whilst not exactly apolitical, poverty theory turned away from "grand" themes such as Marxist understandings of economic transformation and sociological studies of bureaucracy. At stake was a way of comprehending political, economic and social change. Any attempt to grasp the complex relationship between the present and the past becomes difficult if reductionist contrasts between postmodern activism and conventional Marxism dominate discussion. Similar criticisms could be made of other themes in mid-1990s thinking. Hard distinctions between political movements and new social movements or between class-based and identity-based conceptions of politics, produced no real insights.

We can trace these themes through what Cummings has called the "law and organising movement" that flourished in the late 1990s and the early years of the new decade (Cummings and Eagly, 2001, p.447). There was something of a reconsideration of the themes of the new poverty scholarship and a pragmatic engagement with opportunities that had been opened up by Clinton's social policies. Theories of constrained legalism sought to reject "utopianism" whilst maintaining a cautious belief in "legal avenues of transformation" (Buchanan and Trubek, 1992, p.691). In other words, Cloward and Piven were out whilst those theorists and practitioners who struggled to find the correct role for the lawyer were in. The key theme was the need to "encourag[e] organization and collective efforts by clients" – a kind of Wexler/Bellow thesis for new times (Buchanan and Trubek, 1992, p.691). Lawyers might not be at the centre but they were certainly not irrelevant. Lawyers could contribute to the objectives of community organisations through assisting with public education programmes, advising on strategy, and building capacity with allied institutions and organisations. This led to a certain strain in the lawyers' role. For instance, was it strategically correct for a lawyer to be doing organising work when there was unmet need for legal advice? Fears of client domination and professional ethics also limited what a lawyer could do. Reflections on organising practices showed a new understanding of professionalism as a restraint on the power of lawyers even if professional rules had the tendency to limit the very kind of social relations that might be conducive to navigating the tensions that came out of people with different class backgrounds working alongside each other.

So, it was not as if organising went away. If anything, activists innovated new solutions to old problems. Admittedly the "large-scale organising" of the late 1960s and early 1970s was over but "less confrontational local strategies" were viable, and organisations began to appear that campaigned around such issues as the impact of "declining public services and increasing urban and rural poverty" (Cummings and Eagly, 2001, p.464). Moreover, the 1990s had seen a shift in focus to identity-based movements and engagements with "the plight of immigrants and low waged workers, environmental law and community development"

(Cummings and Eagly, 2001, p.469). The Long Island Workplace Project is often held up as a particularly successful innovation in providing help to low-waged, non-unionised workers and developing good working practices between lawyers, workers and organisers. The Coalition for Human Immigration Rights in Los Angeles scored a notable success in marrying together advocacy against labour ordinances with activism on issues around low-waged work. Successful grass-roots movements also showed that pressure could be brought to bear on government and industry seeking to site hazardous and polluting activities in poor communities. The California Rural Legal Assistance Foundation, the Golden Gate Law and Justice Clinic, and the Pennsylvania Initiative, all found ways of coordinating lawyers and activists to achieve their objectives.

One central theme was the emphasis on community development projects. Although community economic development projects had been put in place by both Reagan and Bush, the Community Economy Development (CED) initiatives of the 1990s were key to third-way thinking about poverty. These initiatives were rooted in new governance theory. New governance theory recommended privatisation and decentralisation as a way of creating responsive, locally based programmes. Freed from the heavy hand of central government, private actors, local government agencies and community groups would be able to deliver creative solutions to social problems. Replacing notions of legal regulation that had characterised the war on poverty, new governance theory sought to encourage "experimentalist enterprise" (Bach, 2010, p.256). There was broad support for CEDs from across the political spectrum. The neo-liberals agreed with the emphasis on market-orientated solutions and the left found in new governance theory a form of "public, deliberative participation" (Fung and Wright, 2003, p.3). Rising budget surpluses provided the means to put ambitious plans into action.

The New Markets Initiative (NMI), central to the CED programme, represented a profound shift from war on poverty thinking. The NMI assumed the centrality of the market in securing alleviation of the worst effects of poverty. Indeed, the theory behind the NMI saw the reason for the persistence of poverty as the failure of market development. The solution was clear: federal funds, tax incentives, loans and government action were to be focused on programmes that would encourage the development of new markets in "discrete low-income neighbourhoods" (Cummings, 2001, p.401). Lawyers working with CED programmes began to develop a new set of skills as it appeared that the focus of poverty law had changed profoundly. CEDs were themselves complex and multi-faceted, bringing together partnerships at national and state levels, as well as networks of community groups, businesses and other civil society organisations. Community organisations needed help to encourage CED investment, in particular the attraction of businesses and the delivery of local infrastructure, investment and microfinance schemes for small businesses. One particular area in which lawyers were active was in the area of private construction of affordable housing pursuant to the Low-Income Housing Tax Credit (LIHTC) scheme. The LIHTC enabled construction firms to become eligible for tax breaks if housing schemes contained a certain number of affordable properties. Alongside the LIHTC, the 1994 Community Development Financial Institutions Act sought to enable further investment in poor areas and promote financial services for low-waged people.

What sense can we make of the CED? Melish aligns the new poverty governance agenda with developments in social movement strategy. In place of the "non-negotiable material demands and mass confrontation", CED programmes operate within a "framework of political accountability" where the poor could find a "recognized and secure voice" (Melish, 2010, p.10). However, Melish allows that the governance regime around the PRWORA effectively marginalised voices of the poor who took to "extra institutional spaces" to protest (Melish, 2010, p.12). This was not a replay of the NWRO. Activism focused on the Poor People's Economic Human Rights Campaign (PPEHRC). The PPEHRC was the realisation of a new way of using human rights towards a "new accountability". Moving away from the narrow strategies of the 1960s/70s, and even the more explicitly political use of human rights in the anti-globalisation agenda, the new human rights activism operated with the idea that government "serve[s]" as "a manager of accountability processes between private actors" and ensures the "coordinating [of] the outputs of performance-based accountability processes" with human rights principles at their centre (Melish, 2010, p.75). But criticisms of human rights-based activism were also developing.

Evidence began to emerge that the CEDs were not as effective in poverty alleviation as their proponents had claimed. Studies of various projects suggested that the primary beneficiaries of tax breaks and cheap loans were businesses rather than communities. It also emerged that many of the jobs created were neither sustainable nor sufficiently remunerative. The LIHTC might have encouraged housing construction but on the whole the scheme had created properties for competitive market rents rather than for the low waged or for those in need of public housing. A similar pattern emerges with the financial development programmes. Although the success of some microfinance schemes could be proved, the general pattern was one of long-term failure. One report concluded by denying the central principles of the NMI: "the market economy" could not "provide subsistence for everyone who chooses to participate". Greater government intervention was necessary to build capacity in education, and create jobs and training that "foster business success" (Cummings, 2001, p.450). Moreover, the CED had not encouraged the kind of political participation that, at least in the past, had enabled communities to achieve some control over the decisions that affected them. Reflecting on experiences of community organising in 2008, Gary Delgado suggested that a new sense of political vision was now necessary, not some tepid "lowest common denominator" approach or the avowed localism of the CED. Renewed political vision would have to address the structural reasons for the persistence of racism and poverty (Delgado, 2009, p.6).

New work addressed related difficulties. Bach's work on the Center for Economic Opportunity in New York suggested that the administrative structures put in place were unaccountable to "poor communities" (Bach, 2010, p.241).

Examining the relative success of a community action project in Durham, North Carolina, Bach argued that the governance mechanisms of the "new accountability" were but a "weak nod" towards the kind of "participatory democracy" that might enable poor communities to gain some sort of traction over schemes designed to "help" them (Bach, 2012). Drawing an opposite conclusion to that of Melish about the history of the NWRO, Bach advocated a new militancy to ensure that "governing structures" served "the ends of affected communities" (Bach, 2012, p.157). A study of urban economic redevelopment projects came to similar conclusions. The relevant models of participation were "insufficient" to ensure that benefits flowed to poor people; in fact, the participation model served to "perpetuate structures of inequality and a cruel economic caste system" (Bezdek, 2013, p.17).

These critiques fed into the creation of a new energy that looked back to earlier currents of organisational thought and activity. One model that proved inspirational was George Wiley's Movement for Economic Justice. Wiley had been central to the NWRO and had sought to generalise welfare militancy. His untimely death and the political changes of the 1980s and 1990s meant that this vision was never properly realised. The Association of Community Organizations for Reform Now (ACORN), set up by NWRO activists and coordinated by Wade Rathke (a colleague of Wiley's), provided an important reference point. Organisers and lawyers began to build coalitions bringing together organised labour, poor and low-waged people, immigrants and faith groups (Cummings, 2001, pp.463–464). Commentators started to appreciate the parallels between the emergent forms of organisation and the lessons of earlier times.[11] The fundamental link was an emphasis on notions of economic justice. Organising focused on struggles for a living wage, labour rights and cooperative businesses. There was also a growing awareness of globalisation. It was no longer possible to think of local economies. Activists began to appreciate the role that free trade and international supply chains had on work and worklessness.[12] Themes of political mobilisation thus

11 See Melish (2010).

12 As commentators have suggested, the anti-globalisation struggles that erupted in the later 1990s opened up a new phase of radical politics. These struggles had their immediate roots in the "cross border organising" by groups such as the Direct Action Network (Broad and Heckscher, 2003, pp.713–714). Gaining inspiration from the Ejército Zapatista de Liberación Nacional in Mexico and the growing international links between diverse groups, radical politics became increasingly focused on "direct action tactics" (Kelly and Lefkowitz, 2003, p.95). Analyses of the social costs of neoliberal market reforms opened up new themes. Resistance to globalisation was defined by the Seattle demonstrations of 1999. Around 30,000 people came to Seattle (Bello, 2001). Many commentators noted that anti-globalisation protests represented a point of continuity with the 1960s and a new beginning. Tom Hayden wrote that Seattle showed "a new generation of rebels accomplish[ing] something bigger … than … Chicago in 1968" (Tom Hayden, "The Battle in Seattle", *Washington Post*, 5 December 1999, www.portaec.net/library/mai_wto/tom_hayden_on_the_battle_in.html).

came firmly back into focus; and concerns with social justice reappeared in legal scholarship (Troutt, 2014).

Passing by

We need to sketch out the political changes that formed the background of the latter periods of the scholarship on poverty, law and organising. Our intention is not to weigh up the presidencies of George W. Bush or Barack Obama in any detail. In the next short section of this chapter, we want to merely outline the peculiar shifts in welfare thinking over the last 16 years, and set the scene for our engagement with LatCrit in the last section of the chapter. We also need to engage briefly with the Trump presidency as it threatens "the single biggest attack on antipoverty programs" in recent history.[13] Contemporary critical legal thinking on poverty will have to take into account this profound shift in American politics.

President George W. Bush's inaugural address pressed into service themes that returned to the rhetoric of his father's presidency. Bush praised the "compassion" of the American people: in the "quiet" of its "conscience" Americans knew that "persistent poverty" was "unworthy" of the "Nation's promise." This confrontation with poverty was shorn of the rhetoric of New Deal liberalism, or even the language of the New Democrats. Bush employed a biblical rhetoric. Americans would not walk by "the wounded traveller on the road to Jericho". These striking phrases signalled a new direction in welfare policy. The notion of compassionate conservatism enabled a reinvigorated right-wing ideology to confront Clinton's legacy.[14]

Despite the deep-seated reforms of PRWORA, a great deal of the federal welfare and social security structure was still in place, and radical Republicans were keen to push forward with the Reagan revolution. Charity and churches were more efficient than the state in providing welfare. Given the correct forms of assistance, individuals could lift themselves out of poverty. The task of government is to ensure that individuals look to the "free" market to provide private insurance and savings, and to limit their own efforts to the provision of a safety net for those unable to help themselves. Such an approach is entirely consistent with PRWORA. Bush himself expressed his satisfaction with the legislation, mentioning that since 1996 caseloads had fallen by 50%, lifting "5.4 million people" out of poverty and "chang[ing] lives in a positive way".

A difficult question, to be weighed up by future historians, is that of the political direction of Obama's presidency. Certainly, the election of President Obama in 2008 suggested the opening of a new "progressive" era (Dreier, 2008, p.684). Obama himself came out of the organising tradition and in various speeches and writing identified himself with its energies and political direction. At the same

13 Rebecca Vallas, cited in www.bloomberg.com/politics/articles/2017-03-16/trump-budget-plan-declares-war-on-war-on-poverty-programs.

14 See www.presidency.ucsb.edu/ws/?pid=25853.

time, there was a sense of the enormity of the task faced by a progressive president in difficult economic circumstances. Certainly, the early years of the administration took some bold steps.[15] Dreier spoke of the need for "a contemporary version of the Progressive and New Deal tradition" with government regulation of capitalism through banking reform, revised "workplace safety laws", an enhanced minimum wage and progressive reform of welfare (Dreier, 2008, p.720). Certainly, the Occupy protests after the banking crisis of 2008 suggested that a new mood of militancy was developing.[16] The question for us is the impact of these changes on

15 The American Recovery and Reinvestment Act of 2009 contained some provisions to help the poor, raising benefits to those on the food stamp programme and other nutrition programmes. The Act also extended healthcare entitlements to the unemployed and encouraged states to increase unemployment benefits for those on low wages or working part time. Other provisions covered housing and childcare, and reversed at least some of the reductions made by previous administrations (Piven, 2009, p.47). Significant changes were also made to TANF that were designed to provide higher levels of financial assistance to families and to undo some of the more "draconian" elements of Clinton's legislation (Piven, 2009, p.4748). Qualification for child tax funds was also changed, reversing another principle of workfare (which was premised on ensuring that those on low earnings did not qualify for tax credits). Piven argues that although such changes were welcome, they came nowhere near a meaningful intervention into the structural reasons for poverty. Moreover, they pale into insignificance when compared with the funds made available for corporate rescue packages. Other critics were crueller: "[t]he point, then, is that the nomination of Obama is great news for American liberals, who love equality when it comes to race and gender, but are not so keen when it comes to money" (Michaels, 2008, p.35). The Patient Protection and Affordable Care Act may stand as an example of bipartisan legislation that extended the coverage of Medicare and Medicaid programmes. Although the provisions of the Act have their complexities, a leading voice in grass-roots healthcare activism has described it as part of an "aspirational vision" for "collective demands for economic security, racial justice, gender equality and a fairer distribution of wealth" (Rome, 2013). See also Edelman (2012, p.74): "[w]hat Obama has accomplished" with Medicare and Medicaid is "truly historic". Whilst this may be the case, others, although supportive of healthcare reform, see the Act as flawed in principle, building as it does on earlier neo-liberal proposals for a market in healthcare (Gordon, 2013).

16 Signals that all was not well in financial markets came with the collapse of Enron and WorldCom, one of the major hedge fund management companies (Harvey, 2010, pp.7–8). Rates of repossession had been increasingly steadily from 1998 onwards and moving from low-income groups to the middle classes. Once securities proved to be more or less worthless, the insurance companies that had covered the risks had to be rescued by government funds. Other institutional investors – pension funds, banks and even local governments – also found that the value of their investments had collapsed. One of the most pressing features of the crisis and one that distinguished it from the earlier, more "localised" affairs was the speed and the extent of its development through global markets (Harvey, 2010, p.6). The main reasons for this can be traced back to the "mountain of 'toxic' mortgage-backed securities held by the banks or marketed to unsuspecting investors all around the world" (Harvey, 2010, p.4). On the International Monetary Fund's calculations, the reduction in value of assets was equivalent to "the value of one year's total global output of goods and services" (Harvey, 2010, p.6).

understanding and re-framings of poverty law. Before we can engage with this concern, though, we need to deal with more recent events: a kind of coda to the war on poverty.

Before he was elected to office, Trump had big ideas about welfare reform. It says something about the hangover from the Clinton era, that the president-to-be could frame his thinking on welfare as furthering the basic idea behind the 1996 Act: the rub was that the Welfare Reform Act only applied to the AFDC. Conditionalities should apply to all other welfare programmes on the principle that "[b]enefits should have strings attached". Trump praised the Welfare Reform Act of 2011, which had changed the law on food stamps, requiring recipients to take part in "work activation programs" (as well as limiting spending on abortions).[17] However, what is most interesting from our point of view is the rhetoric in which poverty reform is presented. It is as if themes from Harrington come back but in a mangled, distorted revision. The tough big idea in Trump's tough-talking *Time to get Tough* is that America itself is now the basket case, the impoverished ruin of a once-great nation. Poverty has spread like rot through the polity. The American dream is "in hock" and the "shining city on the hill" is a "car wreck" (Trump, 2011, p.4). As the "deal maker in chief" the president's job is to let the market work its magic – a "president doesn't create jobs, only businesses can do that". Sadly, this truth was lost on the "community organizer" Barack Obama, who had never run a business in his life and presided over a government that "shakes down taxpayers" to provide funds for "special interest groups" (Trump, 2011, p.5). Would it be wrong to suggest that in the call to "be smart and get tough" because there is "no time to waste", you can hear the dim, dying echoes of Dewey's call for creative democracy (Trump, 2011, p.8)? Pragmatism's desire to get things done has become the invective of ignorance armed.[18]

If there is no time to waste, it is felt most acutely by those organising the resistance against Trump. This is no hyperbole. It is worth remembering that 2017 was marked by another return, another memory of the movement. Narrowly

17 See www.congress.gov/bill/112th-congress/house-bill/1167.

18 Trump's inaugural address contained a statement of intent on welfare reform. Welfare reform was also a main theme in his address to the American Conservative Association. Hardly surprisingly, the controlling idea is that work pays; and, as such, welfare reform has to be seen in the context of dealing with the perceived obstacles to the rewards of honesty and hard work. Central planks in policy include reform of the tax system to free up investment for jobs, and immigration reforms that will create and sustain employment for Americans. Critics have suggested that the proposed tax cuts effectively shift the tax burden to the poor, and, with no real evidence of trickle down, cannot be seen as effective tools in anti-poverty policy. At the time of writing, it also appears that promised reform of the Affordable Care Act has stalled. However, the first Trump budget's package of cuts to federal programmes will effectively "pull the rug" from under the feet of many poor and low-waged families (www.washingtonpost.com/news/wonk/wp/2017/03/16/if-youre-a-poor-person-in-america-trumps-budget-is-not-for-you/?utm_term=.fbd6159802ce). The budget effectively brings to an end many of the surviving programmes set up in the war on poverty.

missing the democratic nomination, Bernie Sanders's campaign opened up politics to agendas that drew explicitly on ideas long exiled from the democratic left. A veteran of the civil liberties struggles and a self-confessed socialist, Sanders has put forward a clear sense of an alternative politics. Whether or not inspired by Sanders, there is a fair amount of evidence that the political paralysis that produced Trump is invigorating American grass-roots democracy. On the day of the president's inauguration, half a million women marched in Washington, and an estimated 4 million people took part in protests throughout the country. Town hall meetings pulled together all those who would be effected by the repeal of Obamacare and contributed to Republican frustrations over healthcare reform. Mass demonstrations against the presidential order restricting travel from predominantly Muslim countries also showed the degree of public anger over immigration policy.[19] Against this background, we want to examine one particularly interesting new development in critical legal thinking. Although this predates the Trump presidency, it might provide a way of engaging with grand theory: a new focus on old ideas.

LatCrit: the new breed plugs in

LatCrit represented a re-focusing of critical ideas with a self-assurance reminiscent of the new left. Acknowledging their debt to CRT, and the split of CRT from CLS, LatCrit scholars argued it was necessary to repeat this move, to critique the critique in order to understand race beyond the black-white binary, and to engage with the histories and experiences of many different ethnicities. For us this theme has a very specific cutting edge. Bearing in mind the analyses of the ClassCrits in Chapter 5, we can appreciate why LatCrit is an effective re-working of themes of postmodern scholarship with emphasis on an analysis of material culture and power. It is worth stressing that the LatCrit concern with multiple identities and heterogeneous experiences articulates the terms in which a viable, contemporary analysis can make sense.[20]

LatCrit poverty thinking takes into account the "internationalisation" of race and the study of economic migrants, refugees and other cross-border movements of people. Scholars were active in tracing the links between these phenomena and issues around low-waged work, the absence of labour rights, homelessness and poverty. Recently, LatCrit has extended beyond the interface of race, class

19 See www.newyorker.com/news/john-cassidy/the-trump-resistance-a-progress-report; and www.theguardian.com/us-news/2017/apr/24/100-days-of-trump-resistance-wins-so-far-battles-to-come.

20 The specific contribution of LatCrit to the critique of consciousness is to see it as irremediably plural. As Harris's foundational statement of this theme put it: "we are not born with a 'self,' but rather are composed of a welter of partial, sometimes contradictory, or even antithetical selves" (Harris, 1990, p.584). Harris is arguing that selves are not fixed, nor reducible to distinctions between black and white or the norms of heterosexuality. On homophobia, see Valdes (1997a). On poverty and homosexuality, see Heinze (1995).

and gender to produce alliances with queer theorists and the developing scholarship around transgender issues. The LatCrits label their method multi-dimensionality, which is as good a name as anything for non-reductive thinking. Serious engagement with these themes takes us to the distinctive nature of LatCrit methodology, a desire to articulate an understanding of praxis that is authentic to its engagement with poverty as a fundamentally political problem. Understandings of praxis stress collective engagement and experiments with collective writing around a canon of broadly shared principles. Thus LatCrit "grounds the production of knowledge in the performance of a living and learning community-building process" (Iglesias and Valdes, 2001, p.1248). This is thought that is sure enough to risk moments of crises:

> The commitment to engage difference – as a community building practice – is a major and continuing challenge to each and all of us, both collectively and individually, precisely because it inevitably triggers moments of risk: one never can foretell for sure what the cauldron of diversities and perspectives that we call "LatCrit" will cook up.
>
> (Iglesias and Valdes, 2001, p.1248)

LatCrit sees itself as a movement and from the assurance that this brings, acknowledges that thinking and acting require faith and strength. The worst thing is to retreat to "the 'safety' of sameness" when what is required is a kind of permanent revolution, an ongoing examination of the relevance of its key tenets to the work of those scholars and activists who have committed themselves to the cause (Iglesias and Valdes, 2001, p.1249).[21] The concern with self-examination gives this thinking its anima. Valdes explicitly links praxis to "democratic conceptions and egalitarian practices" (Valdes, 2009, p.145). Unless you lay hold of the way that one thinks, you are trapped in categories created by others. Modes of identity have to be made conscious and, if necessary, rethought.

We can appreciate that Valdes is writing within a tradition that resonates with notions of alienation and reification. The notion of critical "legal knowledge production" taking place around "democratic conceptions" and "egalitarian

21 For instance, Lawson argues that CRT must "expand its scope beyond the boundaries of academia" and affirms that CRT has the potential to achieve this end because of the dynamic relationship it has established between the experiences of its practitioners and their writing (Lawson, 1995, p.368). Lawson locates her work alongside that of Margaret M. Russell, who has an understanding that the "progressive practitioner" can learn from CRT and "embrace a broader and more eclectic vision of lawyering for social change" (see Russell, 1992). Yamamoto has a slightly different version of CRT praxis: "[c]ritical race praxis seeks to bridge at least partially both the 'gap of chasmic proportions' between race theory and political lawyering and the growing divide of law from racial justice" (Yamamoto, 1997, pp.866–867). The fundamental problem is the limitation of CRT to the duality of white and black, which has made it blind to issues of justice between ethnic minorities. In a similar vein to Lawson, Yamamoto speaks of "reconstructive writing" or a "practical turn" to LatCrit (Yamamoto, 1997, p.872).

practices" suggests that resistance to reification can only come from actively engaged thought. With the degeneration of democracy into a narrow idea of proceduralism, it is necessary to renew faith in political agency. Valdes is very much an inheritor of Dewey's notions of democratic character. LatCrit is a peculiarly American response to poverty as a failure of democracy.

Piomelli's understanding of democratic lawyering provides a focus for these themes (Piomelli, 2006, 2009). For some, democratic lawyering may simply be another way of describing rebellious or collaborative lawyering. In terms of our argument it has a particular resonance going back to new left notions of participatory democracy. This new coinage reminds us of a quality that has slipped out of recent theorisations of poverty law. The language of the client-lawyer relationship is now described as one between "fellow citizens" and rooted in an "egalitarian" practice of poverty law (Piomelli, 2009, pp.1385–1388).[22] Democratic lawyering refers back to the work of Ella Baker of the SNCC that was grounded in grass-roots organising. This returns us to a classic concern: those who work together do so against the alienating effects of bureaucracy, racism and hierarchy. Dewey returns as a specific point of reference. Piomelli argues that participatory democracy is central to a complex of ways of living that perform the "value" of the human being. Political engagement with the likeminded creates authentic ways of living and thinking.

It is indeed interesting that these sources of participatory democracy have been rediscovered by scholars associated with LatCrit. We have come across a sophisticated reappraisal of the lexicon of the new left. If the movement was about "our ability to grasp ... the wholeness of what was going on and what was to be done",[23] then the intersectional thinking of LatCrit is a contemporary expression of creative democracy. LatCrit urges the scholar-activist to "get out there" – to bring together theory and practice because justice is "something experienced". Justice is rooted in a "visceral" response to a specific situation (Yamamoto, 1997, p.875). With this in mind, we can confront the question that has haunted us throughout the last three chapters: how can we understand an ethics of poverty law?

Conclusion

This chapter has concerned itself with the changing forms of poverty law activism and theory in the long decades since the end of the 1960s. We have examined how the spirit of the movement has been passed forward.

22 Such a presentation of democratic lawyering locates within the vocabularies and ideas that we have been studying and brings back something forgotten. If one is not careful, democracy becomes just another language of choice. For instance, in Schumpeter's influential account, voting merely expresses the personal, private preferences of a largely apolitical electorate that acts as a kind of brake on the activities of an elite who, as the naturally most talented, are the most suited to govern. Needless to say this thin account of democracy contrasts with the thicker accounts of civil engagement and active participation.

23 Michael Rossman, "Notes from a SDS Reunion", www.sds-1960s.org/Rossman.htm.

One thing that can be saved from the ashes of the new left is the idea of a broad coalition bringing together the precariat, the young, the old and the disenchanted middle classes. Occupy's revolting bodies – and the resisters against Trump – are the descendants of the SDS's faith in the power of the people. Bernie Sanders, although never a member of the SDS, worked alongside Congress of Racial Equality and the SNCC. His presidential campaign had echoes of Port Huron: American democracy must be reinvigorated to take back control from the billionaires in whose interests the system operates. These ideals feed into the new initiatives and forms of solidarity: sanctuary cities and universities, plans to register as Muslims should a register become law and mass protests against the travel ban. Intriguingly, the SDS re-formed in 2006 and its chapters are active in the resistance.

Is the nightmare of Trump waking US radicalism from its slumbers?

Reviewing the last quarter of a century of poverty law thinking, we have argued that the energies that flowed through CLS terminate in LatCrit. LatCrit can be understood as an inheritor of key themes around creative democracy and ethical praxis. LatCrit inherits notions of double consciousness, intersectional thinking and a profound anxiety over its own constitution. We have pointed out that LatCrit scholarship has produced a model of political lawyering that returns explicitly to ideas drawn from the new left.

We now need to pick up on our long-delayed engagement with an ethics of poverty law.

Chapter 9

Diving for dear life

Poverty law and the broken middle

> The aim of all education, even in a law school, is to encourage a process of continuous self-learning that involves the mind, spirit and body of the whole person. This cannot be done unless larger questions of truth and meaning are directly faced.
>
> (Cramton, 1978, p.263)

> We need no more lawyers defending the status quo. We need revolutionaries.
>
> (Quigley, 2007, p.168)

Introduction

The previous chapter engaged with a particular history of poverty law and offered a brief account of the transformation of a tradition over the last four decades. We concluded with an analysis of LatCrit's non-reductive and intersectional approach to creative democracy. Now we want to turn to a final set of themes that focus on our concerns with the "reproduction of lawyering" (Goodrich, 2004, p.392). The reproduction of lawyering will be linked to the sustenance of a radical sensibility. We will return to the concept of "being with" the poor, and to Addams's work in order to find an "origin" for poverty law as the broken middle, located precariously between law and social justice. The broken middle will provide an articulation of an anxiety that finds its authentic expression in ethical praxis.

Social justice and the ethics of poverty law

Despite the attempts of critics to sideline or banish poverty law from the law school, the subject haunts legal thought and practice. If we go back to the roots of contemporary jurisprudence, we can see that poverty law was presented in different ways. Some scholars presented it as the personal commitment to work with the poor,[1] others stressed its importance as an area of

1 This is an old theme within the literature. An early text points out that "there is something radically wrong [with] … unequal distribution of wealth, with such unequal opportunities as everywhere stare us in the face. In the midst of the greatest wealth and

study.[2] Poverty law was also understood to be a development in judicial philosophy.[3] More recently, these disparate approaches have tended to coalesce into a view of poverty law as a realisation of social justice. Whilst this is a productive way of approaching the subject, and we would certainly not want to reject it, there is an awkwardness about the relationship between poverty law and justice. This theme has a pedigree and can certainly be traced back to realism and legal sociology. For instance, Pound spoke of "the backwardness of the law with respect to social problems" (Pound, 1921, p.117).[4] Llewellyn agreed, sharing the sense that "[l]aw does not exist for the corporation executives alone" (Davies, 1993, pp.17–18). However, like Pound, Llewellyn saw no easy relationship between law

progress, exists the deepest poverty" (Anonymous, 1890, p.212). Anxieties about the "muffled discontent" and the "murmur of the masses" encouraged lawyers to provide services for poor clients (Brackett, 1887). Founded in New York in 1876, the Legal Aid Society was, first of all, an organisation aimed at helping poor German immigrants. It became more broadly focused on providing aid and general support in the last years of the century. The Legal Aid Society offered legal advice and help to the new immigrants in the slum tenements of Manhattan's Lower East Side. In the 1900s, the legal profession began to offer more support to the Legal Aid Society, partly because initial fears about competition for clients and lucrative civil litigation had been allayed, but also because legal aid to poor immigrants was seen as a form of cultural induction that would encourage respect for the law.

2 For instance, sociological jurisprudence challenged the dominant laissez-faire model of economics that made for a limited understanding of law. Sociological jurisprudence argued that law should ensure the coherence of society by giving form to social interests and reconciling conflicts between them.

3 In Holmes's work the concern with the judicial failure to weigh "considerations of social advantage" took place in the context of an analysis of the "socialism" that "frightened" the "comfortable classes" (Holmes, 1897, p.21). Holmes urged judges to understand that "they were taking sides upon debatable and often burning questions". When he was nominated to the Supreme Court by Theodore Roosevelt, Holmes showed his sympathies to progressive politics in a marked way. In *Hammer v Dagenhart* 247 U.S. 251, Holmes's dissent asserted that the regulation of child labour was constitutional. He also famously showed his credentials in a dissenting judgment in *Lochner v New York* 198 U.S. 45. Admittedly neither of these cases shows that Holmes was carrying a brief for the poor but his critique of laissez-faire economics resonated with wider understandings of the causes of poverty. Pound associated Holmes with the "progressives" of "two decades ago" and praised him for rooting legal reasoning in an engagement with the reality of social problems rather than "deductions from liberty" (Pound, 1921, p.452).

4 Pound distinguished the narrow forms of legal justice from those pressed into service by sociologists, and was particularly critical of the influence of Herbert Spencer's notions of market liberty on American law. Pound made a sympathetic reference to Commons's notion that justice was not "merely fair play between individuals … [but] … fair play between social classes" (Pound, 1912, p.455). He also showed his sympathy for progressive causes in his engagement with the trial of Sacco and Vanzetti. Pound was not alone in these endeavours. Consider, for example, the notorious address to the University of Michigan Law School where Supreme Court Justice Harlan F. Stone denounced the way in which "the learned profession" had been "tainted with the morals and manner of the market" (Stone, 1934, p.7).

and social justice. Social justice has nothing to do with law or legal reform. It is "a yearning that the less pleasant attributes of men ... might disappear, [so that] something other and better might be substituted for them". Indeed, no scheme of justice can be properly realised: "society [always] has had to compromise with much which is plain injustice" (Llewellyn, 1939, p.6). When he returned to this theme a few years later, Llewellyn saw the achievement of justice as a matter of social organisation. It is a "group job" that calls for "organization, discipline, leadership, and leaders" who can address the problems suffered by the "disadvantaged". The leaders who take on this struggle must be guided by "fairness" and "the dignity of human beings". Llewellyn does not go much further. Other than observing that justice operates "under the principles of scarcity", he leaves his account somewhat vague, an appeal to a pragmatic sense of what, in a given context, appears to be the best way of proceeding (Llewellyn, 1942, p.257).

These views have filtered through into contemporary questions about the nature of poverty law, its place in the law school and its value to a legal education. How can we celebrate the awkwardness of poverty law? Perhaps social justice and poverty law should make the law school uncomfortable. This is not to downplay its usefulness. Quite the opposite. To understand why this location of poverty law is important we need to appreciate how poverty law expresses an enduring anxiety at the gap between law and justice. Poverty law is the nightmare of law's bad conscience.

Failinger's work is an important point of reference for the development of this theme. She describes poverty law practice as "at once zealous and broken-hearted" – defined by strange paradoxes and a contrast between the compromises of everyday lawyering and a vision of hope for a "Beloved Community" that recognises the essential "humanity" of the poor (Failinger, 1999, p.2071). The theory of poverty law must address these gaps and separations with a particular complex in mind, the question of "[h]ow can we act" in order to help poor people "who imagine their lives not as they now are" (Failinger, 1999, p.2073)? The emphasis in on the word *act* – not *act for* – and thus resonates with the extended understanding of poverty law as a legal and ethical practice.

Whilst Failinger is correct to place this question of ethics at the centre of her investigations, do we agree that we need to think of the poor as "solitary" and "vulnerable" – unable to assert their own political agency? Does this approach not return to discredited "culture of poverty" arguments? In whatever way we set up our understanding of a "heartbroken" ethics, it has to take this problem seriously.

What do we mean by ethics? We are not concerned with the model rules of the American Bar Association, with "adversarial processes, regulatory frameworks or organisational structures" (Rhode, 1985, p.591). Nor are we after an ethics where lawyers assume "greater personal responsibility for the consequences of their personal actions" (Rhode, 1985, p.592). Our focus is not on professional ethics at all but with a different understanding of the term. Certainly, it touches on themes that one would find within the ethics literature. The argument thus far has indeed examined "restraints of role" but we have understood this theme to relate to the peculiar anxieties that come out of radical lawyering (Rhode, 1985, p.623).

In order to further discussion of this point, we will look in a little more detail at Failinger's argument. She sketches out the four main positions that seek to define poverty law ethics. One builds on Fried's celebrated notion of the lawyer as "friend" to justify a decision to represent clients on the basis that they are "valuable and valuing agent[s]" (Failinger, 1999, p.2079). The second position gestures towards Luban's work on "ethical dialogue" and suggests that lawyers may wrongly lead clients to courses of action through subtle rhetorical strategies that operate despite belief in a client's autonomy (Failinger, 1999, pp.2083–2084). The third example is a variation on this theme. Despite a lawyer's attempts to "manipulate" his or her client, there is the possibility that lawyer and client can "open themselves to each other" (Failinger, 1999, p.2084). These positions show how modern and post-modern understandings of ethics based either on the autonomy of the lawyer or the "canons of respect and dialogue" emerge in critical thought.

The fourth position illustrates something similar to the ethics of the encounter. Failinger returns to an incident related by Alfieri in his discussion of community organising. She suggests that the meeting between Alfieri and "the stranger" "characterises" the "moment in which poverty law ethicists find themselves today" (Failinger, 1999, p.2085). Leaving a community meeting, Alfieri falls into a conversation with a shadowy figure. Rather than engage in discussions about "coordinating outreach" and analyses of the "community's problems", the stranger merely laughs and comments that "in the sixties they called it urban renewal. They kick you out of your house, move you away from your neighbourhood, and put you up in a high-rise where you don't know anybody". The stranger then turns and walks away. Alfieri's "world of reflective practice" and "collective action" are "shattered" by the "Stranger's own world" which is "practical, needy, proud [and] bitter".

Failinger uses Alfieri's story to point towards an argument about the relevance of Levinas's ethics of alterity for poverty law. Unlike forms of ethics which stress autonomy, care or even dialogue, the ethics of alterity begins with the face of the other. The demand opened up by the face of the other cannot be understood in terms of the other's autonomy. Neither can it be described on the basis of a relational sense of care or even a postmodern notion of respect. Levinas's ethics require a response to a unique person with a singular problem. In responding to the other's demand, the lawyer might fall back on his/her professional role but the "ethical relationship" must be located "in" the moment of encounter which could very well deliver a "threat" to a lawyer's "self-worth" (Failinger, 1999, pp.2108–2109). Responsibility begins with this "freedom, paralysis and fear", an argument that is reminiscent of themes discussed in our reading of Stringfellow (Failinger, 1999, p.2109). The nature of the encounter may be such that it is difficult or even impossible to put into words. Making sense of the ethical encounter may be one of discovering a "second best language" (Failinger, 1999, p.2111). But this is to run ahead with the argument. We need to take stock.

We are examining the ethics of alterity to try to understand how we might frame the theory of poverty law. Our concern is with a way of thinking that can address the peculiar "edgy" situations in which poverty lawyers find themselves. Suffice to say it requires us to go beyond the conventional sense of legal ethics. We can also see from the argument above that we need to be critical of what has passed for both modern and postmodern accounts of ethics. This gives us something to go on. We have not (and will not) make use of alterity to develop our argument. Instead, we want to stress that there is at least some relationship between Failinger's disruption of our "at-homeness" and Stringfellow's work. The ethics of alterity disturbs mundane ideas about the lawyer-client relationship. The encounter between the lawyer and the client is a provocative "moment of unfamiliarity" – the opening of a "space between strangers" (Failinger, 1999, p.2073).[5] Failinger's argument is consistent with the critique of reification and alienation that has run throughout this book. To respond to the demand of the face of the other is to engage with what lies "behind" social scripts. If there was any contemporary re-articulation of classic themes in the theory of alienation, it would appear that they are to be found in this kind of thinking. However, we need to be somewhat critical of an ethics of alterity. Why?

In part this is to do with Failinger's presentation of ethics. She argues that: "ethics is not a thought process engaged in by an autonomous subject about his potential actions toward another, his object. Rather, ethics is the relation established in the face-to-face, nurtured but not constituted by communication" (Failinger, 1999, p.2078). The first sentence provides a useful way of thinking, but the second offers a stark, perhaps too stark choice. Ethics is either a thought process engaged in by autonomous subjects, communicative and dialogic, or it is opened by the "face to face" that relates to, but is not reduced to, communication. Slightly re-working this definition gestures towards an ethics that locates itself in dialectical relationships between people. This dialectical relationship involves the self and the other, but thinking in terms of the self "held hostage" by the alterity of the other may not be best way of understanding social practices of recognition. Finally, power cannot simply be seen in terms of communication, but as we argued in Chapter 5 must take account of commodification, the social reproduction of capital as well as the disciplinary functioning of welfare institutions. Relying on a moment of intense demand in a face-to-face relationship does not transcend power. The question, as we will see, is how we can engage with power relations in an honest way. This might have been precisely what Alfieri's stranger was talking about. Praxis, we might say, cannot be reduced to dialogue and requires a much broader understanding of "encounters" between people. Moreover, praxis does

5 Failinger urges lawyers to turn to Levinas's work where we can find "the vision: the ethics of encounter" (Failinger, 1999, p.2073). Such is the force of the encounter with the other, it "threatens to leave us paralyzed, mute". Looking into the face of the other, with its demand for our help, leaves one with "no words, no articulable way" to decide what to do whilst at the same time being compelled to act (Failinger, 1999, pp.2074–2075). Clearly this experience does not map onto other accounts of ethics, legal or otherwise. Indeed, Failinger confesses that it is hard to know exactly what it means.

not need to be based on the possibility of a successful dialectical resolution of viewpoints. Praxis is always something of a failure, an awkward and ongoing experiment with difficult actions and choices.

As we are taking stock it is also worth elaborating how themes from the previous chapter fit into the present argument. Towards the end of the last chapter, we made much of LatCrit's practical way of thinking. From within the LatCrit stable, Yamamoto usefully sketches out the basic terms of an understanding of praxis as a process that moves from "experience" through "thinking" to "engagement". The "translation" of experience into thought and action is bound up with values that come out of this extended work on the self. This engagement is a "performance" that takes us to the actor him- or herself. As we have always intimated, this is inseparable from an ethical question that we have framed in terms of character or sensibility (Yamamoto, 1997, p.880). Whilst this is not consistent with Rawls's theory of the moral subject that was examined in Chapter 4, it is not entirely unrelated. It is as if the theory of the performance is generated by the "doing" rather than through the application of principles that somehow pre-existed the action.

Social ethics and "being with" the poor

So, we need to take a step back into history and link contemporary poverty theory with an intellectual and ethical engagement that took place early in the twentieth century.[6] The response to poverty that interests us the most is the settlement house movement (O'Connor, 2001, p.26). The settlement house movement sought to bring together the socially engaged middle classes with those living in poverty. Drawing on British ideas, Addams saw settlement houses as a "solution of the social and industrial problems which are engendered by the modern conditions of life in a great city" (Addams, 1910, p.126). Hull House, which Addams established in Chicago in 1889, sought to provide "solutions" to "social

6 These themes are marked in the progressive period: nineteenth-century views of poverty were "by no means devoid of care for [society's] less fortunate members". Concern for the poor expressed itself in the "voluntary measures" of the "propertied classes" rather than any explicit sense that the state itself was under any obligation to care for sections of the population fallen on hard times (O'Connor, 2001, p.237). See also Jacob Riis's *How the Other Half Lives* (1890). Riis drew attention to the scale and depth of urban poverty. The rotting, overcrowded tenements of New York were "the hot-beds of the epidemics that carry death to rich and poor alike" (Riis, 1890, p.5). Hunter's *Poverty* (1904), like Harrington's *The Other America*, showed how most Americans were ignorant of the depth and impact of poverty. Herbert Croly's *The Promise of American Life* (1909) took up the progressive theme of poverty amidst plenty. Croly noted that "grinding poverty" constituted a "grave social danger" threatening the "integrity" of America unless it was possible to "guarantee to every male adult a certain minimum of economic power and responsibility". Those suffering from extreme poverty and destitution "lack the first essential of individual freedom" and were unable to "escape from a condition of economic dependence" (Croly, 1909).

problems" that were due in part to the separation of the educated from the "masses of people" that constituted the labouring classes (Addams, 1910, pp.115–116). Coming together in the supportive environment of a settlement house was the best way of realising "the democratic ideal". We thus come upon an earlier version of themes that reappeared in ERAP. A long time before *The Port Huron Statement*, Addams appreciated that poverty destroyed the "social organism" that was an expression of "common intercourse", "fellowship" and the "reciprocal" relationship between people (Addams, 1892, pp.1, 3).

Addams's audience were unhappy souls, the socially engaged and educated middle classes who were suffering from "maladjustment" – a sense of divergence between "their conscience and their conduct" (Addams, 1902, p.4). For these concerned souls, it was necessary to address "the moral experience of the many" in order to work from authentic "motives" (Addams, 1902, p.5). Addams spoke of the "socialized virtues" to stress the difficulties of a process through which an ethical response to poverty came from engaging with the worlds of the poor (Addams, 1902, p.79). Socialising virtue required effort. It was necessary to move away from the old tradition of charity visiting. Even though the young, well-meaning charity visitor might be committed to helping poor families, her virtue counted for little unless she actually understood that she was just a spectator on the lives of others.

Addams understood that all ethics are rooted in context. Indeed, she made a point of contrasting the "organic" sympathy that the poor showed to each other with the high moral principles of charity workers. Moreover, what distinguishes this desire for a new code of social experience from the efforts of an earlier generation of well-meaning ladies is a profound sympathy for the poor, an ability to understand how the response to poverty may not take the form that a middle-class charity visitor might favour. Social ethics, in this important sense, meant a challenge to the self, a rethinking of one's worldview whilst engaged with the social worlds of the poor.

Our argument is that we can find in Addams a peculiar notion of "going to" and "being with" the poor. The prevalent themes of "going to" and "being with" are therefore difficulty, self-questioning and adaptation. The poor are not "objects" to be improved by virtuous young men and young ladies. Social ethics, we might say, are rooted in democratic encounters between the classes. This gives onto a sense of democracy as the "creed which believes in the essential dignity and equality of all men" and "which affords a rule of living as well as a test of faith" (Addams, 1902, p.6). If we bring together these ideas of democracy and "being with" the poor, we arrive at the core of Addams's ethics. What Addams calls "social experience" is the test of how one lives.[7] In summary, the ethics of "being

7 Adler's ethical philosophy offers some interesting points of comparison with Addams's work. Adler wrote of the need to "preserve the sacred right of individual differences intact, and yet to combine with our fellow-men for the loftiest and purest ends" (Adler, 1880, p.10). He went on to argue that "the welfare of others – moral as well as external – [was as] much our concern as our own" (Adler, 1905, p.73). In *The Essentials of Spirituality* (1905), Adler developed another distinctive theme. Our "spirituality" is inexorably linked to "tutoring ourselves to regard the welfare of others".

with" the poor require "social perspective and sanity of judgment [that] come only from contact with social experience" (Addams, 1902, p.7).

This takes us back Dewey's comments on the "fundamental role of character in moral life" (Dewey and Tufts, 1932, p.255). Character is somewhat hidden or recondite and has to be manifested through action. Not all actions direct us to the specific sense of moral character. Crudely, the important factor is that of discrimination – the need to determine the course between incompatible ends (Dewey and Tufts, 1932, p.207). As soon as we are concerned with this kind of "agency", we are addressing a "moral situation" (Dewey and Tufts, 1932, p.207). The distinction between ends brings with it a question of conflict between values. We don't need to get hung up on this word. It signifies a process of argumentation or choice between ends. The true end is the one chosen within those situations where we deal with "practical problems" (Dewey and Tufts, 1932, p.212). Distinction requires skill, which in turn requires education. The individual must become "habituated" to achieving "good ends" in order to be able to "delight in them". It follows that one can be "immature" and not able to "really know" what is "good" (Dewey and Tufts, 1932, p.217). Distinction thus takes us back to the nature of character or those "active tendencies" which can make someone "warm" to "certain aims" and "cold" to others. If, in moral decision making, our concern is with ends, then character relates to the "prevailing motive" that any given agent is willing to "accept or tolerate". Dewey, writing with Tufts, relates the end of moral decision making to "the social good". One must "fin[d] one's good in the good of others" (Dewey and Tufts, 1932, p.295).

To be able to understand how one's good might be found in the good of another involves something of a dialectic. One needs to see things from the other side. One needs to be able to put oneself in the position of the other. But this is not "the Other" – the distant (or most close) impossible Other of Levinas's ethics. It is the perspective of those others one is with. Thus, "the good moral character" is "active" to the extent that it comes out of the labour, the work on the self (Dewey and Tufts, 1932, p.298). The good moral actor is a person of action involved in doings. His or her "happiness or satisfaction" is focused upon practices "irrespective of the particular pleasures and pains" that they might occasion. This

This "doctrine" was based on the "indefeasible worth" that must regulate the way that we relate to "our fellow men". Adler was willing to indict a society where "many lives are indirectly sacrificed because of the lack of sufficient food" (Adler, 1908, p.34). We get a clear sense of a form of social philosophy that runs parallel to that of Addams if we relate these arguments to passages in *An Ethical Philosophy of Life* (1908), where Adler notes that, having been sent on "errands of charity" as a child, he had always appreciated the "duty of respecting the dignity of the poor while ministering sympathetically to their needs" (Adler, 1905, p.12). Strangely anticipating some of Roberto Unger's arguments, Adler links the notion of personality to the "inherent dignity" of the "human being". Thus, "[t]he sting in poverty is not so much the hardships suffered, as the contempt for the manhood of the poor" (Adler, 1905, p.45). Adler, like Unger, has a strong sense of the way in which poverty crushes an individual's dignity and perception of the good.

cannot be described as sympathy. The sentiment that Dewey is describing goes beyond this particular affective relationship because it is not a natural or spontaneous desire to work for the good of others. It is a form of training and reflection. The correct attitude, tempered by the means of correct training, becomes an ongoing examination of how one should act to further "socialised interests" (Dewey and Tufts, 1932, p.300).

This is not easy. Many people act morally but the special appreciation of socialised interests comes from hard work and a sense of calling. One also needs courage. It is necessary to achieve some sort of standpoint and from that standpoint "accommodate one's ends to those of others", but also to know when to stand one's ground. The whole problem in this regard is that acting for the social good is dangerously similar to having an "aristocratic" temperament. An aristocratic sentiment sees its glory in bestowing goods upon others. The vision of "social welfare" that motivates such acts is not one shared between donor and donee but simply affirmed by the donor. This sentiment is also rooted in a desire to direct others (who should be grateful for such inspired leadership). Understanding social ends is entirely different from these forms of arrogance and selfishness to the degree that it is rooted in "the principle" of democratic morals.

What sense can we make of this argument? Addams and Dewey can help us to re-work our ideas of "being with" the poor. We can see "being with" as a general description of how the creation of character may be linked to working with others towards a shared sense of the social good. However, we don't want to suggest that some general concept of "being with" can be "applied" in order to explain the experiences of poverty lawyers. This would itself be a reification of the dynamics of experience. We can, though, make a limited use of "being with" and further elaborate what we mean by going back to our opening arguments about poverty law as the "in between". These ideas can be brought together to think about poverty law theory as the "broken middle". The broken middle carries forward this sense of a specifically demo*cratic* ethics. We are stressing *cratic* to indicate the root meaning of the suffix *kratos*, which can be taken back to the word *kar* or *ker*. The sense of this small word can in turn be traced to meanings in Old English and other European languages that carry the idea not of strength but of difficulty, exertion or endurance. We want to work with the sense that a democratic ethics of being with the poor must be a difficult self-questioning. "Being with" is to be endured or worked through. In the next section we will develop the argument that poverty law theory is precisely this difficult, ongoing attempt to work at this intersection of law and social struggle.

In the broken middle

How is self-questioning also an engagement with the world of others? There is no "model" for this anxious questioning and it cannot be captured by opposing regnant or rebellious lawyering, a theory of hermeneutics, narrative theory or humanistic practice. Which is not to say that these ways of thinking do not have their uses. They are ways of getting at something that runs through them all. Something we now want to outline.

Towards the end of Chapter 8, we found in Piomelli's work a concern with the work on the self. Ethics is understood as a form of self-fashioning or a way of determining a sensibility, a way of acting in the world. Given that we are not using Foucault as a main reference point, there is no need to labour this point.[8] We can carry forward a sense in which ethics is a style of living. Ethics relate to a set of choices one makes about the person that one is compelled to be. From the perspective of the poverty lawyer, this is inseparable from at least some understanding of the thought and styles of radical traditions. Our argument can be developed by focusing on a concern essential to accounts of the reproduction of lawyering: the point when the radical enters law school. The radical manifests a sense of attraction and repulsion to law and legal training, the complex Goodrich has identified as the "critic's love of the law" (Goodrich, 1999). This complex expresses itself in the anxious realisation of the potential and limits of the law as a vehicle for social change.

Entering law school in search of a professional education, the radical endeavours to build those skills that can be used in social and political struggles. Whilst acknowledging that professional training might involve some degree of compromise with ideals, the law school is anticipated as a place of informed debate. Writers on these themes have attested to the sudden movement from enthusiasm through boredom to despair. Certainly, in the late 1970s, the intellectual, moral and political sterility of the law school was a major theme:

> [o]ur indifference to values confines legal education to the "what is" and neglects the promise of "what might be." It confirms a bias deeply engrained in many law students – that law school is a training ground for technicians who want to function efficiently within the status quo.
>
> (Cramton, 1978, p.262)

Cramton identifies this strange, dizzying moment when one realises that gap between how the law is understood, practised and taught, and what the law might become. One could call this experience the creative alienation of the law school radical, aware that legal training requires the "infantilising" rituals of hierarchy (as if the student needs to be humiliated in order to pass some kind of threshold and

8 It would perhaps be stretching the style of LatCrit thinking to say that it engages with anything analogous to the forms of pastoral power that were so important in Foucault's understanding of ethics. However, some of the ideas and practices of LatCrit thinkers are not entirely unrelated to Foucault's concerns with self-questioning and self-creation. As might be evident from the section above on Addams's social ethics, and indeed the forms of direct democracy practised by the new left (to say nothing of the practices of the Black Panthers touched upon in Chapter 2), our notion of praxis is a long way from Foucault's interests in the self-governance of sexual pleasure.

become a proper lawyer). These are the sentiments of Kelman's spirited denunciations of law school: "fucking oppression" (Kelman, 1984, p.321).

Whilst these trenchant critiques certainly suggest the spirit of those malcontents who objected to the law schools of the 1970s and 1980s, would we be wrong to suggest that, given the profound changes in legal education, poverty lawyers (students and teachers) are still marginalised, unhappy souls? For instance, one can point to creative and innovative poverty law programmes. The fact that poverty law is "ghettoized" in some schools does not mean that a commitment to poverty law is absent from modern legal education (Hornstein, 2009, p.1072). Perhaps there is another way of putting it. Poverty law is important precisely because it is problematic. The subject is, quite correctly, a portal open to dark meditations:

> We want to believe that we are open to the chaos the Indigent lugs with her like mismatched luggage ... Yet, we hold our arm out to stop her from coming too close, from overpowering us with her Need; we retreat into the office, desperately needing to be with others who understand and prize our addiction to orderliness.
>
> (Failinger, 2010, p.122)

Poverty law still confronts the lawyer and the law school with a profound sense of dis-ease.[9] The metaphor of the indigent is particularly striking. This figure of the displaced, the migrant and the traveller (recall Jeanette Washington's poem) is a reminder of all that law would like to hold at arm's length, those messy, chaotic lives on the edges of society. This point relates to our argument about the very nature of poverty law and poverty law theory. For Failinger, as for Cramton, the question is what is "not" taught at law school or the kind of clients that are "absent" from law's versions of the social world (Shalleck, 1993, p.1731). The poverty lawyer realises that law itself operates as the barrier that keeps the poor at a safe distance: "we withdraw from the complications" that acting for the poor occasions (Failinger, 2010, p.130). This is perhaps the perennial dilemma of the poverty lawyer not at home in the law. Divided between two worlds. As Quigley puts it, the poverty lawyer must be prepared to be "uncomfortable" and "unlearn" more or less everything taught in law school (Quigley, 2007, pp.15, 148). The theory of poverty law needs to take this unlearning seriously (Gearey, 2017).

Poverty law cannot quite be accommodated by the law school. Even the most innovative poverty law course cannot quite comprehend the realities of working for the poor. This is not necessarily a bad thing. As we observed above, what gives poverty law its particular quality is the profound realisation that it is on the edges of law as taught. The poverty lawyer must engage in experience. Any understanding of poverty law theory cannot set up an opposition between law in theory and law in practice. It is a question of how one learns from doing. This takes us back to anxiety. Anxiety is the mark of a peculiar subjectivity that finds itself

9 See McDiarmid (1990), Gaber (1998) and Raphael (2000).

struggling for a viable sense of its own being. The self, we might say, is always in between other people, in the midst of the social world even to the extent to which the self is interrupted by others. This is the self that appears in Failinger's writing. However, as we have already suggested, we cannot follow Failinger's argument about alterity in understanding the "in between". We do not want to fetishise others as Other. The other is certainly the limit of the self but in the encounter with others one comes up against a self that is, in certain respects at least, like one's self. The encounter with the other at the limit of the self always makes one anxious precisely if one is concerned with its meaning; the way in which one's settled ways, one's practices might be disturbed (why else should the figure of the stranger be so significant for modern thought?).

The radical sensibility is created in this "in between" where convention is "intersected" by the question of how best to act. In Addams's social ethics this was the token of a proper maladjustment. To take social consciousness seriously is to be challenged, troubled by the "way that things are". There is for all its lived sense of embodiment and solidity, a kind of chimerical quality of the self. It is entirely contingent that one is who one is: "[e]very human being … is thrust into the world by change … the recipient of unearned privilege or undeserved suffering or both" (Ayres, 2001, p.25). Poverty appears as the great cleavage in social being. That the other person is poor and I am not can be understood as the parcelling out of being (to use James's expression). We could all end up poor or fall into poverty. The political/existential radical finds it impossible to go with the "they" and believe that the poor are different and distant. One could easily be amongst them. The withering of self-respect and dignity, the diminishing of one's sense of self, can come about very easily.

Consciousness grapples with what it knows of the world, a world in which it does not feel at home. How can one work to make the world otherwise? With whom can one work? In "being with" these others something is risked. This might be a break with a rigid social script and a sense of how things should be done. What can we call this cast of thought, this struggle against the terms of the given world? To be at the broken middle is to find oneself "in between" or with others having committed to work alongside them. One way of getting at this concern is the concept of solidarity.

Solidarity certainly offers a way of marrying together the response to a specific, unique other with what Blasi has called the "larger stories of collective resistance and community building" (Blasi, 1994, p.1090). It also resonates with Failinger's understanding of how mutual support and reciprocity become politically important (Failinger, 2010, p.2112). We can even perhaps find other authorities for the authenticity of this sense of shared fate. Whilst these senses of solidarity are important and cannot be rejected, no matter how subtly one thinks about this "kernel" of "responsibility" it is not an entirely apt description for "being with" (Unger, 1986, p.82). A too hasty commitment to solidarity raises profound problems, especially if it brings all together under the power of some (the "white ally"). Social ethics addresses this difficulty. Being with others is frustrating.

"Being with" requires endless negotiations and compromises and comes out of the world of pain and hurt that the SDS activists of the ERAP programmes spoke about.

This takes us to the ethical subject wrestling with the difficult question of how to act well. The best recent description of this troubled soul is provided by Wolcher. Wolcher is trying to get at what we were grappling with: how we can understand the conscience of the embodied, thinking, acting individual. We need to be "inside" experience rather than working as a "social critic or moral theorist" might, "from the outside". The outside can be understood as those various modes of description or observation that do not deal with an individual's own understanding of his/her experience. Wolcher is thus engaging with a hidden etymology concealed in the word "theory" which takes us to the notion that theorising might involve knowing how someone "keeps going" or follows a course of action. Any proper account of this mysterious sense of commitment requires us to talk about places difficult to access: soul, sensibility, interiority.

Wolcher's "inside" addresses a kind of thinking that can engage with a particular way of asking the question of the meaning of one's deeds. This does not make any necessary claim to a "doer" behind deeds that plunges us back into a thick ontology of the subject as the self-defining actor. The "ethical question par excellence" is "[w]ho am I"? The anxious question the self asks of itself is that of the subject articulated through their being with others, the subject who "is" how others perceive him/her. The "do-er" is a singularity, a contingent collection of memories and becomings that are the contours of a life lived in the world (Wolcher, 2012). If this is the case, then the broken middle is the sense in which the ethical subject is always in *media res*, in the thick of things, "thrown" into projects that are (in part) defined by understandings of history and tradition. The peculiar singularity of the self and its projects invites and resists articulation in a kind of shuttling between the present, the past and the future. Ethical experience is rooted in the quiddity of the everyday. Its articulation requires one to put into words what can be shared with others who are involved in similar investigations.[10]

10 To understand the in between, we can make reference to Ortega's work. Whilst it is important to respect the precise location of this account of the self, we can borrow a specific theme. The Latina self is located in a borderland that is more than a geographical location; it is an "in between" – an existence between cultures, and even perhaps between languages and histories (Ortega, 2016, p.50). This account sees the self as constantly interrupted, suffering "ruptures" in experience that force a particular kind of reflexivity that is itself to do with cultural dislocation. Ortega speaks of Latina consciousness as "not being at ease". "Not being at ease" describes being in a world characterised by contradiction and ambiguity. "Not being at ease" runs from "contradiction" through to a more acute sense of dread that captures the experiences of those whose daily lives are characterised by "marginalisation" and "oppression", and indeed "alienation" (Ortega, 2016, pp.50, 51). However, this aspect of Ortega's analysis has to be placed in the context of her consideration of the multiplicitous self. There are two important elements to Ortega's appropriation of *Dasein* as a way of thinking about this form of consciousness. Chicana conciousness comes out of being "in between" –

To get at this broken middle of our being with others we need to focus on the fundamental sense that any theory of poverty law must be one that works on the quiddity of the "in between". Poverty law theory is located in a constant learning and shifting of positions. This process takes place against the background of a degraded culture where certain people have been reified and alienated (and one indeed may be alienated from "being a lawyer"). Understanding this alienation, obtaining a creative, critical perspective, is the dialectical play that defines the work on the self and the forging of character. We might then say, again following Louis Wolcher, that the ethics invoked is "a kind of unbearable vigilance" that "bear[s] witness" to the suffering of the poor (Wolcher, 2004, p.147). The broken middle lies at this fracture between law and a broader, more vital sense of a decent life for all.

At this point in our argument, we can return to a line that has passed through William Stringfellow's work and into latter-day champions of social justice like Robert E. Rodes and William Quigley. That these thinkers locate themselves in a Catholic tradition of social justice should not alarm us. For Rodes, the Christian engages with the world in a way that shows regard for the poor. Rodes articulates the very "in between" that we have been analysing. His concept of "pilgrim law" describes the "bridge" between "the society we would like to be and the society we are", or the passage "between our values and their realization" (Rodes, 1995, p.255).[11] There is no dialectic resolving this tension. It is not as if regard for the poor comes into tension with cruel laws, to be resolved in better laws. There is a permanent mismatch between value and realisation, or rather, there is a "mystery" (Rodes, 1995, p.263). This does not let law off the hook or descend into some endless meditation on the subjective nature of values. The "mystery" is another name for the encounter with others. It is the problematic of the "human encounter and [the] common life" that cannot be foreclosed.

existing between cultures, and even perhaps between languages and histories. In between is also *mestizaje* – the self is itself multiple by virtue of its being "between worlds". In this account the self is still experienced as such – as something "felt" – without becoming anything as substantial as Husserl's "primacy of experience" or a "substance" vulnerable to Butler's critique that selves are constructed by experiences, rather than a substratum, a subject which remains the same, coherent to itself (Ortega, 2016, pp.7–8). The present work offers a slightly different location for the self in pragmatism, but arguably there is enough shared between this tradition and the feminist tradition in which Ortega is working for these approaches to complement each other. In terms of the technical analysis of *Dasein*, then, we are concerned with Being that is both "between worlds" and "in worlds" – where being in between and being in discloses to *Dasein* the possibilities of itself (Ortega, 2016, p.68). Ortega's work is important as it makes use of the Heideggerian link between alienation and anxiety, stressing, as this text does, the "negative" and "positive" aspects of this phenomenon of experience. Anxiety may lead to paralysis, but it is also the spur to make choices. There may therefore be the sense in which anxiety or "not being at ease" is a more general experience of a consciousness struggling with the need to take action in solidarity with others.

11 What else is a pilgrim but a traveller and a wanderer?

In the mystery we are subject to imitations and "primordial" longings. To return to an earlier metaphor, examined in the context of Stringfellow's work, we are "called". As we have suggested, the call is heard in "being with" – in human encounter and the common life. The mystery is bound up in the call to a "new state of being" that is "foreign to our experience", "foreign to our thought" and "radically unknowable" (Rodes, 1995, p.263). Precisely because we cannot know, we need to keep experimenting and sustain those encounters with others that open us to ever-new perspectives. This does not lead to an assemblage of the whole, to perfect knowledge of social being. Pilgrim law is a law from elsewhere, foreign to these parts. It is what we learn from the stranger or the refugee, the migrant or the one alongside whom we work. From our "being with" we can perhaps also recuperate a concealed tension within the word theory. The theory with which we are engaged is not that of the spectator, but thought that comes out of social action, the endless difficulty of action with others towards shared ends.

Chapter 10

Kick out the jams

Poverty and critical legal theory

Introduction

This final chapter brings together the various elements of our argument to define a radical sensibility inherited from the new left, the NWRO, radical constitutionalism, CRT and LatCrit: a complex of theory/praxis that informs contemporary critical legal theory.

The first part of the chapter will address radical constitutionalism; a reappraisal of themes linked to welfare rights and filtered through progressive constitutionalism. Welfare rights have returned to haunt the progressive imagination. They "will not die down, but [are not] exactly alive" (Forbath, 2001, p.1825).[1] These spirits beckon us towards another strange encounter: a meeting of radical and progressive constitutionalism that takes us to an engagement with Roberto Unger and a notion of radical sensibility. The second part of the chapter builds on

1 However, the memory of the NWRO has not been to the fore in some approaches to democratic and popular constitutionalism. Post and Siegel (2007) argue that democratic constitutionalism rests on the public perception that constitutional "legitimacy" is "sustained" by "traditions of popular engagement" that enable "citizens" to challenge the government through "constitutional law making, electoral politics, and the institutions of civil society" (Post and Siegel, 2007, p.374). Democratic constitutionalism describes the way in which the "meaning" of the constitution negotiates "popular belief" and law's "integrity" (Post and Siegel, 2007, p.376). Post and Siegel focus on popular mobilisation around *Roe v Wade* 410 U.S. 113 (1973), but they do not consider the NWRO. Kramer's notion of popular constitutionalism also leaves out the NWRO, though the welfare rights movement was an exemplification of the idea that "authoritative legal interpretation" is not just a matter for the court but also the proper province of the "community at large" (Kramer, 2006, p.700). Forbath's notion of progressive constitutionalism goes some way to set the record straight. Progressive constitutionalism is an exercise in the recovery of a narrative about the constitution that can counter the right's domination of the cultural debate. Forbath invokes "an opposite tradition: the rich, reform-minded *distributive* tradition" that taps into popular concern with "poverty and want" (Forbath, 2011, p.1117). In a ringing formulation of the basic insight of the reform tradition Forbath states that "gross economic inequality produces gross political inequality", which demeans the very idea of a "constitutional republic" (Forbath, 2011, p.1118). Forbath locates the welfare rights movement in this context (Forbath, 2011, p.2011).

these arguments and moves towards a study of CLS as a style of thought and a disposition of character. The failure of the movement has bequeathed us critical legal theory. Critical legal theory is an engagement with the problems of the midnight fiction and honourable speech that we elaborated in Chapter 3, an issue that returns us to the fraught question of the relationship between white radicals and "black" thought.

From this perspective it might be possible to hazard a certain thesis about the relationship of poverty to being with – or, to put this in slightly different terms, the ontological effects of poverty on social recognition within market societies. Our concluding comments address an idea of critical legal theory that comes out of the encounter with poverty and activism. As McCluskey has sagely pointed out, it is necessary to be "bold" in bringing together the various fragments of critical legal analysis (McCluskey, 2007, p.1196). Indeed, West and Smiley (2011) have called for a democratic revolution against poverty. It may even be that in seizing the problem of poverty, critical legal theory becomes part of this new movement. As a democratic character, the radical lawyer takes Stringfellow's injunction seriously: to be with others one needs "to substitute voyeurism and academic colonialism for fully human relationships" (Stringfellow, 1962, p.42). How can we think through such matters? If critical legal studies can sustain its energies, then perhaps its anima is a wild mercury amalgam of doubt, pessimism and joy.

Radical constitutionalism

We broke off our analysis of progressive constitutionalism in Chapter 4. We now want to engage with the return of something like a welfare rights position in radical constitutional scholarship. In Chapter 3, we argued that the cultural hold of the ascendant right compelled progressive scholars to change their position and to move away from the notion of a survival income. As the idea of welfare rights was too limited, the concept of equal citizenship came to the fore. However, problems with the equal citizenship argument soon also became clear. Forbath's work addresses these issues. He argues that it is now necessary to adopt a broad understanding of traditions of social citizenship and economic democracy that can be traced back to the New Deal. Progressives have made the strategic mistake of decoupling welfare arguments from those about decent work and wages, a separation unacceptable to the social citizenship tradition which aims at "assuring decent work opportunities and decent livelihoods for all" (Forbath, 2001, pp.1871–1872). The "material base of citizenship" is not provided by "public assistance" but by "some socially recognized contribution on a person's part to the common enterprise" (Forbath, 2001, p.1886).[2] Forbath thus moves towards the

2 Despite its modest desire to reframe equality arguments around minimum protection and just needs, Michelman's reading of Rawls falls into error (Forbath, 2001, p.1870). Michelman loads more onto the notion of welfare rights than the concept can bear (Forbath, 2001, p.1873). A better approach might have been to extrapolate from *A*

conception of a democratic relationship between work and politics. The guiding theme is the question of what a "constitutionally fair opportunity to act as citizen participants" requires. This translates into arguments for basic income, the control of the workplace, and access to education and training. Forbath also shows how poorly paid, precarious jobs make it impossible for people to work their way out of poverty.

The work of Stephen Loffredo also provides a particularly interesting site where lines from the past meet future possibilities. Loffredo argues that any appeal to the inclusion of poor citizens to public debates on welfare is bound to fail as political processes have become so skewed by wealth and corporate lobbies that the case for welfare rights will not be given a proper hearing. Any appeal to the legislature as the correct forum for the articulation of a consensus is unlikely to succeed. Social or doctrinal developments that allow the case for the poor to be made must rest on addressing the distortions of political culture.[3] Given the limitations of

Theory of Justice "constitutional baselines respecting work and participation in the economic order" (Forbath, 2001, p.1875). Central Rawlsian notions such as "self-respect and mutual respect" are grounded in ideas of "commitment and consent" to a "social enterprise" characterised by just economic arrangements. These extend well beyond welfare to "meaningful work in free associations with others" (Forbath, 2001, p.1875). Social citizenship arguments are thus much more expansive than those presented by Rawls.

3 Reviewing the relevant jurisprudence, Loffredo concludes that "the political marginalization of poor people ought to be recognized as a fundamentally undemocratic phenomenon that demands judicial attention" (Loffredo, 1993, p.1379). At the centre of the argument is *Austin v Michigan Chamber of Commerce* 494 U.S. 652 (1990), a case in which "economic capture" of the "political process" was formally acknowledged. The Rehnquist court recognised that "inequalities of private economic power" distort politics and "displace legitimate democratic governance" to the extent that they must be regulated even if this intrudes upon the First Amendment (Loffredo, 1993, p.1285). From *Austin*, we can conclude that "wealth-based distribution of political power is ... democratically illegitimate" (Loffredo, 1993, p.1286). This analysis relies on a process understanding of the constitution and does not present itself as a substantive critique of constitutional values. In short, it is a theory of "democratic legitimacy" based on the principle that "democracy entails some irreducible quantum of political equality" (Loffredo, 1993, p.1303). The Burger court turned against these principles. For instance, in *Dandridge v Williams* 397 U.S. 471 (1970), the court did not invalidate a provision that reduced eligibility for AFDC benefits for large families. Refusing to consider the poor a marginalised minority, the court argued that as race was not involved, the constitution was not engaged. A similar result followed in *James v Valtierra* 402 U.S. 137 (1971). The case involved state law that required local referenda before the building of low-income housing could take place, a restriction not placed on any other housing scheme and thus discriminatory against poor and low-waged people. The court refused to invalidate the provision. These cases "accep[t], if not welcom[e], the political isolation of the poor" (Loffredo, 1993, p.1367). How, though, does *Austin* fit in? For the argument to work, it must provide a return to the "quantum of political equality" principle. *Austin* links back to the cases that saw restriction on formal voting rights and extends the principle to "functional political effectiveness". Taking these points together, it can be suggested that "the political

constitutional doctrine that we have studied, it seems reasonable to follow Loffredo in concluding that the only hope is the creation of a properly "democratic politics" that would "fully enfranchis[e] all citizens regardless of economic station".[4] Certainly the currents of community organising that surfaced in the mid-1990s suggested a renewal of energies (Loffredo, 2001, pp.1278–1279).[5] However, a transfer of energy from the streets to the academy does not appear to have taken place as "liberal constitutional theorists [have] largely abandoned the poor" (Loffredo, 2007, p.1243). In conversation with Frances Fox Piven, Loffredo's mood was dark. He suggested that the "disconnect" between the lower class and "the broader community" was "constitutionally troubling" (Loffredo and Piven, 2007, p.16).[6] Above all it was necessary to re-open arguments about a consistent access to justice strategy in the wake of the "worst recession since the Great Depression" (Engler, 2010, p.473).

So, if welfare rights or social citizenship arguments are to become generally acceptable, it is necessary to intervene in political culture. To pick up on an insight of Sylvia Law's, it is as if the constitution has "alienated people from their own experience" (Law, 1984a, p.955). The analysis of class that we touched upon in earlier chapters has now become a broader discussion of political agency and alliance. Certainly those working with Forbath's and Fishkin's ideas have put forward an analysis of the "material structure of power" – and, in particular, "the political-economic conditions of constitutional discourse". It is worth noting that a study of the "political-economic conditions" also requires a study of "anti-constitutional and anti-capitalist social movements" (Kessler, 2016, p.1537). Although Kessler

marginalization of poor people ought to be recognized as a fundamentally undemocratic phenomenon that demands judicial attention" (Loffredo, 1993, p.1379). Loffredo goes on to suggest that *Austin* requires the state to "mitigat[e] … the effects of concentrated wealth in the political sphere". The case "pierces" the myth that the poor are well represented in the political system, and that therefore the court should be deferential to political decisions made about their interests (Loffredo, 1993, p.1388).

4 Given the role that the influence of wealth plays in politics, the court has erred in proceeding on the basis that the poor are not a "suspect category" that requires "extraordinary protection from the majoritarian political process". The key case is *San Antonio Independent School District v Rodriguez* 411 U.S. 1, 28 (1973). The relevant test asks "whether a group" is "relegated to such a position of political powerlessness as to command extraordinary protection from the majoritarian political process".

5 There is indeed a marked sense in which Loffredo's work has been picked up in the wake of the Occupy movement. The Occupy movement is used as a focus for the critique of the role of the Supreme Court in "helping to protect a very powerful minority at the expense of the majority" (Gilman, 2014, p.393). Re-working the inherent confusions in the test for suspect categories of persons, Stephanopoulos proposes a more rigorous approach that would not only clarify the terms in which the test applied to existing categories of people, but would bring poor people within the protection offered by the doctrine (Stephanopoulos, 2015, p.1557). After all, "if any group is powerless, it is the poor" (Stephanopoulos, 2015, p.1579).

6 One response to this situation was to pursue innovative strategies at a state level and encourage state courts to take up arguments based on positive and socio-economic rights (Loffredo and Hershkoff, 2011, p.925).

does not concern himself with the NWRO, could an account of the anti-oligarchic constitution be one of the portals through which something returns? There are certainly other scholars of constitution history who are willing to conclude that "a gendered and racially unequal pro-capitalist socio-economy has profoundly shaped the 'neutral' laws surrounding welfare policy" (Baldwin, 2008, p.4). In furthering this approach, recent work has also begun to develop tenBroek's thesis on the "dual rules of constitutional law" and the failure to protect the interests of the poor (Nice, 2008, p.631). It is important that class *and* race *and* gender *and* sexual orientation are understood as an irresolvable complex that defines identity. This is indeed how we explained the politics of the NWRO: a form of resistance to the reification and alienation of poverty. Is there a way of bringing together the various strands of argument?

Roberto Unger offers a way forward. Why? Unger is a figure who mediates between progressive constitutional thought and radical and critical traditions.[7] Unger's concern with character and personality allows us to link arguments about economic democracy with an idea of a radical sensibility (Unger, 2007, p.23). Unger's notion of personality explains why lawyers went into the ghettos and why they still commit to critical thought and practice. To develop these points, we will take one step back to go two steps forward. Unger's philosophy has at its core a form of "radicalisation of experimentalism". Remaining authentic to this theme means that Unger's own approach must constantly re-think itself to get at the idea of the social actor. The social actor is frustrated by the compromises of daily life but able to transcend his/her social constitution (Unger, 2007, p.7). Unger has noted that this idea owes a debt to Dewey's "doctrine of experience" (Unger, 2007, p.31). However, Unger is also careful to state that he is not out to "rescue or reinvent" pragmatism (Unger, 2007). Unger is indeed right to reject a form of "imperial pragmatism". His position is largely in keeping with the current of pragmatism that flows into Jane Addams's work and communicates with our arguments drawn from Buber and Stringfellow.

For Unger our imagination must begin with "what is" but creative thought is not limited by its context. Unger refers to this vision of the active agent as a conjunction of "thought and practice" (Unger, 2007). The key point of contact between our arguments and those of Unger is that praxis "unfreezes" dead routines and ways of being. There are, however, still unanswered questions. Precisely how does praxis unfreeze frozen versions of the world? If nothing else, Unger's grasp of praxis shows the complicated and fraught nature of social recognition. We need to explore this important idea in a little more depth.

We might say that Unger is concerned with the constitution of the self. The social self is dependent on others, by turns inspired and trapped by this very

7 For a further elaboration of this argument, see Cornel West (1987, p.945). West is certainly correct to place Unger between Dewey and Gramsci. The position presented in the present text, however, does not necessarily subscribe to West's notion of "left romanticism", nor to his overall location of CLS.

dependency. This "fundamental contradiction" provides a revisionary way of approaching more over-enthusiastic notions of creative democracy where individuals come together in some ecstasy of democratic self-making. Rather like D.H. Lawrence's criticisms of Walt Whitman, Unger reminds us that being with others is difficult. A democratic sensibility cannot just be announced and affirmed. Unger has called this a "free floating anguish" that is inseparable from our "existential groundlessness" (Unger, 2014, pp.21, 12). Looked at in a positive light, this groundlessness is the endless desire to create and re-create ourselves, to "denaturalise" the norms and structures which pass themselves off as givens (Unger, 2007, p.7). In a darker light, it is the way in which we become prisoners of routines and social orders that we lack the imagination and will to challenge. There is no guarantee that opportunities will be propitious for challenging social and institutional norms. In fact, quite the opposite. Unger has a keen understanding of how human beings can be crushed by their circumstances. The "experience of poverty and drudgery, of oppression and belittlement" is "pervasive" (Unger, 2014, p.248). Poverty "undermines equality of respect and opportunity [and] also destroys the practical conditions of self-reliance and self-construction" (Unger, 2014, p.329).

Unger's argument locates the energies of inspired agency in the very places and spaces that we have been thinking about throughout this book. We are working at the level of social experience and the constitution of selves. We must address the "sentiments" through which people define and create themselves in ways that resist dominant norms (Unger, 1976, p.139). This opens onto a different way of conceiving CLS. CLS is not a monolithic, nihilistic bloc. CLS was a movement of ideas involved in the creation and sustenance of what we might call a structure of feeling, a way of relating to others in a spirit of equality. In following this theme through, we can appreciate how Unger's "Promethean" fury of experiment and intervention may perhaps strike some discordant notes. Rather than Unger as a version of Whitman pressing forward with his righteous energy, perhaps we need to calm down a little and not take things "so serious and all".

Kicks joy darkness

Our revisionist approach to CLS corresponds with the way in which those involved in the movement have begun to address recent history. Peter Gabel has written that those who marched and demonstrated together in the 1960s realised that "human relations could be like a vision of a world in which people treated each other with true equality and respect and affection and kindness, and in which people saw each other as fully human and beautiful" (Gabel, 2009, p.515). Gabel notes that although this vision was shared by CLS scholars it became obscured by the failure to assert a moral vision. This left "us in a kind of secular liberal hell of scattered and disconnected individuals with no common passion or direction" (Gabel, 2009, p.515). From this perspective, the renewal of CLS, the refocusing of the vital energies of the 1960s, could come about only through rediscovering the moral or spiritual impulses of the movement (Gabel, 2009, p.515).

This is quite a statement. We would prefer to find a renewal of CLS in a peculiar humour. Whilst this is not quite Goodrich's "satirical legal studies", it does evoke a question of style – and a way of standing back and mocking one's own pretentions (Goodrich, 2004). The desire not to take things too seriously is a strategy that avoids the terrible earnestness that was distinctive of the new left at its worst. It is necessary to open the space or the distance where a tradition can be re-examined. Bob Dylan's career provides a useful analogy for this attitude towards the past. In the face of aggressive student earnestness, he abandoned "protest" and began to develop a more oblique way of communicating. This obliqueness was not so much a disconnection or a refutation of his former self, but a re-presentation: an attempt, perhaps, to become "young" again. It requires wit, self-mockery and the desire to speak differently, to start again in a different way. To hold oneself open to new ideas and to what might happen.

We can find this exemplified in Farley's performance of the spirit of CLS, a spirit that delights in double-ness. Taking a prompting from "How the Law School Fails", Farley identifies the playfulness of the CLS practitioner, the "class turncoat" who wants to turn first-year courses into "utopian proposals" and ways of de-mystifying the law. We need not become so hung up by "questions that kill" as we can dodge the bullet – and, hidden in plain sight, an outsider within the system – find those resources that allow us to "refashion ourselves" (Farley, 2001, p.1016). To see Kennedy as a "religious writer" – perhaps even a religious writer in the vein of William Stringfellow,[8] is to take playful refashioning as a technique for the "critical ontology of the self". Foucault might be invoked, but this is not "theory" or "doctrine". It is an "attitude to life" (Farley, 2001, p.1016). Farley plots out a way of living philosophy. Our own constitution is a symptom of the norms and forces that define us and leave a certain slippage or play where experiment can take place. It is worth remembering that the origins of CLS lie in the failure of the new left. Thus to celebrate experiment, or what we might even call creative democracy, is already to have inherited a particular attitude. At the same time, in carrying forward a certain spirit of the new left, we also carry forward the colour line.

Farley is re-staging Baldwin's concern with the midnight fiction in setting up a reading between CLS and CRT that plots points of continuity and fracture. In the midnight fiction, we perform our differences as strangers to each other, alienated from one another by structures of racism that determine the roles that we will play in social life. The dialectic that might provoke the refashioning of the self is permanently deferred. Such a deferral is fatal to any progressive spirit as it creates a limit compromising any claim to radical sensibility. Was this not the demon with which the new left wrestled? The reality that George Jackson addressed when chiding white radicals for not being revolutionary enough – for failing to liberate themselves from pig Amerika? We have seen how Stringfellow understood the

8 Kennedy has confessed to his own "eccentric religious conviction" (Kennedy, 1997, p.34).

strength of the hatred for the white man in the ghettos of the city. This problem casts a long shadow. In performing the spirit of CLS it is necessary to accept the intense engagement with the colour line and, in particular, the way in which it defines an inner space that may be hard to discover and re-work. In the words of Ellison's *Invisible Man*, confronting the colour line is a necessity in order to go on living. If this process goes on through its own "conflicting phase[s]" it is because it is the dialectic of recognition, tracked down to the very constitution of the self. The dialectic begins with a "[c]onversion to the other" (Farley, 2001, p.1020).

So, the midnight fiction is completely bound up with the very possibility of CLS (Farley, 2001, p.1038). Within the terms of our argument, the internalisation of the other in the self is one way of thinking about alienation. To the extent that one is defined through a fixed colour line, where one's whiteness is defined against the blackness of the other, one is in a situation of both alienation and reification. The play of recognition has shuddered to a halt. The black other – to the degree that s/he accepts this objectification – remains an object, a "spectacle of himself", lacking substantial, self-determined being. The whole play of objectification/subjectification is then covered up or "denied" through a "discourse" which positions whiteness and blackness as "natural categories" rather than mutually defining symbols – ideological counters that are "acted out", made real through social practices (Farley, 1997, p.464). Racism constantly repeats this moment of subordination and dominance (Farley, 1997, p.475). The unfreezing of identity is not achieved by calling for a celebration of essential humanity, but, through the recognition of the difficulty of being with. "Being with" is the ongoing attempt to deal with an historical legacy from the perspective of a future that is not necessarily limited by the past.

This is a difficult one to work out. As Ginsberg notes, "kiss ass is part of the peace" (Ginsberg, 1985, p.496); or, in the terms of *A Critique of Adjudication*, ideas of coherence shelter us from "a kind of terror" that comes from confronting doubts that rest so deeply within you that they are inseparable from your ownmost sense of self (Kennedy, 1997, p.1021). Coherence defines a boundary that plays down double-ness and prevents intersection. The spirit of CLS grapples with the double of the double, the troubled white consciousness, aware that its own transformation means confronting the black other within the self. This is why *A Critique of Adjudication* thinks in terms of bad faith. Bad faith is a version of the fundamental contradiction. At any point our subjectivity is "fixed" and "defined" and "in motion past its apparent fixity, free" (Kennedy, 1997, p.205). The work on the self engages with the internalisation of the norms that have gone in so deep and rested within the self for so long that they appear to constitute one's identity. To be "in motion" is to be in the process of working through, no longer willing to accept that things are the way that they are. Perhaps we should not be so serious, though. We are in pursuit of a spirit of "play" that comes, if it comes at all, in moments of intensity: "[l]oss, nostalgia, yearning, depression, despair"; or, when bored and frustrated, one becomes "buzzed out" by "desired confrontations" (a strange paradox) with others. It remains, after all, "something to do with others of like mind" or with the opening of the mind to like-minded others (Kennedy, 1997, p.346).

Experiments in living

Buzzed out, zapped: modes of "being with" maybe, but certain questions remain. How does this peculiar exercise relate to the thesis of this book? Our closing argument will be that the recuperation of a certain legacy allows us to further expand CLS. We are in pursuit of a moment when CLS becomes critical legal theory rooted in doing and a kind of generous character or sensibility that can – without being crippled by the spirit of gravity – further an affirmatory, democratic, egalitarian living of the world. The theorist is no longer a spectator, but one whose point of view comes out of doing and being with others: an activist.

Thus, critical legal theory, as an expanded CLS, is dedicated to the "recovery of alienated powers" (Kennedy, 1997, p.358). This does not mean that you recover something somehow behind experience, a kind of substratum that was always immanent but concealed. The recovery of powers is a doing – a summoning of creative possibility – where what is thought and talked about with others becomes a spur to action. We might want to call this a "zap", but it would be wrong to call the recovery of powers any one thing. Moreover, nothing suggests that anything will happen to inspire something new, or that the energies that appear are sustainable. Critical legal theory is perhaps "founded" in this equally powerful and fragile sense of vertiginous opening (with a simultaneous risk of collapse). Perhaps it is the moment when the darkness of the midnight fiction begins to lose its hold, but this already sounds too much like a Nietzschean metaphor of dawn light. Too damn heroic. It would be better not to name it. Perhaps it has preconditions or maxims, of which the most important might be "find a friend/collaborator" (Kennedy, 1997, p.376). At the same time, the anima of critical legal theory cannot be fetishised as a formless, inexpressible ecstasy. This too would limit it. Its passion must take (and escape) form. Indeed, the study of radical constitutionalism in the first part of this chapter can be seen as a particular form taken by the critical spirit. In the final section of this chapter, we will return to a way of articulating "the recovery of powers", but there are a couple of preliminary issues of necessary clarification.

We can now reappraise the discussion of poverty and alienation as the degradation of the social world. Critical theory addresses this erasure of human beings. To put this in a slightly different way: the poverty line and the colour line define the great division of the social substance that goes on to determine reified social relations. Thus, as practitioners of the art of thinking/doing, the poverty lawyers that we have studied share the commitment to the idea that all people are creative agents. Law should protect and nurture the creativity of human beings. A commitment to carrying these beliefs into action is what makes the poverty lawyer the exemplar of a particular kind of character. The poverty lawyer lives the frustrations of a personal politics enabled and limited by the professional form of life s/he has chosen. We touched on this point in Chapter 7 in our discussion of the poverty lawyer as existentialist hero. The radical lawyer repeats or affirms the desire to be a radical lawyer. But perhaps this is a little too high sounding. Bad repetition. We might equally say, character is what one does. Poverty law is an exercise in the self-making of the lawyer. Of course this is demanding, but it is neither selfish nor solipsistic. It requires both personal resilience and the opportunities to work on one's self. Thus, to the extent that we have presented poverty as the collapse of meaning or the loss of character, poverty is an index to the existence of profound inequalities that limit access to the resources of self-making. That certain people in poverty are able to re-invent themselves and define their creative agency testifies to the courage and strength of NWRO activists like Beulah Sanders and Johnnie Tillmon. The self-maker is not the lonely philosopher or the poet in the garret. It is the political activist working with others.

From this perspective, we can also appreciate the importance of the problems around the elitism of Critical Legal Studies and critical legal theory. CLS and "theory" are undoubtedly the concerns of a peculiar sub-class of educated professionals. The work of the poverty lawyers might sit uncomfortably in this *milieu*, given their concern with action and working with the poor rather than taking refuge in the relative comfort of academia. Poverty activists – facing the "pain and hurt" of organising – have no time for meditations on negative dialectics or deconstruction. However, we might want to resist such conclusions, studying, as we have been, street philosophers like Huey P. Newton who refused to be limited to a social role assigned to him by a racist culture. The work of Ed Sparer also suggests that one can organise, and read Marx, Hegel and Buber.

These figures might be few and far between, but this should not obscure what is at stake. It is necessary to examine the etymology of the word *elite*. To return to Gramsci. As *The Prison Notebooks* stress, a philosophy of praxis, or the creation of a "[c]ritical self-consciousness", is bound up with the very issue of "an elite who think and act differently from the mass" (Gramsci, 2005, p.334). The root meaning of the term goes back to the Latin *eligere* – to pick out or choose. The work of picking or choosing is the decision to work on one's self. The work on one's self is a rejection of the crippling and limiting assumption that your social role or character is somehow fixed. To consider one's self *elite* is to reject alienation and reification and to recover one's own creative power. Thus, *elite* simply describes those who work in consort because they have chosen their allies. Denouncing ideas is the response of someone lost in their own alienation.

At this point our analysis connects back with the agenda developed by radical constitutional scholarship around equal citizenship as a response to poverty. Poverty is the failure of democracy: the creation of social divisions that are fatal to the democratic character. Thus, poverty and the colour line are the freezing out of the possibilities of authentic "being with": the reification of the social substance. Divisions into classes, or rigid notions of race or gender hierarchy, "educate some into [being] master[s] [and others] into [being] slaves" (Dewey, 1958, p.98). Whether or not Dewey is referring to Hegel is a moot point, but his analysis is very close to Farley's warning about the midnight fiction. It is as if social interaction, the building up of complex social relationships, requires resistance to simplistic divisions. If we lack the strength to contest "common sense" we are condemned to the sterility of a culture that is no more than the repetition of old patterns of thought and stultifying routines.

So, we are in pursuit of a matter of style or a disposition, a way of living well with others. This is perhaps not Gabel's seeker after love but someone who knows how to rub along well with others. The democratic character knows that his or her own sense of meaning is found through a commitment to an end which is a realisation of a shared, common good. At the same time, the democratic character resists dogma. No grandstanding. Conversations rather than monologues. We can appreciate Dewey's observation that the "irony" and "tragedy" of much progressive thought is that it asserts a "common good" through "methods" that are neither "common [n]or good" (Dewey, 1958, p.305).

Can we find this kind of democratic character in critical theory? Arguably, it is exemplified in the creative, imaginative experiment that Collins recommends: ask yourself how it would feel to be someone else. We would need to have something of the self-distancing emotional intelligence that Dewey recommends, or indeed, that we studied in Rich's work in Chapter 3. And this is exactly what can be found in intersectionality. Intersectionality goes after the grain of experience, defining a notion of reflexivity embedded in encounters with others in the world. This is, after all, the democratic political self: "[i]ntersectionality … and multiple consciousness entail analyses that grasp simultaneously the commonalities and peculiarities of any group or person … to better understand the multiple complexities of a particular context" (Valdes, 2005, p.158). From the complex self to the location of the self in a complex reality.[9] Once the boundaries of the key category are disturbed, the issue of its limit must come about. If not the white wo/man of property, then who?

The answer is, in a sense, all of us. Consider the following:

> Imagine how different your life might be if you had been born Black, or White, or poor, or of a different race/class/gender group than the one with which you are most familiar. The institutional treatment you would have received and the symbolic meanings attached to your very existence might differ dramatically from what you now consider to be natural, normal and part

9 We can develop this argument by taking into account some of the themes of Latina phenomenological analysis where the self is *mestizaje* or multiplicitous (Ortega, 2016, p.50). The multiplicitous self responds to others who "are not irrevocably different" by "highlighting similarities, downplaying divergences" (Anzaldúa, 2009, pp.114–115). Perhaps the shuttling between self and other does give us a sense of the self as a "blending" or "intermeshing" of experiences lived as a complexity (Ortega, 2016, p.72). Whilst this accords with Ortega's analysis of how a mestiza consciousness can move between different worlds, we want to suggest a slightly different interpretation. Perhaps there is something else here as well: a kind of given-ness to experience.

> of everyday life. You might be the same, but your personal biography might have been quite different.
>
> (Collins, 1993, p.35)

This is self-examination based on imaginative engagement, a sensibility. As we know from Stringfellow, although you cannot live in someone else's place you can imagine how the world might seem from another's perspective. This can sound a little too abstract. Really engaging with Collins's invitation would require difficult, ongoing and sophisticated thinking. One would have to shuttle between what is closest to the self and what is impossibly distant – the lives of others. What insights do I have into other lives?[10]

We are in a very similar scene to that cast by Kennedy and Farley in the paragraphs above. Perhaps the crucial question is how being buzzed out relates to sympathising with others. To put this a slightly different way, we are engaged with an ethical problem: how to make anxiety creative. In whatever way you work through these demanding questions, you would probably have to assume something like the plasticity of character or self. In this context, the plasticity of the self points towards an emotional and intellectual engagement with what one is and what one could become. Plasticity suggests that you could change the way you think and feel in the light of a new experience or understanding of the world. In other words, this is how you awake from the bad dreams of the midnight fiction. This is also perhaps the feeling of being up against something, at a boundary or on a threshold where the hold of what was taken to be the world begins to weaken, with all the anxious disorientation that this occasions. There is no saying that one does not flee back into old patterns of thought and being, desperately affirming them against the risk of collapse.

Not easy. After all, this is work on the self. We have taken diverse philosophical and literary prompts to outline how the work on the self might be imagined and

10 Openness to experience arguably requires a certain security of self. One might even say a white-ness. What follows is meant as no more than notes on how this problem might be worked out. It is perhaps a fantasia on a theme by Sara Ahmed (2007). The key concern for this book is how "white thinking" can pretend to a radicalism. In most immediate terms, the whiteness of what presents itself as radical thought is inseparable from the whiteness of this paper, which is in turn bound up with white privilege and the commodified form of thinking that is this book. But is this all? The whiteness of this page enables the intercourse between writer and reader: the alienated space of our intersection. If meanings spill out of whatever conveys them, we are not restricted to concepts of commodified knowledge or white privilege. The spaces between us and our non-correspondence enable meanings which are neither anticipated nor desired. Whiteness, as space, is also a space cleared of the self: the self and its words erased and out of view. In this sense, the "ness" of whiteness, its quiddity or quality, erases itself, is no longer itself. Disappearance as the possibility of something else. We are left in a peculiar space of ends and beginnings. One critical response to this line of thinking would be that it is precisely in its erasure of itself that whiteness maintains its power. Maybe.

carried out. In this sense, the midnight fiction is a transferable term, but can only be "used" in other contexts to the extent that one can identify and evoke those specific energies that open up possibilities. Terms like "social recognition" and "being with" are also approximations that urge thought and action to confront the limits and possibilities of social being. We can indeed read Collins's invitation as an imaginative reconstruction of being with. Gines provides the thread that links the resources of continental philosophy to intersectionality as "being with others" (Gines, 2011, p.274). "Being with" experienced in the everyday world is not simply a "levelling down" – a kind of emptying out of meaning in the repeated routines of daily life – but the texture of social experience where one might be surprised, opened to the unexpected or unforeseen. Bringing Gines's and Collins's insights together, we can suggest that the "not" of the self, one's contingent embodiment (I am me not you//you are you not me), provides the very possibility of creative engagements with the experiences of others (even if, as suggested above, one is not strong enough to enter a new world). With intersectional thinking we are in the dialectic of recognition as a mode of being with.

Coming around again

How does this take us to the problem of poverty?

Moynihan's question "why does poverty bother us?" is crucial: it is a primordial question that goes to our being in the world (Moynihan, 1969, p.20). What tentative conclusions might we draw about the "in between" – the social visibility and accessibility of all citizens to each other?

This last section of the chapter does not explicitly return to the opening themes. We are exploring ideas that might provide a "ground" for the kind of arguments that radical constitutionalists are making. Perhaps it would be most accurate to say that we are in pursuit of a way of feeling or theorising. To use Unger's language, we are back with the moulding of the self, and the social anxiety occasioned by the fear of becoming poor, a social death that is ever present and ever possible.

In asking how *we* respond to the poverty of others, we are not focused on how the poor feel about being poor. It may even be that those who are "objectively poor" do not see themselves as such. This is part of the problem, but it is not at the core of our analysis. The fundamental concern is with the meaning of poverty for *us* – where *us* is an expression of being with: a bringing to mind of our constitution through our relationships to others. This bringing to mind could be related to matters studied more properly through statistics and data, but in the present analysis, "poor" and "poverty" are not really matters of social scientific definition. The complex we want to define is limited to an understanding of consciousness appalled by the fate of fellow human beings. One orientating point is the imaginative exercise of standing in another person's place. We could also refer back to the need to confront the magma of terror and dread that lies behind the desire for coherence. Engaging with the poor in this sense should not be confused with the attempt to identify an "essence" of poverty that unites cultures of poverty in "London, Glasgow, Paris, Harlem and Mexico City" (Lewis, 1969, p.25). It is an articulation of anxiety and being with.

But how are we with the poor? There is an "institutional divide" between the poor and the rest of us (West and Smiley, 2011, p.9). Harrington's notion of the invisibility or forgetting of the poor, connects with West and Smiley's "rendering invisible" of the poor and Rainwater's "neutralizing [of] the disinherited" through various tactics of distancing or "othering" (Rainwater, 1967, p.2).[11] The "trait" of poverty, or that which marks someone as poor (culturally specific and knowable) is a form of disappearance – of "not-ness" (not having money; not having opportunity). Distancing the poor thus relates to a certain anxiety about becoming less: of sliding out of view. Poverty lays down a boundary or a shifting frontier: a reminder, for some at least, of the transience of their good fortune. The abyss is never far away. This response to poverty, active in writers like London and Orwell, has largely fallen out of the social scientific literature.[12] It opens onto what we might describe as the existential meaning of becoming poor, of being down and out or nickel and dimed.

The anxiety of becoming poor indicates a particular way in which capitalism is lived. If the "not-ness" of poverty is endemic to capitalism, then the social world defined by capitalism is a world characterised by the proximity of life to being cancelled out. This is why poverty is neutralised, and in such a way one's own possible misfortune kept out of mind. Beneath the surface of consumerism, of material success, or just about managing, is a frightening gulf into which you could fall. Whilst the "fear" of poverty might not be as intense amongst the middle classes as it was in the past, the possibility of becoming poor is open to all. Indeed, it may be one way in which a social "fate" is shared (allowing, of course, the statistical evidence on the greater incidence of poverty amongst women and people of colour). This point can be overdone. Given the numbers of economic migrants and immigrants amongst those classed as poor, the entwining of the poverty line and colour line, it is unlikely that those of higher social and economic status will become poor. However, the gig economy, and the fear of being two pay cheques from disaster, indicates the dynamic of a pervasive social anxiety.

How does this anxiety relate to the concern with social recognition that has run throughout the book? In answering this question, we come back to alienation and double consciousness. Consider the following meditation: "we depend for our self image on the humans immediately around us – to the point of altering our perceptions of the world to fit in with theirs" (Ehrenreich, 2001, p.9). Once the poor demonstrate their own political agency, once they object to their construction as

11 Related to this problem is the idea that the social function of poverty "helps to guarantee the status of the non-poor" (Gans, 1972, p.78). Poverty has a "symbolic" element in the construction of social meaning. We have come across this idea in Chapter 6. For Stringfellow, the poor suffer so that we don't have to. People economically demeaned become a symbol of social suffering that is lived by others as the province of the unfortunate: an inert mass of those who have internalised their own worthlessness.

12 See Gearey (2017).

"the poor", their collective self-assertion re-creates something that was erased or slid out of view. Once we think of the poor as agents it is much harder to exile them from citizenship to a ghetto of slum housing, or to see poverty as a screen on which your own fears of becoming poor play themselves out.

The poor do not need our help. If poverty represents the fundamental social disjuncture that defines being in the world of global markets, and if we are not to neutralise the disinherited, we need to decrease the distances that exist amongst us. At this point we can return to the figure of the radical lawyer who knows that it is necessary to work alongside the poor in the same way that we work alongside any other.

The poor are not the poor. Poverty is itself a reifying category, bound up with the tortuous processes of consciousness working through its own alienation.

Leave the last word to Sparer. Talking to an audience of lawyers, Sparer tells how William Stringfellow "simply set up shop in the worst slum of the greatest city in the world and worked and represented and advocated". Direct address. Listen to me. Poverty law is "good work". But this is not simply a call to action. A reference to Dag Hammarskjöld acts as a kind of charm to ward away a sanctimonious sentimentality and a spirit of gravity. The fate of "our revolution" will be judged by the "kind of people" we will have become (Sparer, 1965, p.61).

If not now, when?

Bibliography

Addams, J 1893, "The Subjective Necessity for Social Settlements", in *Philanthropy and Social Progress*, Ed. H Adams, Thomas Y. Cromwell, New York.

Abel, R 1985, "Law without Politics: Legal Aid under Advanced Capitalism", *UCLA Law Review*, vol. 32, no. 3, pp. 474–642.

Addams, J 1892, "A new impulse to an old gospel", *Forum*, vol. 14, pp. 342–356.

Addams, J 1902, *Democracy and Social Ethics*, Macmillan, London and New York.

Addams, J 1910, *Twenty Years at Hull House*, Macmillan, London and New York.

Addams, J 1912, *Twenty Years at Hull House with Autobiographical Notes*, The Macmillan Company, New York.

Adler, F 1880, *Creed and Deed*, G.P. Putnam's Sons, New York.

Adler, F 1905, *The Essentials of Spirituality*, James Pott, New York.

Adler, F 1908, *An Ethical Philosophy of Life*, Appleton and Co, New York.

Agnew, S 1972, "What's Wrong with the Legal Services Program", *ABA Journal*, vol. 58, no. 9, pp. 930–932.

Ahmed, S 2007, "A Phenomenology of Whiteness", *Feminist Theory*, vol. 8, pp. 149–168.

Alfieri, A V 1987, "The Antinomies of Poverty Law and a Theory of Dialogic Empowerment", *New York University Review of Law & Social Change*, vol. 16, no. 4, pp. 659–712.

Alfieri, A V 1991, "Reconstructive Poverty Law Practice: Learning Lessons of Client Narrative", *Yale Law Journal*, vol. 100, no. 7, pp. 2107–2148.

Alfieri, A V 1993, "Impoverished Practices", *Georgetown Law Journal*, vol. 81, no. 7, pp. 2567–2664.

Alfieri, A V 1996, "Ethical Commitments", *William and Mary Law Review*, vol. 38, no. 1, pp. 199–206.

Alfieri, A 2014, "Objecting to Race", *Georgetown Journal of Legal Ethics*, vol. 27, no. 4, pp. 1129–1162.

Allard, S 2007, "The Changing Face of Welfare During the Bush Administration", *Publius*, vol. 37, no. 3, pp. 304–332.

Allen, T W 1994, "The Invention of the White Race", in *Vol. 1: Racial Oppression and Social Control*, Verso Books, London.

Allen, T W 1997, "The Invention of the White Race", *Vol. 2: The Origin of Racial Oppression in Anglo-America*, Verso Books, London.

Allport, G 1937, "The Functional Autonomy of Motives", *American Journal of Psychology*, vol. 50, pp. 141–156.

Anzaldúa, G 2009, *The Gloria Anzaldúa Reader*, Ed. A Keating, Duke University Press, Durham, NC.

Amott, T 1994, "Eliminating Poverty", in *State of the Union*, Ed. R Caplan and J Feffer, Westview Press, Boulder.

Anonymous1890, "Progress and Poverty", *Current Comment & Legal Miscellany*, vol. 2, no. 4, pp. 208–214.

Anzaldúa, G 2007, *The Anzaldúa Reader*, Ed. A Keating, Duke University Press, Durham.

Appleton, S 1979, "Professor Michelman's Quest for a Constitutional Welfare Right", *Washington University Law Quarterly*, vol. 3, pp. 715–734.

Ayres, B 2001, *Fugitive Days*, Beacon Press, Boston.

Bach, W 2010, "Governance, Accountability, and the New Poverty Agenda", *Wisconsin Law Review*, no. 2, pp. 239–296.

Bach, W 2012, "Mobilization and Poverty Law: Searching for Participatory Democracy Amid the Ashes of the War on Poverty", *Virginia Journal of Social Policy & the Law*, vol. 20, no 1, pp. 96–158.

Baldwin, B 2008, "In Supreme Judgment of the Poor: The Role of the United States Supreme Court in Welfare Law and Policy", *Wisconsin Journal of Law, Gender and Society*, vol. 23, no. 1, pp. 1–40.

Baldwin, J 1965, *This Morning, This Evening, So Soon, in Going to Meet the Man*, Dial Press, New York.

Balkin, J 1997, "Agreements with Hell and Other Objects of Our Faith", *Fordham Law Review*, vol. 65, no. 4, pp. 1703–1738.

Balkin, J 2005, "Deconstruction's Legal Career", *Cardozo Law Review*, vol. 25, no. 2, pp. 720–721.

Baran, P and Sweezy, P 1964, *Monopoly Capital: An Essay on the American Economic and Social Order*, Monthly Review Press, New York.

Baran, P and Sweezy, P 1966, *Monopoly Capital*, Pelican, London.

Barber, D 2006, *A Hard Rain Fell: The SDS and Why it Failed*, University of Mississippi Press, Jackson.

Bauman, R 1988, "The Communitarian Vision of Critical Legal Studies", *McGill Law Journal*, vol. 33, no. 2, pp. 295–356.

Bauman, R 2002, *Ideology and Community in the First Wave of Critical Legal Studies*, University of Toronto Press, Toronto.

Bell, D 1976, *Cultural Contradictions of Capitalism*, Basic Books, New York.

Bello, W 2001, "2000: The Year of Global Protest", *International Socialism*, vol. 12, no. 90, n.p.

Bellow, G 1966, "New Challenges in the Extension of Legal Services", *Student Lawyer Journal*, vol. 12, no. 1 (October), pp. 9–30.

Bellow, G 1977, "Turning Solutions into Problems: The Legal Aid Experience", *National Legal Aid and Defender Association Briefcase*, vol. XXXIV, no. 4, pp. 103–134.

Bellow, G 1980, "Legal Aid in the United States", *Clearinghouse Review*, vol. 14, no. 4, pp. 337–345.

Bellow, G 1996, "Steady Work: A Practitioner's Reflections on Political Lawyering", *Harvard Civil Rights-Civil Liberties Law Review*, vol. 31, no. 2 (Summer), pp. 297–310.

Berman, W 2001, *From the Center to the Edge*, Rowan and Littlefield, Boulder.

Bermúdez, R 2014, "The Chicana Welfare Rights Organization and the Chicano Movement", pp. 95–117, in *The Chicano Movement*, Ed. M Garcia, Routledge, London.

Bernasconi, R and Critchley, S 1991, *Re-Reading Levinas*, Indiana University Press, Bloomington and Indianapolis.

Bernasconi, R and Wood, D 2002, *The Provocation of Levinas*, Routledge, London.
Bernstein, R 1971, *Praxis and Action: Contemporary Philosophies of Human Activity*, University of Pennsylvania Press, Philadelphia.
Bezdek, B 2013, "Citizen Engagement in the Shrinking City: Toward Development Justice in an Era of Growing Inequality", *Saint Louis University Public Law Review*, vol. 33, no. 1, pp. 3–56.
Binder, G 1991, "What's Left?", *Texas Law Review*, vol. 69, no. 7, pp. 1885–2041.
Blasi, G 1994, "What's a Theory For: Notes on Reconstructing Poverty Law Scholarship", *University of Miami Law Review*, vol. 48, no. 5, pp. 1063–1098.
Bork, R 1979, "The Impossibility of Finding Welfare Rights in the Constitution", *Washington University Law Quarterly*, vol. 1979, no. 3, pp. 695–702.
Boyd, D 2015, *White Allies in the Struggle for Racial Justice*, Orbis Books, New York.
Brackett, W 1887, "A Prescription for Poverty", *Chicago Law Times*, vol. 1, no. 2, pp. 123–138.
Brager, G and Purcell, F 1964, *Community Action against Poverty*, College and University Press Publishers, New York.
Brager, G and Purcell, F 1967, *Community Action Against Poverty*, College and University Press, New Haven.
Brauer, C M 1982, "Kennedy, Johnson, and the War on Poverty", *Journal of American History*, vol. 69, no. 1 (June), pp. 98–119.
Breines, W 1988, "Whose New Left?" *The Journal of American History*, vol. 75, no. 2, pp. 528–545.
Breines, W 1989, *Community and Organisation in the New Left*, Rutgers University Press, New Brunswick.
Broad, K 2001, "Critical Borderlands and Interdisciplinary, Intersectional Coalitions", *Denver University Law Review*, vol. 78, no. 4, pp. 1141–1160.
Broad, R and Heckscher, Z 2003, "Before Seattle", *Third World Quarterly*, vol. 24, no. 4, pp. 713–728.
Brooks, G 1963, *Selected Poems*, Harper and Row, New York.
Brown, C S 2002, *Refusing Racism: White Allies and the Struggle for Civil Rights*, Columbia University Press, London and New York.
Buber, M 1958 [1937], *I and Thou*, Charles Scribner's Sons, New York.
Buber, M 1973, *Meetings*, Open Court Pub, Illinois.
Buber, M 1974, *Between Man and Man*, Routledge, London.
Buchanan, R and Trubek, L 1992, "Resistances and Possibilities: A Critical and Practical Look at Public Interest Lawyering", *New York University Review of Law and Social Change*, vol. 19, no. 4, pp. 687–719.
Cahn, E and Cahn, J 1964, "The War on Poverty: A Civilian Perspective", *The Yale Law Journal*, vol. 73, no. 8 (July), pp. 1317–1352.
Calmore, J 1992, "Critical Race Theory, Archie Shepp, and Fire Music: Securing an Authentic Intellectual Life in a Multicultural World", *Southern California Law Review*, vol. 65, no. 5, pp. 2129–2230.
Campbell, B 1984, *Wigan Pier Revisited*, Virago, London.
Castoriadis, C 2005, *The Imaginary Institution of Society*, Polity, London.
Chambon, A S, Irving, A and Epstein, L, Eds 1999, *Reading Foucault for Social Work*, Columbia University Press, Columbia.
Cloward, R and Piven, F 1966, "The Weight of the Poor: A Strategy to End Poverty", *The Nation*, pp. 510–518.

Cohen, A and Alberstein, M 2011, "Progressive Constitutionalism and Alternative Movements in Law", *Ohio State Law Journal*, vol. 72, no. 6, pp. 1083–1114.

Collins, P 1993, "Toward a New Vision: Race, Class, and Gender as Categories of Analysis and Connection", *Race, Sex & Class*, vol. 1, no. 1, pp. 25–45.

Collins, P 2012, "Social Inequality, Power, and Politics: Intersectionality and American Pragmatism in Dialogue", *The Journal of Speculative Philosophy*, vol. 26, no. 2, pp. 442–457.

Collins, P and Bilge, S 2016, *Intersectionality*, Polity Press, London.

Cook, A 1990, "Beyond Critical Legal Studies: The Reconstructive Theology of Dr. Martin Luther King, Jr.", *Harvard Law Review*, vol. 103, no. 5, pp. 985–1044.

Cooley, C 1902, *Human Nature and the Social Order*, Charles Scribner and Sons, New York.

Cornell, D 1985, "Toward a Modern/Postmodern Reconstruction of Ethics", *University of Pennsylvania Law Review*, vol. 133, no. 2, pp. 291–380.

Cornell, D 1986, "Convention and Critique", *Cardozo Law Review*, vol. 7, no. 3, pp. 679–692.

Cramton, R 1978, "The Ordinary Religion of the Law School Classroom", *Journal of Legal Education*, vol. 29, no. 3, pp. 247–263.

Crenshaw, K., Gotanda, N, Peller, G and Thomas, K 1995, *Critical Race Theory*, New Press, New York.

Croly, H 1909, *The Promise of American Life*, Macmillan, New York.

Cummings, S 2001, "Community Economic Development as Progressive Politics: Toward a Grassroots Movement for Economic Justice", *Stanford Law Review*, vol. 54, no. 3, pp. 399–494.

Cummings, S 2007, "Critical Legal Consciousness in Action", *Harvard Law Review Forum*, vol. 120, no. 39, pp. 62–71.

Cummings, S and Eagly, I 2001, "A Critical Reflection on Law and Organizing", *UCLA Law Review*, vol. 48, no. 3, pp. 443–518.

Dalton, H 1987, "The Clouded Prism, Minority Critiques of the Critical Legal Studies Movement", *Harvard Civil Rights-Civil Liberties Law Review*, vol. 22, no. 2, pp. 435–447.

Davies, M 1993, *Brutal Need: Lawyers and the Welfare Rights Movement, 1960–1973*, Yale University Press, London and New Haven.

Davis, A 1997, "Identity Notes Part II: Redeeming the Body Politic", *Harvard Latino Law Review*, vol. 2, pp. 267–278.

Delgado, R 1993, "The Inward Turn in Outsider Jurisprudence", *William and Mary Law Review*, vol. 34, no. 3, pp. 741–768.

Delgado, G 2009, "Reflections on Movement Building & Community Organizing", *Social Policy*, vol. 39, no. 2, pp. 6–15.

Delgado, R 1987, "The Ethereal Scholar: Does Critical Legal Studies Have What Minorities Want?" *Harvard Civil Rights-Civil Liberties Law Review*, pp. 301–322.

Derrida, J 1996, *The Gift of Death*, University of Chicago Press, Chicago.

Dewey, J 1933, "Foreword", in *The Philosophy of Henry George*, G Geiger, The Macmillan Company, New York.

Dewey, J 1958, *Art as Experience*, Capricorn Books, Oakville, Ontario.

Dewey, J 1981, "Creative Democracy" in *The Later Works of John Dewey: 1925–1953*, Ed. J Boydston, Southern Illinois Press, Carbondale.

Dewey, J and Tufts, J 1932 [1908], *Ethics*, Henry Holt, New York.

Diamantides, M, Ed. 2007, *Levinas, Law, Politics*, Routledge-Cavendish, New York.
Douzinas, C 2000, *The End of Human Rights: Critical Legal Thought at the Turn of the Century*, Hart Press, Oxford.
Dreier, P 2008, "The Chicago Sit In: Has Obama's Election Spurred a New Mood of Union Activism", *Dissent*, 17 December.
Du Bois, W 1899, *The Philadelphia Negro*, University of Pennsylvania Press.
Du Bois, W 1903, *The Souls of Black Folk: Essays and Sketches*, A.C. McClurg, Chicago.
Duxbury, N 1995, *Patterns of American Jurisprudence*, Clarendon, Oxford.
Edelman, P 1987, "The Next Century of Our Constitution: Rethinking Our Duty to the Poor", *The Hastings Law Journal*, vol. 39, no. 1, pp. 1–62.
Edelman, P 2012, *So Rich, So Poor*, The New Press, New York.
Ehrenreich, B 2001, *Nickel and Dimed: Undercover in Low-wage USA*, Granta, London.
Ellul, J 1964, *The Technological Society*, Vintage Books, New York.
Ellul, J 1976, *The Ethics of Freedom*, William B Eerdmans Publishing Co, Michigan.
Ely, J 1978, "Toward a Representation – Reinforcing Mode of Judicial Review", *Maryland Law Review*, vol. 37, pp. 451–487.
Engler, R 2010, "Pursuing Access to Justice and Civil Right to Counsel in a Time of Economic Crisis", *Roger Williams University Law Review*, vol. 15, no. 2, pp. 472–498.
Espada, M 1996, *Imagine the Angels of Bread*, W.W. Norton, New York.
Evans, S 1980, *Personal Politics: The Roots of the Women's Liberation Movement in the Civil Rights Movement and the New Left*, Random House, New York.
Failinger, M 1999, "Face-ing the Other: An Ethics of Encounter and Solidarity in Legal Services Practice", *Fordham Law Review*, vol. 67, pp. 2071–2122.
Failinger, M 2010, "Levinas, Law Schools and the Poor: They Stand over Us", *Oklahoma City University Law Review*, vol. 35, no. 1, pp. 115–130.
Fanon, F 1986, *Black Skin White Mask*, Pluto, London.
Farley, A 1997, "The Black Body as Fetish Object", *Oregon Law Review*, vol. 76, no. 3, pp. 457–474.
Farley, A 2001, "Lilies of the Field: A Critique of Adjudication", *Cardozo Law Review*, vol. 22, no. 3–4, pp. 1013–1060.
Feldman, M 1995, "Political Lessons: Legal Services for the Poor", *Georgetown Law Journal*, vol. 83, no. 4, pp. 1529–1632.
Feur, L 1969, *The Conflict of Generations*, New York.
Feuerlicht, I 1978, *Alienation*, Greenwood Press, Westport.
Fisher, D, Ed., 1980, *The Third Woman, Minority Woman Writers of the United States*, Houghton Mifflin Company, Boston.
Fisher, G 1992, "The Development and History of the Poverty Thresholds", *Social Security Bulletin*, vol. 55, no. 4, pp. 3–14.
Fiss, O 1976, "The Fate of an Idea Whose Time Has Come: Antidiscrimination Law in the Second Decade after Brown v. Board of Education", *University of Chicago Law Review*, vol. 41, no. 4, pp. 742–773.
Flacks, R 1966, "On the Uses of Participatory Democracy", *Dissent*, vol. 13.
Forbath, W 2001, "Constitutional Welfare Rights: A History, Critique and Reconstruction", *Fordham Law Review*, vol. 69, no. 5, pp. 1821–1892.
Forbath, W 2004, "Not So Simple Justice: Frank Michelman on Social Rights, 1969–Present" *Tulsa Law Review*, vol. 39, no. 3, pp. 597–638.
Forbath, W 2011, "The Distributive Constitution and Workers' Rights", *Ohio State Law Journal*, vol. 72, no. 6, pp. 1115–1158.

Freire, P 2017, *Pedagogy of the Oppressed*, Penguin Books, London.
Frelich-Appleton, S 1979, "Professor Michelman's Quest for a Constitutional Welfare Right", *Washington University Law Quarterly*, vol. 1979, no. 3, pp. 715–734.
Fried, C 1976, "The Lawyer as Friend: The Moral Foundations of the Lawyer-Client Relation", *Yale Law Journal*, vol. 85, no. 8, pp. 1077–1078.
Friedenberg, E 1994, "Paul Goodman", *Prospects: The Quarterly Review of Comparative Education*, vol. XXIII, no. 3/4, pp. 575–595.
Fromm, E 1955, *The Sane Society*, Routledge, London and New York.
Frost, F 2002, *An Interracial Movement of the Poor*, New York University Press, New York.
Frost, J 2001, *An Interracial Movement of the Poor: Community Organizing and the New Left in the 1960s*, New York University Press, New York and London.
Frug, M 1992, "Progressive Feminist Legal Scholarship: Can We Claim a Different Voice", *Harvard Women's Law Journal*, vol. 15, pp. 37–64.
Fung, A and Wright, E 2003, *Deepening Democracy*, Verso, London.
Gabel, P 1984, "Phenomenology of Rights-Consciousness and the Pact of the Withdrawn Selves", *Texas Law Review*, vol. 62, no. 8, pp. 1563–1600.
Gabel, P 2009, "Critical Legal Studies as a Spiritual Practice", *Pepperdine Law Review*, vol. 36, pp. 515–534.
Gabel, P and Harris, P 1982, "Building Power and Breaking Images: Critical Legal Theory and the Practice of Law", *New York University Review of Law and Social Change*, vol. 11, no. 3, pp. 369–412.
Gabel, P and Kennedy, D 1984, "Roll Over Beethoven", *Stanford Law Review*, vol. 36, nos. 1 & 2, pp. 1–56.
Gaber, P 1998, "Just Trying to be Human in This Place: The Legal Education of Twenty Women", *Yale Journal of Law and Feminism*, vol. 10, no. 2, pp. 165–276.
Galbraith, K 1958, *The Affluent Society*, Hamish Hamilton, London.
Gans, H 1972, "The Positive Functions of Poverty", *American Journal of Sociology*, vol. 78, no. 2, pp. 275–289.
Garcia, M 2014, *The Chicano Movement: Contemporary Perspectives*, Routledge, London and New York.
Gearey, A 2012, *Justice as Welfare*, Bloomsbury, London.
Gearey, A 2017, "You May Find Yourselves Changed in Unexpected Ways: Literature and Poverty Law", *Law & Literature*, vol. 29, no. 3, pp. 405–423.
Gilbert, B and Tenney, G 1967, *Praxis*.
Gilbert, D, Gottlieb, R and Tenney, G 2011, "Towards a Theory of Social Change: The Port Authority Statement", in *Revolutionary Youth and the New Working Class*, Ed. C Davidson, Lulu/Changemaker.
Gilman, M 2014, "A Court for the One Percent: How the Supreme Court Contributes to Economic Inequality", *Utah Law Review*, no. 3, pp. 389–464.
Gines, K 2011, "Black Feminism and Intersectional Analyses", *Philosophy Today*, vol. 55, pp. 275–284.
Gines, K 2013, "Introduction: Critical Philosophy of Race Beyond the Black/White Binary", *Critical Philosophy of Race*, vol. 1, no. 1, pp. 28–37.
Ginsberg, A 1985, *Collected Poems 1947–80*, Harper and Row, New York.
Gitlin, T 1993, *Years of Hope, Days of Rage*, Bantam Books, New York.
Goldfarb, P 1992, "From the Worlds of Others: Minority and Feminist Responses to Critical Legal Studies", *New England Law Review*, vol. 26, no. 3, pp. 683–710.

Goodman, P 1960, *Communities: Means of Livelihood and Ways of Life*, with P Goodman, Vintage Books, New York.
Goodrich, P 1993, "Sleeping with the Enemy: An Essay on the Politics of Critical Legal Studies in America", *New York University Law Review*, vol. 68, no. 2, pp. 389–426.
Goodrich, P 1999, "The Critic's Love of the Law", *Law and Critique*, vol. 10, no. 3, pp. 343–360.
Goodrich, P 2004, "Satirical Legal Studies: From the Legists to the Lizard", *Michigan Law Review*, vol. 103, no. 3, pp. 397–517.
Gordon, C 2013, "The Irony and Limits of the Affordable Care Act", *Dissent*, 15 October.
Gordon, L 1997, *Existence in Black: An Anthology of Black Existential Philosophy*, Routledge, London.
Gordon, L 2014, "Black Existence in Philosophy of Culture", *Diogenes*, vol. 59, nos. 3–4, pp. 96–105.
Gordon, R 1982, "Some Critical Theories of Law and Their Critics", in *The Politics of Law*, Ed. D Kairys, Basic Books, New York.
Gosse, V 2005, *Re-Thinking the New Left*, Palgrave Macmillan, New York.
Grahn-Farley, M 2008, "Race and Class: More than a Liberal Paradox", *Buffalo Law Review*, vol. 56, no. 4, pp. 935–952.
Gramsci, A 2005, *Selections from the Prison Notebooks*, Lawrence and Wishart, London.
Gunn, T 1973, *The Sense of Movement*, Faber and Faber, London.
Gutiérrez, G 1973, *A Theology of Liberation: History, Politics, and Salvation*, Orbis, Maryknoll.
Habermas, J 1989, "The Crisis of the Welfare State", in *Jurgen Habermas on Society and Politics*, Ed. S Seidman, Beacon Press, Massachusetts.
Hall, S 1986, "Gramsci's Relevance for the Study of Race and Ethnicity", *Journal of Communication Inquiry*, vol. 10, no. 2, pp. 5–27.
Handler, J 1992, "Postmodernism, Protest and the New Social Movements", *Law and Society Review*, vol. 42, no. 2, pp. 697–732.
Harrington, M 1962, *The Other America*, Macmillan, New York.
Harris, A 1990, "Race and essentialism in feminist legal theory", *Stanford Law Review*, vol. 42, no. 3, pp. 581–616.
Harvey, D 2010, *The Enigma of Capital*, Profile Books, London.
Hegel, G 1967, *The Phenomenology of Mind*, trans. J B Baillie, Harper, New York.
Heidegger, M 1962, *Being and Time*, Blackwells, Oxford.
Heinze, E 1995, "Gay and Poor", *Howard Law Journal*, vol. 38, no. 2, pp. 433–448.
Heller, A 1984, *Everyday Life*, Routledge, London.
Hernández, T 2000, "An Exploration of the Efficacy of Class-Based Approaches to Racial Justice: The Cuban Context", *U.C. Davis Law Review*, vol. 33, no. 4, pp. 1135–1172.
Hernandez-Truyol, B, Harris, A and Valdes, F 2015, "Beyond the First Decade: A Forward-Looking History of LatCrit Theory, Community and Praxis", *La Raza Law Journal*, vol. 17, no. 1, pp. 169–216.
Hirst, P 2007, "Althusser and the Theory of Ideology", *Economy and Society*, vol. 4, pp. 385–412.
Holmes, O 1897, "The Path of Law", *Harvard Law Review*, vol. 10, pp. 457–473.
Honneth, A 2008, *Reification*, Oxford University Press, Oxford.
Hornstein, R 2009, "Teaching Law Students to Comfort the Troubled and Trouble the Comfortable: An Essay on the Place of Poverty Law in the Law School Curriculum", *William Mitchell Law Review*, vol. 35, no. 3, pp. 1057–1083.

Hudson, S 2010, "Intersubjectivity of Mutual Recognition and the I-Thou: a Comparative Analysis of Hegel and Buber", *Minerva*, pp. 140–155.

Hunter, R 1905, *Poverty*, Macmillan, New York.

Hyppolite, J 1974, *Genesis and Structure of Hegel's Phenomenology of Spirit*, Northwestern University Press, Evanston.

Iglesias, E and Valdes, F 1998, "Afterword: Religion, Gender, Sexuality, Race and Class in Coalitional Theory: A Critical and Self-Critical Analysis of LatCrit Social Justice Agendas", *Chicano-Latino Law Review*, vol. 19, pp. 574–582.

Iglesias, E and Valdes, F 2001, "Afterword to LatCrit V Symposium: LatCrit at Five: Institutionalizing a Post-Subordination Future", *Denver University Law Review*, vol. 78, pp. 1249–1329.

Ignatiev, N and Allen, T 1969, *White Blindspots, Detroit: The Radical Education Project and New York*, NYC Revolutionary Youth Movement.

Illich, I 1980, "Vernacular Values", *Philosophica*, vol. 26, no. 2, pp. 47–102.

Israel, J 1979, *Alienation from Marx to Modern Sociology*, Humanities Press, New Jersey.

Jackson, T 2007, *From Civil Rights to Human Rights: Martin Luther King Jr. and the Struggle for Economic Justice*, University of Pennsylvania Press, Philadelphia.

Jaeggi, R 2014, *Alienation*, Columbia, New York.

James, S 1973, *Sex, Race and Class*, Petroleuse Press, New York.

James, W 1910, *The Self, Psychology: The Briefer Course*, Henry Holt and Co, New York.

Jewula, A 2013, "The Call and the Response: Martin Heidegger and Martin Buber on Responsibility", *Argument*, vol. 3, no. 2, pp. 323–338.

Johnson, K 1990, "Lawyering for Social Change: What's a Lawyer to Do", *Michigan Journal of Race & Law*, vol. 5, no. 1, pp. 201–228.

Johnson, K 1997, "Some Thoughts on the Future of Latino Legal Scholarship", *Harvard Latino Law Review*, vol. 2, pp. 101–144.

Joint Economic Committee1959, *Congress of the United States, 86th Congress 1st Session*, US Government Printing Office, Washington.

Kardnier, A and Ovesey, L 1951, *The Mark of Oppression*, World Publishing Company, New York.

Katz, J 1982, *Poor People's Lawyers in Transition*, Rutgers University Press, New Brunswick.

Katz, M 1996, *In the Shadow of the Poor House: A Social History of Welfare in America*, Basic Books, New York.

Katz, M 2013, *The Undeserving Poor: America's Enduring Confrontation with Poverty*, Oxford University Press, Oxford.

Kaufman, W 1973, *Without Guilt and Justice*, P. H. Wyden, New York.

Kelly, C and Lefkowitz, J 2003, "Radical and Pragmatic: United Students against Sweat Shops", in *Teamsters and Turtles?: U.S. Progressive Political Movements in the 21st Century*, Ed. J Berg, Rowan and Littlefield, Boulder.

Kelman, M 1984, *A Guide to Critical Legal Studies*, Harvard University Press, Harvard.

Kendall, F 2013, *Understanding White Privilege*, Routledge, London and New York.

Kennedy, D 1971, "How the Law School Fails", *Yale Review of Law and Social Action*, vol. 1, no. 1, pp. 71–90.

Kennedy, D 1997, *A Critique of Adjudication*, Harvard University Press, Harvard.

Kessler, J 2016, "The Political Economy of Constitutional Political Economy", *Texas Law Review*, vol. 94, no. 7, pp. 1527–1554.

Kessler, T 1995, "PPI, Patriarchy, and the Schizophrenic View of Women: A Feminist Analysis of Welfare Reform in Maryland", *Maryland Journal of Contemporary Legal Issues*, vol. 6, no. 2, pp. 317–376.

Kessler, T 2008, "Getting Class", *Buffalo Law Review*, vol. 56, no. 4, pp. 915–934.

Kornbluh, F 2007, *The Battle for Welfare Rights: Politics and Poverty in Modern America*, University of Pennsylvania Press, Philadelphia.

Kramer, L 2006, "The Interest of the Man: James Madison, Popular Constitutionalism, and the Theory of Deliberative Democracy", *Valparaiso University Law Review*, vol. 41, no. 2, pp. 697–754.

Laclau, E and Mouffe, C 2001, *Hegemony and Socialist Strategy*, Verso, London.

Laerow, J and Williams, Y 2006, *In Search of the Black Panther Party: New Perspectives on a Revolutionary Movement*, Duke University Press, Durham.

Law, S 1983, "Women, Work, Welfare, and the Preservation of Patriarchy", *University of Pennsylvania Law Review*, vol. 131, no. 6, pp. 1249–1340.

Law, S 1984, "Edward V. Sparer", *University of Pennsylvania Law Review*, vol. 132, no. 3, pp. 425–429.

Law, S 1984a, "Rethinking Sex and the Constitution", *University of Pennsylvania Law Review*, vol. 132, no. 5, pp. 955–1040.

Lawson, R 1995, "Critical Race Theory as Praxis: A View from Outside the Outside", *Howard Law Journal*, vol. 38, no. 2, pp. 353–370.

Lebowitz, M 2003, *Beyond Capital*, Palgrave, London.

Lee, K 2012, "Rethinking with Patricia Hill Collins: A Note Toward Intersectionality as Interlocutory Interstitiality", *The Journal of Speculative Philosophy*, vol. 26, no. 2, pp. 466–473.

Lefebvre, H 2002, *Critique of Everyday Life*, Volume 1, Verso, London.

Lewis, A 2009, *The Shadows of Youth: The Remarkable Journey of the Civil Rights Generation*, Hill and Wang, New York.

Lewis, O 1969, "Culture of Poverty", in *On Understanding Poverty: Perspectives from the Social Sciences*, Ed. D P Moynihan, Basic Books, New York, pp. 187–220.

Liebow, E 1967, *Tally's Corner*, Little Brown and Co., Boston.

Lipkin, R 1999, "Progressivism as Communitarian Democracy", *Widener Law Symposium Journal*, vol. 4, pp. 229–272.

Liu, G 2008, "Rethinking Constitutional Welfare Rights", *Stanford Law Review*, vol. 61, no. 2, pp. 203–270.

Llewellyn, K 1939, "One Realist's View of Natural Law for Judges", *Notre Dame Lawyer*, vol. 15, no. 1, pp. 3–8.

Llewellyn, K 1942, "On the Good, the True, the Beautiful in Law", *Chicago University Law Review*, vol. 9, pp. 202–204.

Loffredo, S 1993, "Poverty, Democracy and Constitutional Law", *University of Pennsylvania Law Review*, vol. 141, no. 4, pp. 1277–1390.

Loffredo, S 2001, "Poverty Law and Community Activism: Notes from a Law School Clinic", *University of Pennsylvania Law Review*, vol. 150, no. 1, pp. 173–204.

Loffredo, S 2007, "Poverty, Inequality, and Class in the Structural Constitutional Law Course", *Fordham Urban Law Journal*, vol. 34, no. 4, pp. 1239–1268.

Loffredo, S 2009, "Gideon Meets Goldberg: The Case for a Qualified Right to Counsel in Welfare Hearings", *Touro Law Review*, vol. 25, no. 1, pp. 273–346.

Loffredo, S and Hershkoff, H 2011, "State Courts and Constitutional Socio-Economic Rights: Exploring the Underutilization Thesis", *Penn State Law Review*, vol. 115, no. 4, pp. 923–982.

Loffredo, S and Piven, F 2007, "A Discussion of Poverty, Class, and Economic Justice", *New York City Law Review*, vol. 11, no. 1, pp. 3–23.

Lopez, G 1987, "The Idea of a Constitution in the Chicano Tradition", *Journal of Legal Education*, vol. 37, no. 2, pp. 162–166.

Lopez, G 1989, "Reconceiving Civil Rights Practice: Seven Weeks in the Life of a Rebellious Collaboration", *Georgetown Law Journal*, vol. 77, no. 4, pp. 1603–1718.

Lopez, G 1989a, "The Work We Know So Little about", *Stanford Law Review*, vol. 42, no. 1, pp. 1–14.

Lopez, G 1996, "An Aversion to Clients: Loving Humanity and Hating Human Beings", *Harvard Civil Rights-Civil Liberties Law Review*, vol. 31, no. 2, pp. 315–324.

Lopez, G 2004, "Shaping Community Problem Solving around Community Knowledge", *New York University Law Review*, vol. 79, no. 1, pp. 59–114.

Lopez, G 2005, "Living and Lawyering Rebelliously", *Fordham Law Review*, vol. 73, no. 5, pp. 2041–2054.

Lopez, G 2009, "Changing Systems, Changing Ourselves", *Harvard Latino Law Review*, vol. 12, no. 1, pp. 15–40.

Löwith, K 1982, *Max Weber and Karl Marx*, Controversies in Sociology, HarperCollins.

Löwy, M 2017, "Martin Buber's Socialism", *The Journal of Jewish Thought and Philosophy*, vol. 25, no. 1, pp. 95–104.

Lukács, G 1967/1968, *History and Class Consciousness*, Merlin Press, London.

Luna, G 1999, "On the Complexities of Race: The Treaty of Guadalupe Hidalgo and Dred Scott v. Sandford", *University of Miami Law Review*, vol. 53, no. 4, pp. 691–716.

MacDonald, D 1963, "Our Invisible Poor", *The New Yorker*, 19 January.

Mack, R 1995, "Critical Race Theory as Praxis", *Howard Law Journal*, vol. 38, no. 2, pp. 353–370.

MacKinnon, C 1987, *Feminism Unmodified*, Harvard University Press, Harvard.

Mahoney, M 1999, "Constructing Solidarity: Interest and White Workers", *University of Pennsylvania Journal of Labor and Employment Law*, vol. 2, no. 4, pp. 747–772.

Mahoney, M 2009, "What's Left of Solidarity – Reflections on Law, Race, and Labor History", *Buffalo Law Review*, vol. 57, no. 5, pp. 1515–1596.

Manderson, D 2006/2007, *Proximity, Levinas and the Soul of the Law*, McGill-Queen's University Press, Montreal.

Mantler, G 2013, *Power to the Poor: Black-Brown Coalition and the Fight for Economic Justice, 1960–1974*, University of North Carolina Press, Chapel Hill.

Marcuse, H 1955, *Eros and Civilisation*, Beacon Press, New York.

Marcuse, H 1964, *One Dimensional Man*, Beacon Press, New York.

Marcuse, H 2003, *One Dimensional Man*, Routledge, London.

Marcuse, H 2005, *The New Left and the 1960s*, Routledge, London and New York.

Marx, K 1954, *Capital Vol. III*, Lawrence and Wishart, London.

Marx, K 1973, *Grundrisse*, Penguin, London.

Marx, K 1975, *Capital: Volume 1*, Progress Publishers, Moscow.

Marx, K 1977, *Economic and Philosophical Manuscripts of 1844*, Progress Publishers, Moscow.

Matsuda, M 1987, "Looking to the Bottom: Critical Legal Studies and Reparations Minority Critiques of the Critical Legal Studies Movement", *Harvard Civil Rights-Civil Liberties Law Review*, vol. 22, no. 2, pp. 232–399.

McCluskey, M 2003, "Efficiency and Social Citizenship: Challenging the Neoliberal Attack on the Welfare State", *Indiana Law Journal*, vol. 78, no. 2, pp. 783–876.

McCluskey, M 2007, "Thinking with Wolves: Left Legal Theory after the Right's Rise", *Buffalo Law Review*, vol. 54, no. 4, pp. 1191–1298.

McDiarmid, M 1990, "What's Going on Down There in the Basement: In-House Clinics Expand Their Beachhead", *New York Law School Law Review*, vol. 35, no. 1, pp. 239–292.

McThenia, A W 2004 [1995], *A Radical Christian and Exemplary Lawyer: Honoring William Stringfellow*, Wipf and Stock, Eugene.

Mead, L 1992, *The New Politics of Poverty*, Basic Books, New York.

Melhem, D 2005, *New York Poems*, Syracuse University Press, Syracuse.

Melish, T 2010, "Maximum Feasible Participation of the Poor: New Accountability, and a 21' Century War on the Sources of Poverty", *Yale Human Rights and Development Law Journal*, vol. 13, no. 1, pp. 1–134.

Menkel-Meadow, C 1988, "Feminist Legal Theory, Critical Legal Studies, and Legal Education Or the Fem-Crits Go to Law School", *Journal of Legal Education*, vol. 38, no. 1, pp. 61–86.

Menkel-Meadow, C 1994, "Culture Clash in the Quality of Life in the Law: Changes in the Economics, Diversification and Organization of Lawyering", *Case Western Reserve Law Review*, vol. 44, no. 2, pp. 621–664.

Mészáros, I 2005/1970, *Marx's Theory of Alienation*, Merlin Press, London.

Michaels, W 2008, "Against Diversity", *New Left Review*, vol. 52, pp. 33–36.

Michelman, F 1969, "Foreword: On Protecting the Poor through the Fourteenth Amendment", *Harvard Law Review*, vol. 83, no. 1, pp. 7–59.

Michelman, F 1973, "In Pursuit of Constitutional Welfare Rights: One View of Rawls' Theory of Justice", *University of Pennsylvania Law Review*, vol. 121, no. 5, pp. 962–1019.

Michelman, F 1979, "Welfare Rights in a Constitutional Democracy", *Washington University Law Quarterly*, no. 3, pp. 659–694.

Michelman, F 1986, "Foreword: Traces of Self-Government", *Harvard Law Review*, vol. 100, no. 1 (November), pp. 4–77.

Michelman, F 1988, "Law's Republic", *Yale Law Journal*, vol. 97, no. 8, pp. 1493–1538.

Michelman, F 1999, "What (if Anything) is Progressive-Liberal Democratic Constitutionalism", *Widener Law Symposium Journal*, vol. 4, pp. 181–200.

Michelman, F 2011, "Liberal Constitutionalism, Property Rights, and the Assault on Poverty", *Stellenbosch Law Review*, vol. 22, no. 3, pp. 706–723.

Michelman, F 2014, "Why Not Just Say No: An Essay on the Obduracy of Constitution Fixation", *Boston University Law Review*, vol. 94, no. 3, pp. 1141–1158.

Midgely, J 1992, "American Social Policy and the Reagan Legacy", *Journal of Sociology and Social Welfare*, vol. 19, no. 1, pp. 13–28.

Mobilization for Youth (MFY)1966, *Action on the Lower East Side: Progress Report and Proposal July 1962–June 1964*, Mobilization for Youth, New York.

Moffat, K 1999, "Surveillance and the Government of the Welfare Recipient", in *Reading Foucault for Social Work*, Ed. A S Chambon, Columbia University Press, Columbia.

Moran, R 1997, "Neither Black Nor White", *Harvard Latino Law Review*, vol. 2, pp. 61–100.

Movement for Youth (MFY)1962, *Action on the Lower East Side; Progress Report and Proposal*, MFY, New York.

Moynihan, D 1969, *Maximum Feasible Misunderstanding: Community Action in the War on Poverty*, Free Press, New York.

Mutua, A 2001, "Why Retire the Feminization of Poverty Construct", *Denver University Law Review*, vol. 78, no. 4, pp. 1179–1210.

Mutua, A 2008, "Introducing ClassCrits: From Class Blindness to a Critical Legal Analysis of Economic Inequality", *Buffalo Law Review*, vol. 56, no. 4, pp. 859–914.

Mutua, M 2008a, "Human Rights and Powerlessness: Pathologies of Choice and Substance", *Buffalo Law Review*, vol. 56, no. 4, pp. 1027–1034.

Nadasen, P 2005, *Welfare Warriors: The Welfare Rights Movement in the United States*, Routledge, New York.

Nancy, J-L 2000, *Being Singular Plural*, Stanford University Press, Stanford.

Newton, H P 1973, *Revolutionary Suicide*, Harcourt Brace Jovanovich.

Nice, J 2008, "No Scrutiny Whatsoever: Deconstitutionalization of Poverty Law, Dual Rules of Law, & Dialogic Default", *Fordham Urban Law Journal*, vol. 35, no. 3, pp. 629–672.

Nixon, R 1992, *Seize the Moment*, Simon & Schuster.

Noble, C 1997, *Welfare as We Know It*, Oxford University Press, Oxford.

Novak, D 1985, "Buber's Critique of Heidegger", *Modern Judaism*, vol. 5, no. 2, pp. 125–140.

O'Connor, A 2001, *Poverty Knowledge: Social Science, Social Policy, and the Poor in Twentieth-Century U.S. History*, Princeton University Press, Princeton.

Office of the Assistant Secretary for Planning and Evaluation2000, *Reasons for Measuring Poverty in the United States in the Context of Public Policy – A Historical Review, 1916–1995. The Period Leading Up to the War on Poverty*, available at https://aspe.hhs.gov/report/reasons-measuring-poverty-united-states-context-public-policy-%E2%80%94-historical-review-1916–1995/period-leading-war-poverty.

Ollman, B 1971, *Alienation: Marx's Conception of Man in Capitalist Society*, Cambridge University Press, Cambridge.

Ollman, B 2003, *The Dance of the Dialectic: Steps in Marx's Method*, University of Illinois Press, Champaign.

Olsen, F 1983, "The Family and the Market: A Study of Ideology and Legal Reform", *Harvard Law Review*, vol. 96, no. 7 (May), pp. 1497–1578.

Orleck, A 2005, *Storming Caesar's Palace: How Black Mothers Fought Their Own War on Poverty*, Beacon Press, New York.

Orshansky, M 1967, "Demography and Ecology of Poverty", in *Proceedings of a Conference on Research on Poverty*, submitted to The Center for the Study of Social Problems, National Institute of Mental Health, Bureau of Social Science Research, Washington, DC.

Ortega, O 2016, *In Between Latina Phenomenology, Multiplicity and the Self*, State University of New York Press, Albany.

Park, L 2001, "Perpetuation of Poverty through Public Charge", *Denver University Law Review*, vol. 78, no. 4, pp. 1161–1178.

Patterson, J 1981, *America's Struggle Against Poverty in the Twentieth Century*, Harvard University Press, Harvard.

Perls, F, Hefferline, R and Goodman, P 1951, *Gestalt Therapy: Excitement and Growth in Human Personality*, Julian Press, New York.

Piomelli, A 2000, "Appreciating Collaborative Lawyering", *Clinical Law Review*, vol. 6, no. 2, pp. 427–516.

Piomelli, A 2006, "The Democratic Roots of Collaborative Lawyering", *Clinical Law Review*, vol. 12, no. 2, pp. 541–614.

Piomelli, A 2009, "The Challenge of Democratic Lawyering", *Fordham Law Review*, vol. 77, no. 4, pp. 1383–1408.
Piomelli, A 2013, "Sensibilities for Social Justice Lawyers", *Hastings Race and Poverty Law Journal*, vol. 10, no. 2, pp. 177–190.
Pitkin, H 1981, "Justice: On Relating the Public and the Private", *Political Theory*, vol. 9, no. 3, pp. 327–352.
Piven, F 2009, "Poor Relief: Does Obama Have a Poverty Policy?" *New Labor Forum*, vol. 18, no. 3, pp. 47–52.
Piven, F and Cloward, R 1972, *Regulating the Poor: The Functions of Public Welfare*, Vintage, New York.
Post, R and Siegel, R 2007, "Roe Rage: Democratic Constitutionalism and Backlash", *Harvard Civil Rights Civil Liberties Law Review*, vol. 42, pp. 374–376.
Pound, R 1907, "The Need of a Sociological Jurisprudence", *Green Bag*, vol. 19, pp. 607–615.
Pound, R 1912, "Social Justice and Legal Justice", *Central Law Journal*, vol. 75, no. 20, pp. 455–463.
Pound, R 1914, "Justice According to Law", *Columbia Law Review*, vol. 13, no. 8, pp. 696–713.
Pound, R 1921, "Judge Holmes's Contributions to the Science of Law", *Harvard Law Review*, vol. 34, no. 5, pp. 449–453.
Quigley, B 2007, "Human Rights Trump Property Rights – Lawyers are Called to Become Revolutionaries", *Guild Practitioner*, vol. 64, no. 2, pp. 95–105.
Radin, M and Michelman, F 1990, "Pragmatist and Poststructuralist Critical Legal Practice", *University of Pennsylvania Law Review*, vol. 139, no. 4, pp. 1019–1058.
Rainwater, L 1967, "The Problem of Lower Class Culture and Poverty War Strategy", in *On Understanding Poverty*, Ed. D Moynihan, Basic Books, New York.
Raphael, J 2000, *Saving Bernice: Battered Women, Welfare and Poverty*, Northeastern Press, Lebanon, New Hampshire.
Reich, C 1964, "The New Property", *The Yale Law Journal*, vol. 73, no. 5 (April), pp. 733–787.
Reyes, B 2004, "Changes in Trip Duration for Mexican Immigrants to the United States", *Population Research and Policy Review*, vol. 23, no. 3, pp. 235–257.
Reznikoff, C 2005, *The Poems of Charles Reznikoff*, Ed. S Conney, Black Sparrow Press, Boston.
Rhode, D 1985, "Ethical Perspectives on Legal Practice", *Stanford Law Review*, vol. 37, no. 2, pp. 589–652.
Rich, A 1979, *On Lies Secrets and Silence*, WW Norton and Co., New York.
Rifkin, J 1980, "Toward a Theory of Law and Patriarchy", *Harvard Women's Law Journal*, vol. 3, no. 1, pp. 83–95.
Riis, J 1890, *How the Other Half Lives*, Charles Scribner's Sons, New York.
Rodes, R 1995, "Pilgrim Law", *Journal of Law and Religion*, vol. 11, no. 1, pp. 255–266.
Rodriguez, O 1977, *The Politics of Chicano Liberation*, Pathfinder, New York.
Rome, E 2013, "Can Progressives Do Big Things? Obama Care is the Test", *Dissent*, 25 July.
Rose, G 1981, *Hegel Contra Sociology*, Verso, London.
Rossinow, D 1994, *The Politics of Authenticity*, Columbia University Press, Columbia.
Rotenstreich, N 1989, *Alienation: The Concept and its Reception*, E.J. Brill, Leiden.
Rothstein, R 1965, "A Short History of ERAP", *SDS Bulletin*, 4, available at www.sds-1960s.org/documents.htm.

Russell, M 1992, "Entering Great America: Reflections on Race and the Convergence of Progressive Legal Theory and Practice", *Hastings Law Journal*, vol. 43, pp. 749–767.

Saad-Filho, A and Fine, B 2004, *Marx's Capital*, Pluto Press, London.

Sager, K 1994, "Justice in Plain Clothes: Reflections on the Thinness of Constitutional Law", *Northwestern University Law Review*, vol. 88, no. 1, pp. 410–435.

Sager, L 1993, "Justice in Plain Clothes: Reflections on the Thinness of Constitutional Law", *Northwestern University Law Review*, vol. 88, no. 1, pp. 410–435.

Sale, K 1973, *SDS*, Vintage Books, New York.

Salerno, R 2003, *Landscapes of Abandonment; Capitalism, Modernity and Estrangement*, SUNY, New York.

Sarat, A 1990, "The Law is All Over: Power, Resistance and the Legal Consciousness of the Welfare Poor", *Yale Journal of Law & the Humanities*, vol. 2, no. 2, pp. 343–380.

Sarat, A and Scheingold, S 1998, *Cause Lawyering: Political Commitments and Professional Responsibilities*, Oxford University Press, New York.

Sayers, S 2011, *Marx and Alienation: Essays on Hegelian Themes*, Palgrave Macmillan, London.

Schacht, R 1971, *Alienation*, Allen and Unwin, London.

Schaff, A 1980, *Alienation as a Social Phenomenon*, Pergamon Press, London.

Schneider, E 1986, "The Dialectic of Rights and Politics: Perspectives from the Women's Movement", *New York University Law Review*, vol. 61, pp. 589–610.

Seeman, C 1961, "On the Meaning of Alienation", *American Sociological Review*, vol. 26, pp. 753–758.

Shalleck, A 1993, "Constructions of the Client within Legal Education", *Stanford Law Review*, vol. 45, no. 6, pp. 1731–1754.

Sheehan, S 1976, *A Welfare Mother*, Houghton Mifflin Company, Boston.

Simon, W 1990, "The Rule of Law and the Two Realms of Welfare Administration", *Brooklyn Law Review*, vol. 56, no. 3, pp. 777–788.

Smith, D 1987, "An Analysis of Ideological Structures and How Women are Excluded: Considerations for Academic Women", *Canadian Review of Sociology and Anthropology*, vol. 12, no. 4, pp. 131–154.

Sparer, E 1965, "The New Legal Aid as an Instrument of Social Change", *University of Illinois Law Forum*, no. 1, pp. 57–62.

Sparer, E 1984, "Fundamental Human Rights, Legal Entitlements, and the Social Struggle: A Friendly Critique of the Critical Legal Studies Movement", *Stanford Law Review*, vol. 36, no. 1 & 2, pp. 509–574.

Sparer, E, Thorkelson, H and Weiss, J 1966, "The Lay Advocate", *University of Detroit Law Journal*, vol. 43, no. 4 (April), pp. 493–516.

Spindelman, M 2011, "Progressive Constitutionalism Considered", *Ohio State Law Journal*, vol. 72, no. 6, pp. 1069–1072.

Stephanopoulos, N 2015, "Political Powerlessness", *New York University Law Review*, vol. 90, no. 5, pp. 1527–1608.

Stone, H 1934, "The Public Influence of the Bar", *Harvard Law Review*, vol. 48, no. 1, pp. 1–14.

Stone, M 2016, *Levinas, Ethics and Law*, Edinburgh University Press, Edinburgh.

Stringfellow, W 1957, "Lawyer as Churchman", *Vanderbilt Law Review*, vol. 10, no. 5, pp. 939–966.

Stringfellow, W 1962, *A Public and Private Faith*, Eerdmans Publishing Co., Grand Rapids, MI.

Stringfellow, W 1966, *Dissenter in a Great Society*, Reinhart and Winston, New York.

Stringfellow, W 2005 [1964], *My People is the Enemy*, Wipf and Stock, New York.

Stringfellow, W and Towne, A 1971, *Suspect Tenderness*, Holt Reinhart and Wilson, New York.

Students for a Democratic Society (SDS)1968, *Take a Step into America: Don't Mourn – Organise*, The Movement Press, San Francisco.

Tabb, W 1971, *The Political Economy of the Black Ghetto*, W.W. Norton, New York.

Tillmon, J 1972, "Welfare is a Women's Issue", *Ms Magazine*, pp. 111–116.

Torres, G 1988, "Local Knowledge Local Color: Critical Legal Studies and the Law of Race Relations", *San Diego Law Review*, vol. 25, no. 5, pp. 1043–1070.

Tremblay, P 1992, "Rebellious Lawyering, Regnant Lawyering, and Street-Level Bureaucracy", *Hastings Law Journal*, vol. 43, no. 4, pp. 947–970.

Triece, M 2013, *Tell It Like It Is: Women in the National Welfare Rights Movement*, University of South Carolina Press, Columbia, South Carolina.

Trilling, L 1972, *Sincerity and Authenticity*, Harvard University Press, Harvard, Massachusetts.

Trimberger, E 1979, "Women in the Old and New Left", *Feminist Studies*, vol. 5, no. 3, pp. 431–450.

Troutt, D 2014, *The Price of Paradise: The Costs of Inequality and a Vision for a More Equitable America*, New York University Press, New York.

Trubek, L 1994, "Lawyering for Poor People: Revisionist Scholarship and Practice", *University of Miami Law Review*, vol. 48, no. 5, pp. 983–998.

Trubek, L G 2011, "The Worst of Times … and the Best of Times: Lawyering for Poor Clients Today", *Fordham Urban Law Journal*, vol. 22, no. 4, pp. 1123–1140.

Trump, D 2011, *Time to Get Tough*, Regnery Publishing, Washington.

Tushnet, M 1980, "Dia-Tribe", *Michigan Law Review*, vol. 78, no. 5, pp. 694–789.

Tushnet, M 2011, "Progressive Constitutionalism: What Is It", *Ohio State Law Journal*, vol. 72, no. 6, pp. 1073–1082.

Unger, R 1976, *Law in Modern Society*, Free Press, New York.

Unger, R 1986, *Passion: An Essay on Personality*, The Free Press, Boston.

Unger, R 2007, *The Self Awakened: Pragmatism Unbound*, Harvard University Press, Massachusetts.

Unger, R 2014, *The Religion of the Future*, Harvard University Press, Massachusetts.

Valdes, F 1997, "Foreword: Poised at the Cusp: LatCrit Theory, Outsider Jurisprudence and Latina/o Self-Empowerment", *Harvard Latino Law Review*, vol. 2, pp. 1–60.

Valdes, F 1997a, "Queer Margins, Queer Ethics: A Call to Account for Race and Ethnicity in the Law, Theory, and Politics of Sexual Orientation", *Hastings Law Journal*, vol. 48, no. 6, pp. 1293–1342.

Valdes, F 1999, "Theorizing 'OutCrit' Theories: Coalitional Method and Comparative Jurisprudential Experience-RaceCrits, QueerCrits and LatCrits", *University of Miami Law Review*, vol. 53, no. 4, pp. 1265–1322.

Valdes, F 2005, "Legal Reform and Social Justice – An Introduction to LatCrit Theory, Praxis and Community", *Griffith Law Review*, vol. 14, no. 2, pp. 148–173.

Valdes, F 2009, "Rebellious Knowledge Production, Academic Activism, and Outsider Democracy: From Principles to Practices in LatCrit Theory, 1995–2008", *Seattle Journal for Social Justice*, vol. 8, no. 1, pp. 131–172.

Wallace, S 1965, *Skid Row as a Way of Life*, Harper Torch Books, New York.

Webb, B 1926, *My Apprenticeship*, Penguin, London.

Weiners, J 2015, *Supplication: Selected Poems*, Enitharmon Press, London.
West, C 1987, "Between Dewey and Gramsci: Unger's Emancipatory Experimentalism", *Northwestern University Law Review*, vol. 81, no. 4, pp. 941–952.
West, C 1988, "Brendan Brown Lecture: Reassessing the Critical Legal Studies Movement", *Loyola Law Review*, vol. 34, no. 2, pp. 265–276.
West, C 1989, *The American Evasion of Philosophy: A Genealogy of Pragmatism*, University of Wisconsin Press, Madison.
West, C 1991, *The Ethical Dimension of Marxist Thought*, Monthly Review Press, New York.
West, C and Smiley, T 2011, *The Rich and the Rest of Us: A Poverty Manifesto*, Third World Press, Chicago.
West, G 1981, *The National Welfare Rights Movement: The Social Protest of Poor Women*, Praeger, New York.
West, R 1986, "Deconstructing the CLS-FEM Split", *Wisconsin Women's Law Journal*, vol. 2, pp. 85–94.
West, R 1990, "The Role of Law in Progressive Politics", *Vanderbilt Law Review*, vol. 43, no. 6 (November), pp. 1797–1806.
West, R 1999, "Is Progressive Constitutionalism Possible", *Widener Law Symposium Journal*, vol. 4, pp. 1–18.
Wexler, S 1970, "Practicing Law for Poor People", *Yale Law Journal*, vol. 79, no. 6 (May), pp. 1049–1068.
White, G 1971, "From Sociological Jurisprudence to Realism", *Virginia Law Review*, vol. 58, no. 6, pp. 999–1028.
White, L 1987, "Mobilization on the Margins of Litigation: Making Space for Clients to Speak", *New York University Review of Law & Social Change*, vol. 16, no. 4, pp. 535–564.
White, L 1990, "Goldberg v. Kelly on the Paradox of Lawyering for the Poor", *Brooklyn Law Review*, vol. 56, no. 3, pp. 861–887.
White, L 1990a, "Subordination, Rhetorical Survival Skills, and Sunday Shoes: Notes on the Hearing of Mrs. G.", *Buffalo Law Review*, vol. 38, no. 1, pp. 1–58.
White, L 1992 "Paradox, Piece-Work, and Patience", *Hastings Law Journal*, vol. 43, no. 4, pp. 853–860.
White, L 1992a, "Seeking … the Faces of Otherness …: A Response to Professors Sarat Felstiner and Cahn", *Cornell Law Review*, vol. 77, pp. 1499–1511.
White, L 1993, "From a Distance: Responding to the Needs of Others through Law", *Montana Law Review*, vol. 54, no. 1, pp. 1–18.
White, L 1994, "Collaborative Lawyering in the Field – On Mapping the Paths from Rhetoric to Practice", *Clinical Law Review*, vol. 1, no. 1, pp. 157–172.
White, L 1998, "Facing South: Lawyering for Poor Communities in the Twenty-First Century", *Fordham Urban Law Journal*, vol. 25, no. 4, pp. 813–830.
White, L 2002, "In the Interests of Justice", *Fordham Law Review*, vol. 70, no. 5, pp. 1921–1928.
Whitman, W 1885, *Leaves of Grass*, Brooklyn, New York.
Wilkerson, C 2007, *Flying Close to the Sun*, Seven Stories Press, New York.
Williams, R R 2000, "Hegel's Ethics of Recognition", *The Journal of Religion*, vol. 80, no. 3 (July), pp. 531–553.
Williams, W C 1983 [1976], *Selected Poems*, Penguin, Harmondsworth.
Wilson, J 2006, "Invisible Cages: Racialized Politics and the Alliance between the Panthers and the Peace and Freedom Party", in *In Search of the Black Panther Party: New*

Perspectives on a Revolutionary Movement, J Laerow and Y Williams, Duke University Press, Durham.

Wing, A 1991, "Brief Reflections Toward a Multiplicative Theory and Praxis of Being", *Berkeley Women's Law Journal*, vol. 6, no. 1, pp. 181–202.

Wink, W 1992, *Engaging the Powers*, Fortress Press, Minneapolis.

Winter, R 1986, "Poverty, Economic Equality, and the Equal Protection Clause", *Supreme Court Review*, vol. 1972, pp. 41–102.

Wittman, C and Hayden, T 1963, "An Interracial Movement of the Poor?" accessed 20 April 2017, http://michiganintheworld.history.lsa.umich.edu/antivietnamwar/items/show/37.

Wolcher, L 2003, "Ethics, Justice, and Suffering in the Thought of Levinas: The Problem of the Passage", *Law and Critique*, vol. 14, no. 1, pp. 93–116.

Wolcher, L 2004, "A Meditation on Law and Ethics", *Slovenian Law Review*, vol. 1, pp. 139–152.

Wolcher, L 2005, *Beyond Transcendence in Law and Philosophy*, Birkbeck Law Press/Glasshouse, London.

Wolcher, L 2010, "An Inquiry into the Possibility of Ethical Politics", *Rutgers Journal of Law and Religion*, vol. 11, no. 2, pp. 383–405.

Wolcher, L 2012, "The Critical Imperative", *The Crit: A Critical Studies Journal*, vol. 5, no. 2 (Summer), pp. 1–11.

Wolcher, L 2016, *The Ethics of Justice Without Illusions*, Routledge GlassHouse Books, London and New York.

Wright Mills, C 1958, *The Causes of World War III*, New York.

Wright Mills, C 1960, "Letter to the New Left", *New Left Review*, no. 5, pp. 18–23.

Yamamoto, E 1997, "Critical Race Praxis: Race Theory and Political Lawyering Practice in Post-Civil Rights America", *Michigan Law Review*, vol. 95, no. 4, pp. 821–900.

Young, N 1977, *An Infantile Disorder: The Crisis and Decline of the New Left*, Westview Press, Boulder.

Zucker, M 1964, "Citizens Advice Bureaux", paper presented for the Conference on the Extension of Legal Services to the Poor, Washington, DC.

List of cases

Index

For Product Safety Concerns and Information please contact our EU representative GPSR@taylorandfrancis.com Taylor & Francis Verlag GmbH, Kaufingerstraße 24, 80331 München, Germany

Batch number: 10725973

Printed by Printforce, the Netherlands